RESURRECTING THE STREET

Overcoming the Greatest Operational Crisis in History

by Jeff Ingber

RESURRECTING THE STREET: Overcoming the
Greatest Operational Crisis in History

Copyright © 2012 by Jeff Ingber.

Second Edition

ISBN: 978-0-9854100-0-1

First Printing

Printed in the United States of America

This book is sold with the understanding that neither
the Author nor the Publisher is engaged in rendering
legal, accounting or other professional services by
publishing this book.

For Béla and Marika Ingber,

with much love

Table of Contents

"Our people ran out of the Trade Center without a pencil. No trade records. No tickets. The business that we did in the North Tower we backed up in the South Tower, and vice versa. We didn't know where to go the next morning. Or even if there was a firm left."

Ron Purpora, senior executive of Garban Securities LLC[1]

New York City

A: Federal Reserve Bank of New York, 33 Liberty St

B: GSCC, 55 Water St

C: Bank of New York Headquarters, 1 Wall St

D: Bank of New York Main Operations Center, 101 Barclay St

E: Trinity Church, 1 Wall St

F: Bond Market Association, 40 Broad St

G: New York Stock Exchange, 11 Wall St

H: American Stock Exchange, 86 Trinity Pl

I: One Chase Manhattan Plaza

J: Four New York Paza, 107 Broad St

K: One World Trade Center (the "North Tower")

L: Two World Trade Center (the "South Tower")

M: Seven World Trade Center

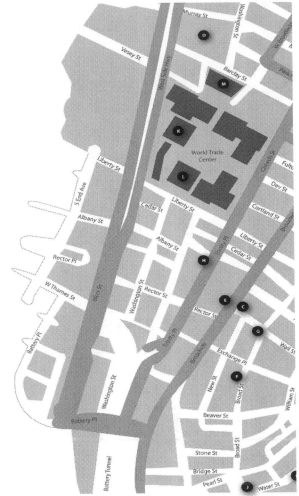

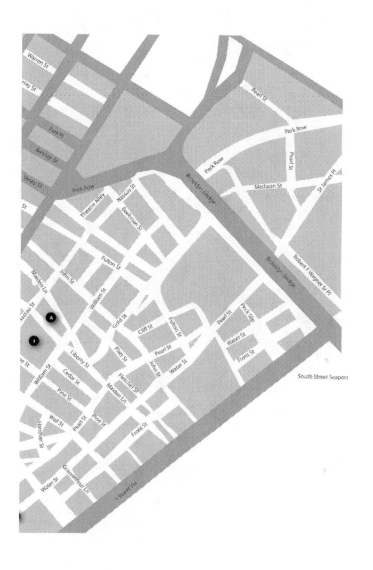

PREFACE

On the morning of September 11, 2001, I was in my office in lower Manhattan, less than a mile from the World Trade Center, when the first plane hit the North Tower. Later I found myself among a throng of evacuees in the street, shocked and disoriented. I struggled to make sense of it all – the smell, the chaos, charred paper flying by, and rumors of widespread destruction.

Standing at the edge of Pier 11, I watched a thick black cloud devour the sky above. All of lower Manhattan was going up in flames, or so it appeared. I turned to look at the Brooklyn shoreline, and tried to convince myself that I could swim there. And then the boats began to arrive and, ever so gradually, calm returned.

The fears I experienced on that morning were trivial compared to the suffering of so many. And I've largely buried my emotions from that day. Except one. I inhaled that cloud of dust and ash and, to this day, it chokes me with rage. Friends and colleagues had been murdered. I would think of Steve Lillianthal, my sister's nephew. Steve was a 38-year-old bond trader, a father of four-year-old twins, and a sweet guy. I had sat next to him at my niece's wedding earlier that year, where he happily spoke about his family and soon-to-be third child. Months later, he was gone. Why?

The idea for this book came to me around the first anniversary of 9/11. Still fresh in our collective consciousness was the unfathomable loss of life and physical devastation. But there was little awareness of the crippling effect the fall of the towers had on the functioning of the U.S. financial markets. When I would hear or read of the impact of 9/11 on Wall Street, the focus invariably was on the effort to restart the equities markets, particularly the New York Stock Exchange. Few understood the harm to the financial system that had otherwise occurred.

Particularly affected was the U.S. government securities market, from both a human and infrastructural perspective. It was revived through the sacrifice and determination of a range of professionals. Many of these individuals easily could have walked away for days or weeks. Or forever. Instead, they talked their way through police lines, slept in unventilated offices, endured difficult physical conditions, scrounged up alternate locations, and overcame personal grief and understandable fears for their own safety to help restore individual companies and the markets as a whole.

There were similar laudable attempts to bring back vital financial exchanges based in lower Manhattan, including the American Stock Exchange, the New York Board of Trade, and the New York

Mercantile Exchange. All of these efforts ultimately were successful, fueled by a spirit of patriotism risen to a level that those of my generation had never experienced.

Unable to express my feelings about that day, any personal account of 9/11 would have been sterile. I found my voice through others. I drove to a local Radio Shack, bought a tape recorder and some audio tapes, and began what would amount over the years to more than 100 interviews.

What became apparent to me during my research was that the days immediately following 9/11 presented the financial industry with the greatest operational crisis in its history; a struggle that required individuals to deal with a uniquely horrific blend of personal and professional difficulties. Key officials had been killed, others could not be located. Primary and backup sites were unavailable or inadequate. Massive amounts of critical data were lost, and there was a crushing inability to communicate, locate, or verify information. Employees could not get to where they needed to be, assuming they even knew where that was. It was not known for a time which firms could participate in the markets and to what degree, nor was it clear to what extent certain markets had been damaged and when they could reopen. Full reconciliation of the securities and funds positions that were affected took two years.

And, even then, many market participants were left with a money difference that had to be written off.

Nor could the human impact of the 9/11 events be divorced from the business issues. Amid the drive to assess the harm to the markets and to address severe disruptions, the first priority had to be to determine the whereabouts of workers, evacuate them, ensure their safety, and comfort them. While this was being done, those grappling to repair the markets had to cope with their own feelings of anxiety, shock and loss. 9/11 should have been just an ordinary work day. Nothing but the mundane was anticipated.

No one who was in the World Trade Center area on that day, who saw a plane fly into a tower or a person fall from one, who had family or friends at risk, or who had his or her own safety endangered, was left unscarred. Most of those involved in the market had no framework for processing that morning's events. As one industry leader noted, "My generation missed Vietnam, and wasn't used to having colleagues die."[2] Each person would handle his or her pain and fears in a private way; many later admitted that the focus on business issues was a welcome distraction.

Everyone in the financial community knew someone who was or might have been in the towers that morning. Far too many had to carry on while coping with the grief of having lost a family member, friend, or colleague. Yet with the pain of this truth ever present, they also sought, as spouses, siblings, children, and friends, to contact loved ones and reassure them of their safety. As parents, they struggled to find the best way to comfort their children, and to explain the incomprehensible. As leaders, their projection of emotional balance was crucial in order to instill confidence in the future of their company and of the financial system.

Whenever the vast story of 9/11 is told, the heart of it is and must always remain the profound loss of life and individual suffering. But part of the complete narrative is the deliberate attack waged on capitalism and the free markets that are fundamental to our society and way of life. This is an account that I was uniquely positioned to help tell, having been at the time the General Counsel of the Government Securities Clearing Corporation, the central utility for the U.S. government securities market. I was a firsthand witness to many of the extraordinary events that occurred.

I also had the good fortune to have known or worked with many who were integrally involved in resolving the crisis. The heroes of 9/11 were the firefighters, police, and emergency and rescue workers, who performed their duties with immeasurable courage. In the financial community, managers and their staff compelled themselves to continue to carry out their responsibilities in the face of unparalleled challenges. In doing so, they collectively sent a message that we would not be defeated.

This book tells of the regeneration of the U.S. markets, day by day, during the time period immediately following 9/11. I wrote most about what I know best, leading me to focus on the U.S. government securities market and, in particular, its clearance and settlement process. The book also provides a brief history and background of that market, which is helpful to understanding how it was affected.

The events of 9/11 brought the most important financial market in the world – the one looked to by investors globally for safety in times of trouble – to the brink of paralysis. The crisis was ultimately resolved through the willpower and wisdom of groups of disparate individuals, accompanied by an unprecedented climate of cooperation among fierce competitors that embodied the American spirit at its finest.[3]

CHAPTER 1

OPERATIONAL DEVASTATION

"The damage to infrastructure was beyond belief. From a practical standpoint, the risk really was on the operational side. A dealer can always figure out a way to trade. Just give him a pencil and piece of paper and another trader and he'll trade. The issue of settlement processing was our main concern."
Brian Roseboro, Assistant Treasury Secretary for Financial Markets [1]

It was and remains the vow of al Qaeda to destroy the U.S. economy, and the financial markets were a deliberate target on 9/11.[2] Almost a third of the firms located in buildings affected by the World Trade Center attacks were in the financial services industry.[3] Close to three-quarters of those killed worked in that industry; many were operations personnel, who are essential to maintaining the "plumbing" of the markets.[4]

The World Trade Center complex consisted of seven buildings in all. Each of its floors took up an entire acre, and the 200,000 tons of structural steel used to build the two towers was more than was needed for the Verrazano Narrows Bridge, which spans from Staten Island to Brooklyn.[5] The collapse of the towers turned daytime into night. It engulfed the surrounding area in dense clouds of dust containing pulverized cement, glass, asbestos and other contaminants and created 1.5 million tons of debris.[6]

At the core of the operational catastrophe was the obliteration of infrastructure. Thirty-five million square feet of office space (a third of it in the Trade Center itself), the equivalent of almost 30 Empire State Buildings, and about 60 percent of the downtown Manhattan "Class-A" commercial real estate, were lost or damaged.[7] An estimated 100,000 employees in 1,300 businesses were displaced.[8] 12,000 buildings in lower Manhattan were left without electricity, and many were also without gas or steam.[9] Thousands of computer servers used by financial firms were lost, and the water supply was temporarily shut off for a wide area.[10] Transportation throughout lower Manhattan stopped; for days, there were restrictions on access to that area and movement within it.

The financial industry is critically dependent on telecommunications. The collapse of Seven World Trade Center in the afternoon of 9/11, which became fodder for conspiracy theorists,[11] sent debris into the adjacent Verizon communications center at 140 West Street, severely damaging it.[12] That center's switching equipment controlled much of lower Manhattan's phone lines. Altogether, 300,000 voice lines and four million data circuits, affecting 14,000 businesses, went down.[13] Many financial institutions believed that they had obtained "redundancy" in their telecommunications capabilities by contracting with multiple providers or by having their communication lines directed over different physical paths, only to find that all those lines had been routed through the same damaged Verizon switching facility.[14]

Disaster recovery, which has the dual goals of enabling the prompt resumption of business and safeguarding transactions and financial information,[15] didn't begin to anticipate the magnitude of the devastation. It was acceptable, indeed common, to have a concentration of resources in one geographic area, based on the assumption that the effect of any unexpected event, such as a fire or flood, would be limited to one building or block. As a result, many companies, to maximize efficiency, had their primary and backup facilities within close proximity to each other, leading them to lose access to both.[16]

Business resumption planning didn't adequately consider the potential for the loss of a significant number of employees or for them being unreachable. It was widespread practice to have all staff members work in the same location, allowing a single event to disrupt and harm much of a firm's workforce. In many cases, there were no comprehensive employee lists containing their contact information; companies that were in the towers spent days trying to track down their staff and determine who had survived.[17]

Nor was it envisioned that backup sites would have to carry the full business for weeks or months. Many market participants used vendors that maintained locations for work space, storage of data, and handling of mainframe computer demands, but those service providers based their resources on the likelihood that only one or two clients would need them at the same time.[18] In numerous cases, vendors were pressed to find desks, communications links, and PCs for a much larger number of workers than was ever anticipated. Compounding the problem was the loss or inaccessibility of key personnel at certain firms who had been designated to handle disaster scenarios.[19] Even for available staff, travel around the New York City area was difficult post-9/11, and getting them to backup sites proved a challenge. Many of those who witnessed the attacks were too traumatized to return to work.

9/11 exposed the industry's widespread weaknesses in record-keeping and document retention. Billions of dollars worth of physical securities, stored in vaults in the Trade Center, were destroyed and had to be painstakingly recreated.[20] Crucial data were lost because firms didn't routinely preserve them remotely or in electronic form. Morgan Stanley had stored at the Trade Center millions of individual client records that it struggled to locate or reconstruct.[21] This flaw wasn't limited to market participants. The Securities and Exchange Commission's (SEC) Northeast regional office was ruined when Seven World Trade Center collapsed. While all 300 SEC employees were evacuated unharmed, hundreds of investigations, including the broad inquiry into initial public sales of stock begun in the late 1990s, were hampered by the loss of notes and files that were kept only in that building.[22]

None of the U.S. financial markets was spared disruption.[23] No U.S. stock, options or futures exchange functioned on 9/11 except for a brief interval at best. Not only were the New York stock markets shut, but stock exchanges in Philadelphia, Chicago, and San Francisco voluntarily closed as well.[24] Even though most of these exchanges escaped direct damage, none reopened until the following Monday, after connectivity (the ability of networks to join computers to one another) had been tested over the weekend and voice and data links restored.[25] This four-business-day hiatus was the longest gap in history in the operation of the U.S. equities markets.[26]

The American Stock Exchange (AMEX) building, just 200 yards south of the Trade Center at 86 Trinity Place, suffered extensive structural damage. The AMEX, which didn't have a backup trading floor, was able to recommence operations on the following Monday only by moving its equities trading operations to the floor of the New York Stock Exchange (NYSE) and its options activities to the Philadelphia Stock Exchange.[27]

On the futures side, one exchange, the New York Board of Trade (NYBOT), which traded commodities such as coffee, sugar, cotton, and orange juice, had its headquarters in Four World Trade Center.[28] The New York Mercantile Exchange (NYMEX), which traded natural gas, crude oil, gold, silver, and other physical commodities in traditional "open outcry" pits in the World Financial Center, across the street from the Trade Center, halted pit activity until the following Monday. In addition to its concern about resuming trading, the NYMEX had to focus on recovering nearly 12 metric tons of gold, then valued at $110 million, buried under Four World Trade Center.

9/11 severely shocked the payments and securities settlement system, which "lubricates and underpins" the financial markets.[29] Some banks were unable to make payments, resulting in an unexpected cash shortfall for other banks.[30] In the market for transactions in "commercial paper" – debt instruments that are essential for large banks and corporations to acquire the money needed to meet short-term obligations such as payroll and utilities – there was a massive failure to settle. There also were breakdowns in the federal funds market and widespread closings of bank branches. Meanwhile, the grounding of airline flights seriously hampered check processing for days.[31]

Prior to 2001, the financial markets had endured other operational emergencies. The closest comparison to the devastation caused on 9/11 came in 1835, when a "Great New York Fire" destroyed the New York Stock Exchange and most of the buildings around Wall Street.[32] Looking to more recent events, during Wall Street's "Paperwork Crisis" from 1968 to 1971, the back-offices of brokerage firms were literally buried in paper, overwhelmed by the processing requirements of increased volumes of securities transactions.[33] This led the equity markets to close on Wednesdays, and to shorten trading hours on other days, to catch up on the backlog.[34]

On "Black Monday," October 19, 1987, when the largest one-day percentage decline in stock market history to that point occurred, there was queuing and clogging in the order routing systems, causing the NYSE difficulty executing its trades.[35] Nearly five years later, in April 1992, around 124 million gallons of the Chicago River poured into the network of freight tunnels under Chicago's central business district. After filling the tunnels, the water rose into the basements of many downtown buildings, knocking out electric power and natural gas service. The Chicago Board of Trade (CBOT) was impacted because its air conditioning system was underwater. A shutdown of its computer systems kept the CBOT closed for days.[36]

But 9/11 was unique in the intensity and swiftness of its devastation, together with the depth of its human tragedy. Particularly in one market, that for U.S. government securities.

CHAPTER 2

TUESDAY MORNING: IN HARM'S WAY

"At one point, I made a list of those I knew who had died. Forty one in all. Two of the five people who I considered my best friends. Each of the forty one I knew well, not just casually. Many from my old neighborhood in the Bronx. Many who I had hired."

Tom Kinnally, repo trader[1]

If there is one constant in the memories of those who think back on September 11, 2001, it is this: after a particularly hot summer, the weather that Tuesday was gorgeous. Pleasantly warm, clear, and radiant. A day to linger outside, to stroll, or to get in a round of golf.

The lives of many who worked in the World Trade Center and surrounding area that morning were relatively unaffected, and in some cases spared, for a number of reasons. The weather might have been one; it was surely a day to play hooky. Summer vacation season hadn't ended. Some were delayed because they took time to vote in the New York City Primary Day election. Others slept later after staying up to watch the Giants lose to the Broncos on Monday Night Football. For many, their work day didn't start until 9 a.m. or later.[2]

When the first plane struck, the U.S. stock markets were still preparing to open. Yet by that time the U.S. government securities market – known as the "Govie" market, where trading in U.S. Treasuries and securities issued by federal agencies occurs – was in full bloom.

The Govie market is a professional one involving buying and selling, in amounts that range up to hundreds of millions of dollars, by expert traders. Looked at globally, this market operates 24 hours a day, with hubs in New York, London, and Tokyo. Activity never truly stops. The disproportionate impact of 9/11 on the Govie market stemmed largely from one factor: local trading begins early. In New York, by the time the attacks began, the market already had been open for over an hour and a half, and more than $500 billion worth of trading had occurred.[3]

The bulk of that early activity was in "repos," short for repurchase and reverse repurchase agreement transactions. In a repo, one party sells securities to acquire cash, and later buys the securities back while also making a payment of interest (Figure 1). A Govie repo is economically equivalent to a short-term loan of cash in exchange for the pledge of government securities as collateral, making it a safe transaction.

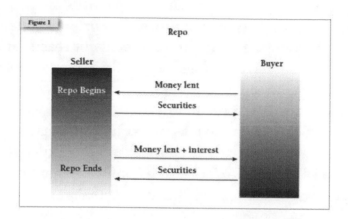

Figure 1

Repos constitute a significant segment of the U.S. government securities market, representing the most important short-term credit market in the United States. Banks and broker-dealers alike depend on short-term financing; repos are their lifeblood. The great majority of repos are traded in the early part of the business day.[4] Repo traders often are at work by 7 a.m., as are their support colleagues who handle operations or finance. The latter are needed to ensure that the trades are recorded and that instructions are generated for the required movements of cash and securities, as well as to prepare the settlements of previous trades.

At 8:46 a.m., while thousands of individuals in the Financial District were at their desks, American Airlines flight 11 flew into floors 93 through 99 of One World Trade Center, known as the "North Tower."

Fragments of the plane erupted out of the south face of the tower, landing as far as five blocks away. The building swayed several times, as burning jet fuel, which poured down stairwells, elevator shafts, and the sides of the building, created thick black smoke that enveloped the upper floors. Hundreds were killed instantly; more than a thousand were trapped.[5]

John Salemmo was working for Morgan Stanley in a financial support area on the 70th floor of Two World Trade Center, the "South Tower." He recalled, "The impact of the plane crashing into the other tower had a ripple effect that shook our building from its foundation."[6] Salemmo had a clear view of the side of the North Tower that overlooked the courtyard: "Windows were blown out. Smoke and fire. Desks and other parts of the office were going out the window. You could see all sorts of debris."[7]

The landing gear of the first plane had pierced the roof of the Marriott World Trade Center Hotel, which sat between the two towers, and crashed into an office next to the swimming pool on the top floor.[8] Barbara Blumberg, a vice president for Standard Chartered Bank, was having breakfast with colleagues from India. Sitting in the Greenhouse Café in the hotel's upper lobby, with its striking fountain and a skylight view of both towers, Blumberg heard an explosion and looked up through the glass ceiling: "We saw the fireball. Then we realized that things like girders were falling off the building and breaking through the glass. Hotel staff were all coming down. The maids were hysterical. There was a gentleman wrapped in a towel with half a face of shaving cream." [9] Blumberg and her coworkers fled.

Not the First Act of Terrorism

World Trade Center workers lived with an awareness that the towers were a focal point for an assault. As the symbol of capitalism and wealth, the entire Wall Street community has long been a target for terrorists. Prior to 2001, the worst assault in U.S. financial history occurred on September 16, 1920, when a horse-drawn buggy loaded with 100 pounds of dynamite and 500 pounds of cast-iron slugs exploded on Wall Street, across from the headquarters of the J.P. Morgan Bank, killing 38 people and injuring hundreds more.

On January 24, 1975, a bomb detonated in Fraunces Tavern, a lower Manhattan landmark where George Washington had bid farewell to his officers at the end of the Revolutionary War. Four people were killed; more than 50 were injured. The Puerto Rican nationalist group FALN, which had set off other bombs in New York City, claimed responsibility, but no one was ever prosecuted.

Less than a decade before 9/11, on Friday, February 26, 1993, at 12:18 p.m., a large explosion ripped through the basement public parking garage of the Trade Center. The cause was a 1,500-pound urea-nitrate bomb packed in a yellow Ford Econoline rental van, which carved out a crater 200 feet by 100 feet wide and several stories deep. Designed to bring down the towers, that bomb killed six persons, injured more than 1,000 (most suffered smoke inhalation), and caused nearly $300 million in property damage.[10]

For those on the top floors, it took more than two hours to walk down to the lobby. The length and difficulty of that trek out of the building was a fact that many in the Trade Center would remember to their advantage eight years later.[11] One of the North Tower's tenants, Cantor Fitzgerald, a financial services firm specializing in bond trading, went through a reconciliation process the following weekend that foreshadowed what the industry would undergo after 9/11. That Saturday, with the Trade Center generally inaccessible, Federal Reserve Bank of New York officials helped a handful of Cantor staff gain permission to reenter the North Tower and scale, with backpacks, more than 100 stories to retrieve trade files. Because brokers had to evacuate before completing trade tickets for many transactions done on the morning of the bombing, many of those tickets were missing key terms, including one or both of the counterparties on each side of the trade. They would need to be completed with the help of records from Chase Manhattan Bank, Cantor's clearing bank.[12]

It wasn't surprising that after the first plane attack, many industry veterans immediately thought back to the 1993 bombing. At that time, Dave Buckmaster had been working at 40 Wall Street, running operations at Carroll McEntee & McGinley, one of the dozens of "primary dealers" that trade directly with the New York Fed.[13] Not only did he hear the bomb, but several people from the industry, covered in soot, later had come over to his shop. On 9/11, Buckmaster was head of planning for the Government Securities Clearing Corporation, based at 55 Water Street in lower Manhattan. Seeing the damage from the impact of the first plane, he turned to a colleague and barked, "Looks like the bastards bombed the Trade Center again!"[14]

Nick Gialanella, director of operations for Refco Securities,[15] whose headquarters were a stone's throw away at One World Financial Center, had an office that faced the towers. "There was this tremendous noise and vibration in the building," he recalled. "I turned and looked out the window and saw a huge fireball coming out of the tower and debris flying everywhere. I immediately thought of what had happened in '93. When the bomb went off then, I happened to be working out in the gym on the top floor of the Vista Hotel. So this was strike two for me."[16]

Murray Pozmanter, managing director in charge of fixed-income operations at Nomura Securities International, a Japanese-owned primary dealer in Two World Financial Center, had an office that looked directly into the side of the North Tower: "I felt the windows rattling and the building shaking. But unlike in 1993, instead of smoke coming up, things were falling down. We realized that something different had happened."[17]

Devastation of the Govie Market

If the terrorists who planned and executed the 9/11 events had wanted to target the Govie marketplace, they couldn't have chosen a more strategic location than the World Trade Center. Not that the Trade Center had a formal role as a hub for the Govie market. No centralized exchange, like a New York Stock Exchange, exists in the fixed-income markets, which include corporate bonds, mortgage-backed securities, fixed-income derivatives, municipal securities and emerging market debt.[18] These are known as "over-the-counter" markets, whose primary participants trade with one another from locations all over the globe on a bilateral basis or through brokers, inter-connected by communications links.

Still, the 9/11 attacks and subsequent widespread damage adversely impacted every key participant or group of participants in the U.S. government securities market (Figure 2). As a result, that marketplace, which was the most important of them all, also was the most devastated.

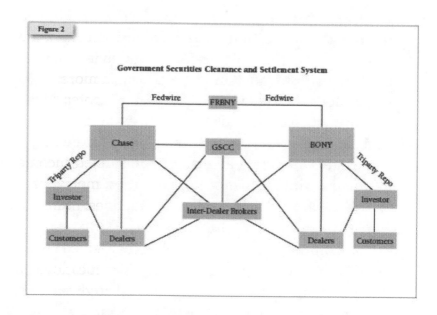

Figure 2

Government Securities Clearance and Settlement System

Along with the large dealers, there were four pillars of the Govie market; each was put in crisis on 9/11. One was the inter-dealer broker community, the group of middlemen through which most non-retail trading in the Govie market was done. Another was the Federal Reserve Bank of New York, whose books hold the records of government securities ownership. Then there were the two "clearing banks" – The Bank of New York and The Chase Manhattan Bank. These were indispensable intermediaries between the New York Fed and Govie market participants that were used by every major broker-dealer and bank, and without whose credit and custodial services the market could not function. Finally, there was the Government Securities Clearing Corporation (GSCC). GSCC ensured that Govie trades were accepted as valid, and then that they were "settled" by the buyers receiving securities and the sellers receiving payment.

For every one of these key segments of the market, lower Manhattan was a crucial location. This was no longer out of necessity but more a vestige of the days when all financial instruments were in paper form and money and securities were exchanged by messengers, requiring all major financial firms to be in close proximity.[19] Thus, the early morning events of 9/11 destroyed the physical foundation of the Govie market.

Compounding the crisis was that, given the large number of Govie market participants located throughout the globe, ensuring they all receive relevant news on a timely basis is challenging even under normal circumstances. On 9/11, this information flow was enormously difficult to conduct and, in many cases, choked off. The standard forum for discussing and resolving industry-wide issues was the Bond Market Association (BMA), the industry's trade group.[20] However, the BMA had its main office at 40 Broad Street, just south of the New York Stock Exchange and less than a half mile from the Trade Center. BMA staff evacuated that office on 9/11, and it was inaccessible all that week.

In the early morning of 9/11, an enormous amount of government securities trading, over 16,000 transactions, had been executed by dealers, brokers, and banks. The records of much of that trading were lost. There was no reset button; those records would have to be painstakingly reconstructed. "Real-time messaging," which would have delivered data on trades within minutes of their execution to a central, secure place, was available at that time, but its use was minimal. The standard was to send all of the day's trade data only at the end of the day.

Despite the massive trade reconciliation problems, the Govie market never fully suspended operation. While trading went on in midtown Manhattan and elsewhere, there was limited ability to fix existing problems, record new trades properly, and determine their legitimacy. Severe imbalances of money and securities positions developed at various firms and between the two key clearing banks; for awhile, proper settlement became impossible.

How badly damaged were those four mainstays of the Govie market?

The Inter-Dealer Brokers

A cornerstone of the Govie market on 9/11 were the nine "inter-dealer brokers" that facilitated the large majority of trading among dealers and banks (as opposed to "broker-dealers," which trade for themselves on a proprietary basis and for retail customers). They were: BrokerTec, Cantor Fitzgerald Securities, Euro Brokers, Garban Securities, GFI, Hilliard Farber & Co., Prebon Securities, Tradition Asiel Securities, and Tullett Liberty Brokerage.

These brokers, in exchange for commission, provided electronic screens that displayed best bid and offer prices for trade execution by the dealers. They were a conduit through which major market participants received price information, enhancing transparency. Conversely, their presence in the middle of the trades allowed the large dealers and banks to conduct their business anonymously, without the disclosure of proprietary positions and trading strategies. Hence, they were also referred to as "blind brokers."

The largest inter-dealer broker, and arguably the most significant participant in the Govie market, was Cantor Fitzgerald. Yet many people outside of the Financial District were unaware of this company until the horror of 9/11. Cantor traced its roots back to 1945, and in 1972 had revolutionized the Govie market by introducing the first electronic screens for U.S. government securities trading. Cantor transacted more in dollar volumes of trades – approximately $50 trillion a year – than the NYSE, AMEX and NASDAQ combined.[21]

Cantor and its new electronic trading network, eSpeed, had their world headquarters on floors 101, 103, 104, and 105 of the North Tower, just below the 40,000-square-foot Windows on the World restaurant.[22] For those in the industry, Cantor was synonymous with the World Trade Center, and the immediate thought of many on seeing or hearing of the attacks was of the effect on both Cantor and the Govie market.[23] All 658 Cantor staff members at work on the top floors of the North Tower at 8:46 a.m. perished.[24] That number would have been even higher had not the success of eSpeed made hundreds of broker jobs obsolete.[25] Cantor's death toll on 9/11 was more than that of any other organization, including the New York City Fire Department.

The next largest Govie inter-dealer broker was Garban Securities LLC, which had more than 700 employees on the 55th floor of the South Tower and on two lower floors of the North Tower. Garban was part of ICAP, a large voice and electronic inter-dealer broker operating world-wide in many markets.[26] Occupying lower floors, Garban was spared human loss except for the death of one staffer, Karen Lyn Seymour-Dietrich. Seymour-Dietrich, who had young twin boys, was attending a financial technology seminar that morning hosted by Risk Waters Group Ltd., a British company, at the Windows on the World conference facility on the 106th floor.[27] Breakfast was being served to conference participants on the 107th floor, in the Wild Blue restaurant, when the first plane struck. Sixteen Risk Waters staff members and 53 conference attendees were killed.[28]

Yet another inter-dealer broker, Euro Brokers Inc., was on the 84th floor of the South Tower.[29] Minutes after the North Tower was impacted, it was announced over the South Tower public-address system that the building was safe and there was no need to evacuate. Given the knowledge available at that moment, the fire safety staff in the South Tower were trying to prevent people from being hurt or killed by falling debris from the North Tower.[30] This PA announcement inadvertently led to hundreds of deaths.[31] Because their floor was in the impact zone of the second airplane, 61 of 280 New York-based Euro Broker staffers died.[32]

These three critical inter-dealer brokers suddenly and unexpectedly lost their principal offices by mid-morning on 9/11. Two of the three firms experienced massive loss of life, including many of their senior officials. Five of the six remaining brokers had their operations disrupted. Even the sixth, BrokerTec, whose main office was in Jersey City's downtown waterfront area, was affected. It had to invest time and incur risk as it shifted its middle and back-office systems, which were run by a vendor, Oasis, out of lower Manhattan. BrokerTec and Oasis staff worked through the night on 9/11 to transfer those systems securely over to Jersey City.[33]

Further crippling the brokered market was that "Tradeweb," an on-line bond trading system that allowed large companies active in the Treasury market to obtain real-time prices and trade with multiple dealers, had its principal offices on the 51st floor of the North Tower. Tradeweb was by far the largest electronic platform for institutional trading in Govies, executing about $20 billion a day in the Treasury market. It would not resume business for two weeks.[34]

Apart from the brokers, many of the largest dealers in the Govie market also had offices in the World Trade Center, including Morgan Stanley, Merrill Lynch, and Lehman Brothers. Morgan Stanley was the biggest Trade Center tenant, with 3,700 staff and 1.3 million square feet of office space in the South

Tower and Five World Trade Center.[35] Merrill Lynch, the world's largest brokerage firm, and Lehman Brothers, another huge market player, each had its global headquarters in the World Financial Center, a group of four towers built in the 1980s directly across from the Trade Center.[36] In addition, numerous other dealer firms active in the market had significant offices in the World Financial Center or otherwise near the Trade Center. All were forced to evacuate, losing access to their facilities. Many couldn't effectively trade or even communicate on 9/11.[37]

The Two Clearing Banks

All the dealers and inter-dealer brokers depended integrally on one of two commercial banks to hold their securities, settle their trades, and finance their positions.[38] These were The Bank of New York (commonly referred to as "BoNY")[39] and The Chase Manhattan Bank (Chase).[40] In their role as the "clearing banks," BoNY and Chase together were responsible for processing and settling virtually all of the *two trillion dollars* in government securities transactions generated by the brokers and dealers daily.[41]

Each bank provided large amounts of credit to their customers – dealers and financial institutions – to fund their intraday and overnight securities positions.[42] Every large dealer also depended on one of the two banks for its tri-party repo arrangements. Tri-party repos, integral to the dealers' financing, involved the bank as custodian of the collateral and provider of other administrative services.[43] Mutual funds relied on the clearing banks to invest securely their funds in repos.

Both BoNY and Chase had to relocate to backup sites because their main centers of operation were just a few blocks from the Trade Center. Chase had three operating sites in lower Manhattan, each of which became temporarily inaccessible. Its Govie clearance function was headed by Al Clark: "When we set up Four New York Plaza [at the corner of Broad and Water Streets] as a backup for One Chase Plaza, which are about eight blocks apart, we took into account the separate power grids, separate telephone grids, generators on both buildings, and uninterrupted power sources in both buildings. Because of that, we thought it was a fail-safe arrangement. Turned out not to be."[44]

BoNY's situation was even more difficult. Nearly half of its 19,000 employees, including those responsible for its main computer center, worked close to the bank's headquarters at One Wall Street.[45] BoNY had to evacuate both its headquarters and its main operations center at 101 Barclay Street (a block north of the Trade Center), which housed its bond clearing and settlement systems; it would eventually lease temporary space in 17 separate locations in New York City.[46] The company experienced communications problems with its customers for days, preventing market participants from timely confirming the status of their bank accounts and

whether delivery of funds or securities to those
accounts had been made.

The New York Fed and GSCC

The Federal Reserve Bank of New York was
affected on 9/11 because of its location at 33 Liberty
Street, just two blocks from the Trade Center.[47] The
New York Fed operates Fedwire, the securities
transfer, settlement and safekeeping system vital to
the Govie market.[48] The Fed's building, a neo-
Florentine fortress that holds the largest accumulation
of gold in the world, went into lock down, with
shotgun-carrying guards stationed at both
entrances.[49] Employees were relocated to the lobby
and below-ground levels.[50] Outside, thick dust and
smoke led officials to turn off the ventilation system
to protect air quality.[51] By Wednesday evening, the
building had to be evacuated because of concern that
One Liberty Plaza, a block away, might collapse.[52]

One other key player in the government
securities market was the Government Securities
Clearing Corporation. The bulk of Govie trading done
by broker-dealers, banks, inter-dealer brokers and
other institutions flowed through GSCC, which
confirmed and helped settle those trades.[53]

GSCC was allowed to stay in its offices at 55
Water Street, but access to lower Manhattan was
severely restricted in the following days.[54] If one left
the area, it was difficult to return, leading many
employees to sleep in their offices for days. Spared
the suffering inflicted on those in and next to the

Trade Center, GSCC staff, like many who worked in lower Manhattan in the days after 9/11, coped with poor conditions including lack of ventilation, uncertain water supply, and limited food sources.

Confusion

That morning, Rich Visco, vice president of trade processing for GSCC, had a unique perspective from the 31st floor. His work space faced west, with an unimpeded view of the North Tower less than a mile away. Plus, Visco had an edge over other observers: "I had binoculars because of the falcons that lived in the area. We would watch them zip by and attack the pigeons. They would tear them apart on top of the buildings."[55] Operations guys also admitted to having used the binoculars to observe any topless rooftop sunbathers they could find.

The sky around Water Street soon became filled with burnt paper floating past the building and across the East River to Brooklyn. Tom Quaranta and Bob Trapani, who together ran GSCC's client services and were in an office facing away from the North Tower, thought they were seeing confetti. Quaranta quipped that the City must be giving the Yankees, who had beaten the Mets in the World Series the year before, another ticker-tape parade, even though the baseball season wasn't over.[56] Close to the Trade Center, there was a sickening gas-like odor caused by the burning jet fuel.[57] Further away, one person described the smell as being like "burning band-aids."[58]

As Visco watched through his binoculars from the west end of the 31st floor, something flew straight down: "Looked like a piece of lint at first. Then I realized – it was a body." Others had a closer view. Nick Gialanella of Refco walked to the corner of the 24th floor of One World Financial Center: "I saw people standing and then jumping from the tower. I thought, 'How bad must it be that people can make that decision?'"

John Salemmo watched from the South Tower: "Some looked like they were just trying to escape. I saw people holding on to the outside columns of the building and a few actually trying to shimmy down to get away from the unbearable heat. The pictures in my head never go away. People falling over 90 stories and exploding like a watermelon when they hit the ground."

Bill Peterson, a senior vice president and associate general counsel in the Morgan Stanley legal department, was on the 65th floor of the South Tower: "Because of the attack in '93, we had been trained repeatedly in what to do should there be a problem. We all hated those exercises, but our security director, Rick Rescorla, insisted on them. [Rescorla, a retired United States Army officer, was the World Trade Center security chief for Morgan Stanley. He implemented evacuation procedures that were credited with saving many lives; all but six of Morgan Stanley's 3,700 Trade Center employees survived.[59]] So at that point, those of us there fell into the mode that we had been drilled into."

While walking down the stairs, Peterson heard the public-address announcement that the South Tower was safe and everyone should go back to their office: "Right after that announcement ended, one of those trader-type voices came wafting up from the stairs below me to the effect of 'Yeah, right!' And everyone kind of giggled and kept going down." Because Peterson ignored the announcement, by the time his building was struck he was in a stairwell below the 44th floor.

Others in offices close to the Trade Center could only guess at what had happened. Jane Buyers, a managing director for Chase, was at her desk at Chase Plaza on the 21st floor: "I heard this loud bang and went to the window, which faced north, overlooking the New York Fed building which had workmen on its roof. They were looking around and all of a sudden glanced over their shoulders. It seemed as if they had seen Satan himself. They went flying off the roof."[60]

Joe Blauvelt was at the Chase repo desk, which he headed, at 270 Park Avenue in Midtown: "All the TVs on the trading floor were showing the visual. We all thought it was a stupid pilot error. But the floors became busy. I immediately tried to cover my positions through futures in Chicago. And the financing desk got long [bought] cash, because cash is king in a crisis."[61]

Many traders first understood that the market wasn't functioning properly when their eSpeed screens went out.[62] But much of the Govie market continued operating fairly normally during the 17 minutes between the two plane attacks, because there was little concrete sense of the situation. Whether it was wishful thinking or not, the predominant belief, consistent with some initial news reports, was that the damage had been caused by an accident involving a small aircraft. Despite the size of the hole in the North Tower and even though the visibility that day was virtually unlimited, this notion was held by most, including President George W. Bush, National Security Advisor Condoleezza Rice, and Mayor Rudolph Giuliani.[63]

Many were reminded of an incident they had either heard or read about happening in 1945, when a B-25 bomber crashed into the Empire State Building.[64] But any illusions about the accidental nature of that morning's events were shattered at 9:03 a.m., when United Airlines flight 175 flew into the South Tower and exploded. What followed was an extraordinary migration out of lower Manhattan.

CHAPTER 3

EVACUATION: BY ANY MEANS POSSIBLE

"An announcement came over the loudspeaker, 'We don't know what's happening. It may not be safe in here anymore. Get out any way you can. God Speed!'"

Ann Marie Hanley, trader, American Stock Exchange[1]

Around 9 a.m., Dave Cosgrove, a vice president in the Government Securities Clearing Corporation's operations area, was poring over a list of members. Sensing that companies would have difficulty staying in the Trade Center, Cosgrove was trying to identify those located in the towers. Something went flitting past the window and caught his eye: "At first, I thought it was the falcon. Then I realized that it was a trade ticket, half-burnt. Still glowing orange. I could think of no explanation for that."

Cosgrove's phone rang. It was a buddy, Adam Arias, from Euro Brokers. Cosgrove asked Arias what he was still doing at work. Arias responded, "I'm an operations guy. I'll be here until the end. They said everything was okay." Cosgrove tried to persuade Arias to come over to 55 Water Street to work there, but Arias was adamant about staying.

Cosgrove had his back to the window while they talked. "A few seconds later, I hear shouting. I turn to look out the window and see a huge fireball. I'm screaming, 'Adam, Adam!' but all I heard was a whooshing sound, and then the line went dead."[2] (Arias survived the second plane crash, and helped many co-workers to safety; later they credited him with having saved their lives. Arias perished outside the South Tower after it collapsed.)[3]

United Airlines flight 175 took a path over New Jersey, Staten Island, and New York Harbor in its final moments.[4] It flew into the south face of floors 77 to 85 of the South Tower, killing about 200 people instantly and trapping hundreds more, some of whom were horribly injured.

Rob Palatnick, head of GSCC technology, was one of the tens of thousands in the immediate area watching: "The plane makes the turn around the corner and accelerates. It hits the building and I scream, as does everyone else."[5] Marc Lackritz, President of the Securities Industry Association, called immediately from Washington D.C. to his New York office at 120 Broad Street to urge his staff to leave: "One of the secretaries, who had seen the second plane from our conference room, grabbed the phone and began crying hysterically. All I could do was repeatedly urge her to go home and tell everyone else to do so. She left, and never returned to work."[6]

Sal Sodano, CEO of the American Stock Exchange at 86 Trinity Place, just south of the Trade Center, was on the exchange floor watching on TV as the second plane struck: "The trading floor quaked, and soon I could see smoke and flames coming in from the north side of the building." With the 9:30 a.m. opening time impending, Sodano called Dick Grasso, Chairman of the nearby New York Stock Exchange, which hadn't suffered any structural damage, to tell him that the AMEX wasn't going to open. Grasso argued against that, until Sodano explained the situation in full. Then Sodano called a contact at the SEC to inform his regulator that the AMEX couldn't open: "He said to me, 'You can't close unless we have verification of your conditions.' I screamed at him and hung up. But he had no clue what was going on. He was just doing his job."[7]

Tom Wipf, who ran Morgan Stanley's financing desk, was in London that day: "I was on the phone, in a cab going to Heathrow, when the second plane hit. My buddies in New York were describing it to me. At first we had a huge argument about what had happened – whether it was just a replay of the first plane. There was a human lack of ability to process." Joe Blauvelt and the Chase repo desk traders in Midtown also were watching the TV screens. "Despite all the usual frenzy, when the next plane hit, the entire floor stopped," Blauvelt recalled. "People put their heads down. We were in disbelief."[8]

Ron Purpora, one of Garban's senior executives, was in his home on Staten Island, packing for a vacation to Italy: "I was standing in front of my TV, wondering whether my staff in the South Tower was alive," Purpora remembered. "I tried to count the floors to see which ones the second plane flew into, but that was impossible."[9]

Some just heard the plane. Jets normally fly over Manhattan at 8,000 feet or more, and planes don't typically approach local airports by flying low over the harbor. Tom Costa, Chief Operating Officer of GSCC, was at his desk when the plane went past the building: "It was an extraordinarily loud roar, almost like when you're on a jet and the pilot has put the throttle wide open. And I instinctively knew that something was wrong."[10]

In the Morgan Stanley offices on the 70th floor of the South Tower, John Salemmo was close to the impact zone: "Within seconds, the drop ceiling panels were collapsing. And the walls were exploding fire from the electrical system. I thought to myself that it was a coin toss whether I was getting out of there or not."

The first staircase door that Salemmo tried didn't open; another one did. He moved quickly down five floors before the staircase became flooded with people: "At least twice, we lost the lights. The building often shook a bit, a repeated tremor effect." Salemmo and others tried to calm those who panicked, urging them to focus on one staircase at a time. Around the 20th floor, those walking down started to pass firefighters going up. "Looking back, it's just devastating," Salemmo recalled. "Those guys had no idea what they were walking into. No chance." After about a half hour, Salemmo made it out of the building.

Bill Peterson, of Morgan Stanley, had reached the concourse level of the South Tower soon after the plane attack. He later described the last part of his walk down:

> "At one point, there was some noise and the whole staircase moved, like a sailboat heeling. The lights went off, then came back on rather quickly. I lost my balance, and some people got knocked off their feet. Everyone started moving a lot quicker. A woman next to me, an employment lawyer who I worked with, said to me, 'Bill, are we gonna die now?' I didn't know what to say, so I decided to play John Wayne and said, 'I hope not!'"[11]

On the concourse level, Peterson saw "burning debris, and charred body parts strewn all over." He was directed by New York City firefighters and Port Authority police to walk through the underground plaza to the northeast side of the Trade Center complex. Standing by the post office on Church Street, Peterson spotted a burning jet engine sitting in the middle of Vesey Street. Several jumpers landed close to him including one person who fell on a firefighter, appearing to kill them both and sending Peterson into a state of shock. Finally, he was chased from the site by police. Peterson walked to Broadway, and got on a pay phone line. Then he heard "the most God-awful creaking sound."

"We Went Out into Thick Gray Smoke"

Just before 10 a.m., as the world watched on TV, the South Tower crumbled, emitting an ear-splitting noise and killing almost everyone who remained in the building as well as many people in the Concourse, in the Marriott Hotel, and on neighboring streets. Huge clouds of pulverized material and contaminants enveloped the area.

Raj Manian, an assistant vice president in operations for Citibank, had been on the last PATH train that made it into the World Trade Center.[12] He walked ten minutes up to his office in the Citi Investment Bank's headquarters at 388 Greenwich Street. By the time Manian arrived, the building was being evacuated. It would be converted for use by the Red Cross as a medical hub, with a mobile hospital in the courtyard.[13]

Manian decided with three of his friends to walk back down West Street to the World Trade Center to help. When they got within two blocks, the South Tower fell. They scrambled behind a parked construction trailer. "You could hear the debris hitting the metal trailer," Manian recounted. "Tat-tat-tat-tat. When the sound stopped, we looked out and saw the rubble of the South Tower. And people in the North Tower panicking."[14]

In the American Stock Exchange building, two short blocks from the World Trade Center, Ann Marie Hanley, a trader, heard a rumbling and then felt the building shake, to the point where she was sure it would collapse. Over a hundred AMEX staffers were left in the building. Hanley and a group of others went to the front exit, on Trinity Place, which was further from the South Tower, but a fire had broken out in a room near that exit and it was barricaded. The group then headed to the back exit, which led onto Greenwich Street across from the Towers, but the doors had been locked and chained by security staff. They ran up to the mezzanine level to a fire exit, which was also blocked. "At that point, people became hysterical," Hanley remembered. "Some were crying and saying their good-byes to each other. I found myself telling several colleagues, 'I love you!'"

One trader, Ryan McHogan, screamed at the crowd to keep a cool head, and led them back down to the rear door. This time, a dozen men working together broke the chains and opened the doors. Hanley followed the throng: "We went out into thick gray smoke that was blinding. We needed to go left, away from the World Trade Center, but at first we couldn't tell which way we were walking. There was dead silence. When the fighter jets flew over, we dove against the building and to the floor."

The crowd walked south on Greenwich Street, which was covered in debris that included landing wheels from one of the planes.[15] Two blocks down, at Rector Street, they were near George's Restaurant, a Greek diner that delivered to office workers in the area, when they passed a candy store with rubble blocking its glass door entrance.[16] They could hear people inside banging and screaming. A group of men stopped to find garbage cans from the street, which they used to break the glass and free those trapped inside.

Further north, on Broadway, Bill Peterson was still waiting in line to use a pay phone. When the South Tower fell, everyone standing in that queue ran. Peterson jumped on the phone and left a voice mail for his wife and his boss. Then he saw the debris cloud rushing toward him and took off. His determination to leave his wife a message saved his family from hours of anguish. Unbeknownst to Peterson, his 12-year old daughter, who had been told at her middle school that the World Trade Center had fallen, was sitting in the administrator's office screaming, "Tell me my daddy isn't dead!"[17]

Nick Gialanella had left the World Financial Center and was standing by the Hudson River when the South Tower fell: "First it was the sound. You didn't know what was happening, but there was this thunderous rumbling. Then people were screaming that the building is collapsing. And you had this vision of this 110 story thing falling on its side, on top of you. Everyone just ran."

At 80 Broadway, Tom Perna, BoNY's executive vice president in charge of government securities clearing, was standing by the floor-to-ceiling windows of BoNY's retail branch when he saw a rush of people running down Broadway. "People were getting thrown against the windows of the branch," he later said. "It was like when you're driving in your car and bugs splatter against the windshield." Perna and others inside hurried to the twin set of revolving doors at the branch's entrance. "It took about 15 minutes for us to get everyone in. In the crush to escape the debris and dust, people squashed against each other, with their arms and legs stuck in the doors."[18]

A maelstrom raced down the side streets surrounding the New York Fed building, with crowds fleeing ahead as in a Grade B horror movie.[19] The Fed's main entrance at 33 Liberty Street was shut. The employees' entrance on Maiden Lane, on the north side of the building, remained open, guarded by protection staff with shotguns. That staff had been instructed to lock the vaults, secure the building's perimeter, and clear the street to ensure that emergency vehicles could get to the Trade Center.[20] Recalled Jamie Stewart, the New York Fed's first vice president, who was in charge, "We assumed that we might be a target because of all the gold in our underground vaults."

Stewart's boss, Bill McDonough, was abroad.[21] Stewart was sitting with his senior team in his 10th floor office, which had become the New York Fed's war room, when he received a call from his security staff telling him that there were people on the street clamoring to enter the building: "My first reaction was that we shouldn't admit unknown persons, but then I heard that some people were smothered in the dust and suffocating from it. I told my staff, in that case, we've got to take care of them."

Panicked and choking men and women were huddled in the alcoves outside the Fed building, devoured by the dense billow, some banging on the doors. As they came in, each turn of the revolving door brought with them thick airborne filth that competed for space.[22] They were first made to hold their arms high, then screened, searched, and doused with water. Some were given treatment by the Fed's small medical staff at a facility inside the entrance, including a man who had broken his leg while running.[23]

Dave Gordon of G.X. Clarke, a small government securities firm, was standing at the north end of Chase Manhattan Plaza, across from the New York Fed building, hanging on to a cyclone fence: "The debris came in waves, it just kept piling on. I thought that any second a girder would hit me in the head. Everything got pitch black. And then it stopped. I had four or five inches of debris covering me. It was so toxic that I started spitting like crazy. I was leaning against the fence with my newspaper still under my arm. When I looked around, it was like a lunar landscape."[24]

"Everything Was Covered in Ash"

At 10:28 a.m., the North Tower collapsed, killing most of those inside and many on the streets below. The tower's fall released another blizzard of filth, which was sucked in by the ventilation systems of nearby buildings.

At the New York Fed, employees on the upper floors were relocated to space below street level. Jim McLaughlin, director for protection operations, had stood outside watching. He then went down to the lower, windowless levels to check on staff. Although he understood little about what was happening, McLaughlin tried to provide reassurance. After getting several strange looks, a friend suggested he go to the men's room. "My hair, face, suit...all were snow white," McLaughlin later said. "I must have seemed like a nut job."

Barry Mandel, a senior vice president in Merrill Lynch's Legal Department, was at 222 Broadway, a block and a half from the World Trade Center. He and his colleagues heard the second plane, and then could see people falling from the North Tower: "That really frightened us. We didn't know what to do, whether to leave or stay. So we stayed. Suddenly, there was a huge cloud coming towards our building, and debris began to hit the windows. No one had any idea what that meant. It became completely dark and again people began to freak out."

Mandel and others decided to evacuate the building. They walked down from the 13th floor, but when they reached the third floor, smoke began traveling up the stairwells. The air was acrid, making it hard to breathe. "We're in the dark and nobody understands what's happening," he recalled. They walked onto the floor, finding a large room with computer equipment and a separate air conditioning system. More than 50 people crowded into that windowless room, where they waited for over an hour. On the way out, Mandel passed a window:

"Everything was covered in ash. It was like a still picture, with the firemen and police just frozen there, and no vehicles moving. When we got to the lobby, it was a complete mess. Ankle deep dust that covered our shoes."[25]

Omer Oztan was a lawyer for the Bond Market Association. Not only did he see the second plane on TV but he also heard it himself. Initially, he remained in his office at 40 Broad Street, assuming that the BMA would need to put out a statement or press release regarding the status of the markets. Within an hour, realizing that staying might be dangerous, he and others took to the staircase, eventually becoming trapped in the lobby. People came in "looking like they were covered in powdered sugar from head to toe." Finally, they left the building, making their way east, then north. They passed the point at which Water Street intersects with Fulton Street, the site of a distinctive fountain with water cascading over a wall. People were bathing in it to wash off the residue covering their bodies.[26] The same scene was occurring just a few blocks north at the fountain at Foley Square.[27]

Sara Kelsey was General Counsel of the New York State Banking Department, located at Two Rector Street, just three blocks south of the Trade Center. She decided to walk with a colleague to the Brooklyn Bridge. "We were holding handkerchiefs to our faces," she remembered. "I had popped my contacts out and put on my glasses, and the lenses quickly became opaque. My friend wore his contacts throughout, and at the end of his trip home he had to go to a hospital emergency room because his eyes were damaged."

Where to Go?

Nick Gialanella and Peter McCarthy, a Refco colleague, both engulfed in soot, ran south along the path paralleling the Hudson River, towards Battery Park. They saw people leaping into the river to escape. Recollected Gialanella, "We ran through a set of hedges in the park, and found this guy who was digging a hole, trying to bury himself in it. He tells us to get in the hole, but we just kept running south." Gialanella and McCarthy ended up at the Americana Café in the Park, where people had broken the windows to take sanctuary.

Barbara Blumberg of Standard Chartered Bank was near Battery Park as well: "It crossed my mind that I might have to swim for it. Then a laundry service truck drove up. They opened the back door and started hurling out all the clean laundry they had. Tablecloths, towels, napkins, whatever they had in the way of linens, to help everyone wipe off the dust and cover themselves up."

Tom Russo, a prominent securities lawyer then Vice Chairman and General Counsel of Lehman Brothers, had watched the horror unfold from Three World Financial Center, the tallest of the Center's towers with a pyramid top. He organized the evacuation of Lehman staff. After leaving the building, Russo walked up the West Side Highway to meet his boss, Dick Fuld, at an office in Midtown. A police officer yelled at Russo to pick up the pace, because he had smelled gas and was worried that the gas mains beneath the pavement might explode. "I couldn't go any faster because I had knee problems and was in agony already," Russo remembered. "I wondered whether I should instead jump into the Hudson River and swim. I had a serious debate with myself, and ended up deciding – by about 51 to 49 percent – to keep going uptown by land."

Jean Donnelly and Murray Pozmanter were in the Nomura Securities operations control area at Two World Financial Center, which was evacuated onto West Street. Waiting by the Hudson River, they had a full view of the Trade Center. Donnelly could see people waiving undershirts, trying to summon help. Told by the police that more planes may be coming, they began to walk north, as a group, on West Street.

When the South Tower fell, Donnelly and Pozmanter were passing Stuyvesant High School, about a half mile from the Trade Center. "We heard a whining and thought it was another plane," said Donnelly later. "We started thinking about where we could take cover. Then we realized that it was the sound of steel melting. People were dropping to their knees and praying. And then there was all this smoke and we ran."[28] As the two continued north, shop owners were handing out water and inviting people to come in and sit down. Donnelly and Pozmanter ended up at Chelsea Piers, near 23rd Street along the

Hudson River, where free ferry service was being offered to New Jersey using World Yacht boats.

Meanwhile, following the second plane attack, the GSCC staff felt vulnerable being in a tall building in lower Manhattan. Some took the elevator, but most walked down 31 flights.[29] Many had no clue where to go. Tom Costa initially waited underneath the FDR Drive underpass: "I watched the buildings burn. There were little pieces of paper floating by me. I plucked some out of the air and recognized the names of the firms on the letterheads." Ultimately, most of the staff congregated across from 55 Water Street in a small covered arcade at Seven Hanover Square, next to Harry's, the famed restaurant they often frequented.

For GSCC's operations staff, the backup location was across the East River in MetroTech, a 16-acre business center in downtown Brooklyn, at the offices of the Securities Industry Automation Corporation (SIAC).[30] SIAC was the technology hub for the securities industry, responsible for running the computer systems and communication networks of the NYSE and AMEX.[31] When Dave Cosgrove stepped outside, he walked over to the Old Slip side of the building, noting that traffic was still moving on the FDR Drive. Cosgrove grabbed one of his staff, Carlos Cardentey. They jumped into Cosgrove's truck and headed to Brooklyn. It was a slow crawl; they were one of the last autos to get across the Brooklyn Bridge before police barred vehicular access to the public.

The rest of the GSCC staff remained at Seven Hanover Square, joined by others who had commuted in later. One of the technology employees arrived in a state of shock, telling his boss, Rob Palatnick, that he'd had to dodge people falling to the ground in front of him as he was exiting the Trade Center.[32] Some employees who were deemed "non-essential" were told they could go home. The decision to let non-essential workers leave was common on Wall Street that day, although a difficult one because management would be releasing staff into a dangerous environment. Early on, some who left buildings near the towers were severely burned when jet fuel poured onto them.

Allison Mansfield, new to the GSCC legal department, left to meet her fiancée who worked nearby. They joined the masses walking north. "The FDR Drive was filled with people," Mansfield remembered. "No one saying a word. Some were completely covered in dust. Many were crying."

The two walked to her apartment in the East 40s, passing residents from apartment buildings who had set up tables to distribute water and help the injured. After changing their clothes, they left to donate blood. The streets were now filled with people heading over the Queensboro Bridge. Both waited two hours to give blood, only to be turned away because the center lacked the resources to process everyone.

June Carey of Citibank's Global Securities Services had evacuated 111 Wall Street, a half block from the FDR. In the lobby of her building, a man had taken off his undershirt, ripped it up, and started handing out the pieces. "When in your right mind would you ever think that you'd take a piece of torn undershirt from a stranger and put it over your mouth? But it was a great idea and I kept it while walking on the FDR," Carey later said.[33]

Bart Schiavo, head of quality assurance for GSCC, joined the thousands on the FDR Drive. With a fine soot raining down that covered everyone to some degree, Schiavo soon gave his handkerchief to a man covered in filth. Many walked to Brooklyn, despite concerns that the bridges themselves might be targets. On the Brooklyn side of the Brooklyn Bridge, a cluster of ambulances and rescue workers had set up an open-air triage center, where police officers restrained sobbing men and women from going to Manhattan to look for their relatives.[34] Schiavo bypassed that bridge and also the Manhattan Bridge, where women prayed in front of a golden Buddha at the Manhattan entrance.[35] Instead, he walked another mile to the Williamsburg Bridge, on which automobile traffic had been stopped except for fire trucks and emergency vehicles heading toward Manhattan.[36]

Fran Glasser, an administrative legal assistant for the Depository Trust & Clearing Corporation, which handled back-office operations for much of the financial industry, had first headed over to Battery Park, her company's designated emergency meeting place. While searching for colleagues, the debris from the South Tower rushed towards her. Despite being in her 70s, she hustled to the FDR Drive: "There were trucks that had stopped with water supplies, handing out water to everyone for free." As she approached the Brooklyn Bridge, the North Tower fell. A black haze threatened above and the crowd walked faster. When U.S. military planes roared overhead, they could not be seen, causing panic. Then order returned and the procession continued, hindered by the discarded high heeled shoes that lay all over the area.[37]

After the second plane crash, word began to spread at the NYSE that the South Tower would collapse. NYSE head Dick Grasso ordered officials in the 23-story main building on Broad Street, known for its six immense Corinthian columns, to leave their offices and assemble on the huge trading floor, in case the tower fell onto the building.[38] He then locked the building down, not allowing staff to leave until around 1pm.[39]

Meanwhile, the GSCC staffers who remained at Seven Hanover Square were trying to piece together what was happening. Cell phone service was sporadic, and the BlackBerry was still somewhat of a novelty.[40] Along with others in the immediate area, they knew less than did TV viewers a continent away. Rumors of even more destruction ran rampant, including a supposed attack on the New York Stock Exchange, a story that was believable because of a giant smoke cloud advancing from that direction.[41]

When a wall of smoke and dust rushed down William Street, it enveloped the GSCC staff, among them Tom Costa: "I started to run, but got overtaken. It was hard to breathe because it wasn't just smoke. There were clumps of dust and crap in the air." Marc Golin, vice president in charge of membership, thought, "This was how I was going to die. I was convinced of it because I couldn't see across the street."[42]

Stranded in the Subway

Before the New York City Transit Authority had halted all subway service at 10:20 a.m., some made the choice to take the subway home. Kate Connelly, a GSCC vice president, walked over to Broadway and Wall Street, rushing onto a departing Lexington Avenue line train headed north, just before the North Tower fell.[43] The train went a hundred feet or so, starting to build momentum, when the brakes slammed and the lights went off. Connelly remembered:

> I was sitting between a Vietnam vet on my left and an NYU film student on my right. The student was around 20 – all excited because he had his camera and was filming the tracks and all the people in the car, giving his personal commentary. Then he asked aloud what all that "snow" was, and I responded that it was ashes. And he said, "Well, now you're scaring me!" All of a sudden his demeanor changed. He realized that this was serious, not just a nice opportunity for a school film project. On the other hand, the vet just sat there trying to read

the paper with the emergency lighting. He said that he had seen worse, and wasn't concerned. I was somewhere between the total calm of the vet and the sudden panic of the student.

Connelly and others walked through the cars to the front of the train, but they found no relief. When some people tried to open the car windows, they were screamed at, as that would just worsen the air quality.

After about 15 minutes came an announcement that the Transit Authority was aware the passengers were there and that someone would come get them. The lights went on briefly, but darkness soon returned. A half hour passed, and then came another announcement that the conductor would try to back up the train to the Wall Street stop. With the subway going only a few feet at a time before lurching to a stop, they eventually arrived at the station and walked out single file, holding hands.

Paul Saltzman, General Counsel of the Bond Market Association, earlier had also been trapped in a subway train that eventually let out at the Wall Street station: "We emerged at Trinity Church. It was all blackness and soot. Papers flying all over the place. Sirens. My first thought was that it was a nuclear attack. But then I saw a patch of blue sky as I looked down Broadway. I covered my face and walked to my office at 40 Broad."[44]

When Kate Connelly reached the subway platform, she was no closer to home than she had been hours earlier. Connelly and her fellow riders were led to the basement of a nearby building. They were asked to remain inside because the rescue vehicles trying to get to the Trade Center had little visibility to spot pedestrians. The group in the basement was calm for the most part, although some wept. One woman who jumped up screaming, "This is the Armageddon!" as predicted in the Book of Revelation, was quieted by others.

"Then all of a sudden, there were boxes of juice," Connelly recalled. "And I thought, if we're getting boxes of juice, we're going to live." Around 1:30 p.m., they were told they could leave. As they walked up Broadway, she noticed the discarded shoes. "They were in the middle of all of the ash, which was about mid-calf high. It seemed that every time you took a step it churned up shoes." Connelly walked several miles to Penn Station and took the Long Island Rail Road home.

Searching for Open Offices

Meanwhile, Rich Visco and Bob Trapani, two industry veterans, had been asked by Tom Costa to go to BoNY's building at One Wall Street. The hope was that BoNY, as well as Chase, would have available contingency space in the area for GSCC staff in case 55 Water Street was inaccessible. "So off we went," recollected Trapani. "Totally in the opposite direction from everyone else." They passed a friend of Visco's who yelled to him, "Dickie, where are you going? Are you out of your mind!" But Visco and

Trapani just laughed. "We were the only two schmucks walking towards the Trade Center," Trapani remembered.

Reaching One Wall Street, Visco stood in front of the building, using his size and strength to keep steady against the sea of humanity surging south down Broadway. Trinity Church was across the street; a solemn presence overshadowed by its surroundings.[45] Visco looked at the clock on the steeple. It was just before 10 a.m.

Trapani stood next to him. Both were already drained from having to walk single file for blocks against the crowd, at times shimmying around scaffolding poles to move forward. Now they were at a place they had been countless times before. But it was unfamiliar. The sky was raining paper, and the towers were on fire. They were searching for someone they knew, anyone who could let them into their bank's offices. It was futile. There was no plan for this. Only the ordinary had been expected that morning.

At first it was the sound: "pop, pop, pop." Metal bursting off a building. The South Tower yielding to superior force. Then Trapani noticed, out of the corner of his eye, the antenna at the top of the tower starting to come down. Suddenly, a cloud of smoke and debris hurtled at them. They started to run, finding separate paths to safety. Trapani sprinted down Broadway past the iconic statue of the bull, using his tie to cover his mouth and just barely staying ahead of the dense mass that chased after him. He reached the lobby of 55 Water covered in filth.

With a horde of others, Visco ducked into the lobby of One Wall Street to wait for the debris to clear and the smoke to subside. He left after about an hour, soon encountering a man walking towards the Trade Center with a bunch of wet towels folded over his arm. The man gave one to Visco to put over his face, and kept going. Visco thought about joining him, but instead headed back to his office to help figure out what was going on.

Some GSCC staff had gone directly from Seven Hanover Square back to their building. Dave Buckmaster was one of the first. The TV in the conference room was on, and a person watching told him that there now was military air cover. Buckmaster sent an email to his colleagues at 10:05 a.m., telling them it was safe to return to the office.[46] It was a gut call by Buckmaster, and a correct one, as staff was better off inside. Concerned about his son, who worked on nearby Pine Street, and his son's fiancée, who worked in the South Tower, he then made calls until he learned that they were safe. When the North Tower collapsed, Buckmaster heard it: "I could feel the souls rushing past me. I was sure there were tens of thousands who had just died." Black smoke encircled the building. Nighttime had come early.

Evacuation by Water

Many Wall Streeters, including Tony Scianna of SunGard, gravitated to Pier 11, just off the FDR Drive: "There were tons of boats coming in, including fishing boats, to take people off the island. So many that they were backed up. No one asked for a ticket or money. Some had medics. People helped you to wash your face off with eye wash. I remember the silence on the boat I was on, except for crying. As we got past the Statue of Liberty, headed to the Atlantic Highlands, at a certain point the sun was shining and the clouds dissipated. We looked back but could only see smoke."[47]

On 9/11, more than 400,000 people were evacuated from Manhattan by water. Most were taken to New Jersey, which could not be reached on foot; the only river crossings from Manhattan to New Jersey (except for the George Washington Bridge, in the far north end of Manhattan), are tunnels.[48] An ad hoc flotilla of tugboats, ferries, fireboats, work boats and private pleasure boats all participated, some acting independently and others under the direction of the Coast Guard. This waterborne procession, characterized as the largest since the evacuation of British soldiers trapped on the beaches of Dunkirk, France in 1940,[49] began minutes after the first plane attack, when the Coast Guard base on Staten Island put out a call for "all available boats."[50]

The use of watercraft was essential to the evacuation effort. By 9:15 a.m., the Port Authority of New York and New Jersey began closing New York City bridges and tunnels, including all five that cross into lower Manhattan, to all but emergency vehicles and pedestrians. Many morning commuters, stuck while approaching the New Jersey entrances to the Holland and Lincoln tunnels, stood outside their cars, watching the towers burn and collapse.[51]

After the South Tower fell, the Brooklyn Battery Tunnel, which connects South Brooklyn with lower Manhattan, lost both lighting and ventilation on the Manhattan side, forcing motorists to abandon their cars in the tunnel as smoke and debris poured in. Many in the tunnel were directed by firefighters to a makeshift triage station on Greenwich Street just south of the Trade Center.[52]

Workers who were headed back to New Jersey faced particular difficulty. Around 10:30 a.m., New Jersey Transit stopped all rail service into Manhattan's Penn Station, and by 10:45 a.m., the PATH train from New Jersey to Manhattan ended its service.[53] Omer Oztan waited for a ferry to New Jersey at Chelsea Piers in a line that stretched for many blocks: "There had to be 150,000 to 200,000 people waiting. Even with the ferries running constantly, it took me over two hours to get on one."

A Million People Fled – But Many Stayed

Around 11 a.m., via a telephone call broadcast on television channel New York 1, Mayor Giuliani urged New Yorkers to remain calm and evacuate lower Manhattan. "If you are south of Canal Street, get out. Walk slowly and carefully. If you can't figure out what else to do, just walk north," he advised.[54]

Manhattan is the most densely populated urban area in the United States, and on 9/11 more than one million people living and working in lower Manhattan fled.[55]

But thousands of Wall Street employees remained in the area. A core group of GSCC staffers made calls to family and friends. Most of Rich Visco's friends from his old neighborhood in Flatbush, Brooklyn were cops or firemen. When Visco called home, his wife told him that his brother, a fireman stationed in Brooklyn, though off duty that day, had been called in after the towers fell. Crying hysterically, she pleaded with Visco to get out of Manhattan. "I kept telling her that the crisis was over, that our planes were in the air," Visco recollected. "Of course, there were rumors that our building was next."

It's estimated that at least 200 people fell to their deaths that morning. Nearly all were from the North Tower, which was struck first and collapsed last. (Fewer than a dozen were from the South Tower.)[56] People on the top floors could no longer cope with the heat generated by the blazing jet fuel. One of those who fell from the North Tower killed Danny Suhr, a 37-year-old firefighter. Suhr worked in Engine Company 216 in the Williamsburg section of Brooklyn. He was the first firefighter to lose his life that day.

By mid-day, Visco had heard this news. Suhr was one of his best friends. "I grew up with him in Brooklyn, playing football together since we were

12," he recounted. "We were pretty tight as kids, always in each other's houses." Suhr had been an outstanding football player – a *New York Daily News* all-city lineman in high school. He and Visco still played together on the Brooklyn Mariners, a semi-pro football team.[57] When he learned of Suhr's death, Visco walked to an isolated area on the floor, sat on a radiator, and held his head in his hands as he wept. Through word of mouth, Dave Buckmaster found him. Visco insisted that he needed to go to the Trade Center to help, but Buckmaster convinced him that he could best be of assistance by staying at work. Visco didn't go home until Friday night, three long days later. As he approached his door and saw his wife, he blurted out, "I can't believe Danny's dead!"[58]

Throughout the morning and afternoon on Tuesday, the evacuation of Manhattan continued, by foot, boat, and auto. As Fran Glasser walked up the FDR Drive, she noticed that cars were stopping to pick people up. Initially reluctant to get into a car with a stranger, Glasser knocked on the window of one, driven by a young insurance broker who lived in Chatham, New Jersey, and asked to hitch a ride. Not being allowed to exit the FDR in Manhattan, they took a much longer route over the Tappan Zee Bridge, which connects Westchester and Rockland Counties in New York, and then drove back down the Palisades Parkway to get home. "We stopped at a rest area to get a bite to eat and use the bathroom," Glasser recalled. "I go in the ladies room and look in the mirror. My hair was snow white. I shook my head and the dust and soot came down my face, which was now white and black."

Meanwhile, the scene on the New Jersey side was chaotic. Jean Donnelly's ferry took her to Weehawken, across the Hudson River from midtown Manhattan. From there she walked south two miles to the Hoboken train terminal: "When we got on the train, there was a bomb scare, so they evacuated us. At that point, we were numb. The bomb-sniffing dogs went in to check. Then we got back on."

Later in the day, the Hoboken terminal was shut down, and converted to use as a triage center. A MASH unit was set up for survivors and rescue workers.[59] June Carey had taken a ferry to Jersey City, landing near the Colgate clock, and then walked north to the Hoboken terminal. By the time she arrived, in the early afternoon, the trains weren't running. Carey took a bus to Newark: "When we got off the bus, the local fire department was there with hoses set up. They were looking at the crowd, and pointed to me and called me over. I'm told that I need to be hosed down, because I was covered in dust. But I said no, because I thought the huge hose would knock me down. They tagged me as someone who wouldn't be de-contaminated. Then they took my blood pressure and let me go on my way."

Nick Gialanella had taken a ferry to the floating dock at the Atlantic Highlands on the north end of the Jersey shore: "People on the boat were filthy and bloody, and trying to get napkins and the like to clean up," he later said. Medical and army personnel were at the ferry terminal, where showers had been set up. "When you came off the boat, people were hugging you. It was like you came back from a war."

The fear caused by the collapse of the two towers reverberated in midtown Manhattan. The burning smell had traveled north, and there were rumors that the Empire State Building, once again the tallest building in the City, was next to be attacked. Larry Lemmon worked for HSBC Bank on 39th Street, near the Empire State Building, which had been shut down by 9:30 a.m.[60] Lemmon later described the environment: "At times, they would ask people to move away from the windows facing the Empire State Building to the other side of the floor. From where I sat, I could see the top of that building, and I couldn't help but feel that, if it fell, it would fall on me."[61]

For those GSCC staffers who remained, much of the day was spent trying to determine the status of member firms and locate colleagues. A group of them slept in the office that night, discomforted to see a view of New Jersey where once the Trade Center had stood. Many camped in their offices for the rest of the week. The first night, Rob Palatnick's young son left a message on his voice mail saying he heard that planes were crashing into buildings and they were falling down, and asking his dad to come home. Palatnick stayed.

Others left in the late afternoon or evening, walking into a desolate landscape. By Tuesday evening, 1,500 National Guardsmen had been mobilized, pervading the downtown area.[62] A panorama of wrecked cars and buses lay near the Trade Center. A figurative snowstorm had descended, leaving inches of burnt paper and other residue on the streets that were sent flying whenever fire trucks and emergency vehicles drove by. Bill Langan, a GSCC vice president, walked over the Brooklyn Bridge and reported that the smoke and soot didn't let up until he was half way across.[63] Steve Greenberg, head of marketing, left the area after sundown: "Very few lights. New luxury vehicles abandoned in the middle of the street with their doors open. And few people other than troopers."[64]

Bob Trapani decided to go home that night, "because my kids didn't grasp the concept that I was okay." He took one of the last ferries to Jersey City, where he was met by volunteers offering comfort and drinks. A woman gave him a ride to the Hoboken train terminal; she told Trapani that she had been shuttling people from the ferry to the train terminal all afternoon. As they reached Washington Street, Hoboken's main drag, Trapani noticed that "people were dining outside with their bottles of wine, as if nothing had happened. A few miles away, you had this catastrophe going on. Weird."

Nikki Poulos, GSCC's associate general counsel, also left late in the day, catching a ferry from Pier 11 to Jersey City. In the evening, when putting her four-year-old son to bed, he asked her, "Why did the building fall? Didn't they put nails in it?"[65]

Around midnight, Jim McLaughlin and his friend Charlie Duffy, a fellow ex-cop also working in Protection at the New York Fed, walked a couple of blocks to the Holiday Inn on Gold Street to see if there were any available rooms. Passing Zeytuna, a deli across from the Fed's building, they saw dozens of pieces of fresh fruit caked in dust, reminiscent of nuclear winter.[66] The lobby of the hotel, dimly lit with emergency power, was thick with guests lying on chairs and on the floor, refusing to go back to upper-floor rooms. The desk clerk told McLaughlin and Duffy that they could have a room free of charge. Instead, they headed to the hotel bar.

Two hours later, McLaughlin, knowing he wouldn't be able to sleep, walked back to 33 Liberty Street. It's an old building; even with all the doors and windows closed, dust and ash had seeped in through the seals.[67] Maintenance staff were busy cleaning the lobby floors. McLaughlin grabbed a vacuum cleaner and joined them.

CHAPTER 4

THE MOST CRUCIAL GLOBAL MARKET

*"The consequences of the failure of the
Treasury market were unfathomable. If it
hadn't come back, the repo market would
have closed. The Government then couldn't
have conducted monetary policy, and the
liquidity premium that the Government
enjoys would have been decimated. Our
ability to restore the marketplace literally
saved the taxpayer billions of dollars."*
Eric Foster, Associate General Counsel,
Bond Market Association[1]

The financial world has changed enormously
since 2001, but the U.S. government securities market
was and remains the single most crucial global
financial market. It is a massive one, with an
aggregate dollar value of trading vastly larger than
that of the equity markets.[2] The Govie market also is
widely regarded to be the most liquid market; the one
with the highest efficiency of pricing and trading. [3]
Dealers and "buy side" entities, such as banks,
insurance companies, and pension funds, use
government securities extensively for funding,
investing, risk mitigation and even speculation.[4]

At the foundation of the Govie market are the
securities issued directly by the Treasury
Department.[5] U.S. Treasuries are the most widely

held debt instrument globally.[6] At the end of 2000, the amount of marketable Treasury securities was $3 trillion.[7] Treasuries are supported by the "full faith and credit" of the U.S. government. Therefore, in times of crisis, the Treasury market typically becomes the focus of investors' "flight to quality" (the rush by investors to buy safe securities). The safety and liquidity of the market allow the Treasury Department to borrow at the lowest possible cost to fund the U.S. government.[8]

U.S. government securities are not just Treasuries.[9] They also include "agency" securities, which are obligations of government-sponsored entities such as Fannie Mae, Freddie Mac, Farmer Mac, and the Federal Home Loan Banks that were established by Congress to facilitate lending for socially-important purposes such as education, agriculture, and housing.[10] On 9/11, agency securities, which included mortgage-backed securities, were popular investments because of the agencies' high credit ratings and the government's sponsorship and supervision.[11] The near equivalence of agency securities to Treasuries would change later in the decade, when the subprime mortgage crash that began in 2007 led regulators to place Fannie Mae and Freddie Mac into conservatorship a year later.

The Govie market encompasses different types of trading,[12] including derivatives transactions, of which the most significant on 9/11 were the Treasury futures traded on the Chicago Board of Trade.[13] The most critical type of government securities activity engaged in on 9/11 was *not* in plain buy and sell transactions but, rather, in "repo" transactions involving government securities as collateral.[14] The buy-and-sell and repo markets are integrally related because repos are the principal method by which dealers fund their inventory and trading positions in government securities.[15]

Repos have been in use for almost a century.[16] They're the means by which broker-dealers tap into the liquidity of cash-rich entities such as mutual funds and pension plans to obtain financing, as well as to invest cash or borrow specific securities.[17] Banks are dependent on short-term financing, and Govie repos are a key source.[18]

The U.S. Govie and global markets are interwoven. Treasuries serve a vital role as "benchmarks" that are used to price other fixed-income securities and to set rates on a range of financial instruments, including mortgages, car loans, student loans, mortgage-backed securities, and structured debt like collateralized debt obligations.[19] And Govies are used extensively by institutions to manage risk by acting as hedges for positions taken in other markets.

The prospect of an operational disconnect between buyers and sellers in the Govie market, even for a brief period of time, was unsettling. Impairment of that market would have left financial institutions without a basic means of obtaining critical short-term funding. Essential risk mitigation would have been limited. The normal method for markets to price and set rates on a wide range of financial instruments might have been lost. And the ability of the federal government to conduct monetary policy and, even more essentially, to fund itself, would have been put in question.

Markets are rational; they anticipate change (such as Y2K), adapt to it, and price for it. But no one forecast 9/11 or the potential for widespread devastation of operational structure. From such unexpectedness and sudden shock can come chaos, and a loss of confidence that underpins the financial markets. A stark example of this came seven years later when, on September 15, 2008, the insolvency of a single large investment bank, Lehman Brothers, even though anticipated by some, led to the seizing up of global funding and credit markets.[20]

In a crisis, investors worldwide seek shelter in U.S. government securities. What if that market isn't functioning? The psychological impact alone would be enormous. The perception of financial well-being and the integrity of the economic system worldwide could be shattered.

How did the Govie market become such a vast and essential one? To understand, we have to look back to its origins.

The First Government Securities

The U.S. national debt originated in 1775 when, within a week of the Battle of Bunker Hill, the Continental Congress authorized the issuance of $2 million in bills of credit, called "continentals," to finance the Revolutionary War.[21] By the end of the war, continentals had become nearly valueless, and repayment to the holders of Revolutionary War bonds and securities was uncertain.

When the Constitution was adopted in 1787, it gave to the new Congress, and deliberately not to the individual states, the power to borrow on the credit of the United States.[22] Two years later, the Department of the Treasury was formed, and Alexander Hamilton became the first Treasury Secretary. On January 9, 1790, Hamilton submitted his "Report on Public Credit" to Congress. In it, he proposed that the new federal government assume all foreign, domestic and state debt (which totaled more than $77 million) as its own obligation, by issuing bonds that would pay interest and eventually be retired. Hamilton insisted that unqualified maintenance of the national debt, with the government having the authority to levy taxes in support of it, was "a matter of high importance to the honour and prosperity of the United States."[23]

However, a group in Congress strongly opposed federal assumption of the states' Revolutionary War debt. Initiating a debate that continues to this day, Thomas Jefferson characterized the national debt as a "monstrous fraud on prosperity."[24] The southern legislators, whose states had relatively small debts, argued that federal assumption would be unjust. [25] Virginia's James Madison, in a debate in the House of Representatives on April 22, 1790, declared that, "if the public debt is a public evil, an assumption of the state debts will enormously increase and, perhaps, perpetuate it."[26]

Ultimately, a compromise was reached. Hamilton agreed to support the move of the nation's capital to the District of Columbia, in exchange for the southerners' support of the state assumption legislation. Thereafter, in the Funding Act of 1790, the Treasury Department consolidated and refinanced all of the remaining debt from the Revolution.[27] This action marked "the birth of the U.S. investment markets."[28] Two years later, the New York Stock Exchange was established, and U.S. government debt became the main type of security traded on that exchange.[29]

Government securities dominated trading in the 1790s, and U.S. debt quickly came to be considered "prime credit," as evidenced by Napoleon's comfort in selling the Louisiana territory to the United States in 1803 for $11.25 million in new Treasury bonds (plus cancellation of certain debts).[30] In the U.S., for much of the 19th century, bonds – both government securities and private debt – were sold door-to-door, with some firms sending salesmen out on bicycles.[31]

The Impact of War

Total Treasury debt remained fairly small in the first half of the 19th century, and for a short time, during the presidency of Andrew Jackson, it was eliminated. Private debt was greater; for much of that time, railroad obligations constituted the largest segment of the long-term bond market.[32] This meant that only a rudimentary government securities market was possible. The trading in government debt that did take place was handled mostly by private banking houses that bought and sold bonds over-the-counter for their own account.[33]

As would be true throughout U.S. history, war created a need for significant additional government bond issuances. To raise funds to fight the War of 1812, President Madison and Treasury Secretary Albert Gallatin used the country's two principal financiers – Stephen Girard of Philadelphia and John Jacob Astor of New York.[34] In May 1846, the United States went to war with Mexico over the annexation of Texas and California, and Congress authorized additional debt to meet these obligations.[35]

The Civil War also was paid for by massive bond issuances. That war cost the nation more than $5 billion in expense, creating an enormous expansion of government debt. As the Civil War dragged on, the federal government was forced to completely overhaul its financial organization to cope with the debt burden.[36]

To sell debt securities, the North needed a currency supply for citizens to pay for them. In 1862, the Legal Tender Act was passed, which authorized the Treasury Department to issue not only $500 million in bonds to fund the war effort but, also, $150 million in Treasury notes, known as "greenbacks."[37] Congress required citizens, banks, and local governments to accept greenbacks as legal tender for public and private debts.[38] Congress then imposed for the first time a federal income tax to help pay for the war,[39] establishing the Internal Revenue Bureau within the Treasury Department to oversee the collection of excise and income taxes.[40]

Once the Civil War was over, the public debt began to be paid down. After 1866, there were 28 continuous years of budget surpluses, as revenues poured in from tariffs and land sales in the West. Thereafter, a financial panic and a decline in tariff revenues took hold, followed by the cost of the Spanish-American War in 1898. During that time, successive Treasury Secretaries redeemed public debt securities to place money back into the economy, often buying securities at a premium in the open market.[41]

The 20th Century

The first modern-day government securities dealer was C. F. Childs & Company, set up in Chicago in 1911. Until that time, brokerage houses, such as J.P. Morgan & Co., transacted in fixed-income securities only as part of their overall activity. They bought and sold those securities on a commission basis, mostly on the New York Stock Exchange.

C. Frederick Childs, born of privilege in Vermont and educated at Yale, believed that he could establish a successful firm that dealt only in federal and local government securities, and that would make its money not on commission but through the spread between bid and ask. The first bond issuance handled by the firm was debt issued at the behest of President Theodore Roosevelt to finance the completion of the Panama Canal. C.F. Childs was so successful that two years later, when the Federal Reserve System was established, the firm's staff members were invited to acquaint Fed personnel with the workings of the Govie market.[42] Within a decade, three new government dealers had been established – Salomon Brothers & Hutzler, Discount Corporation of New York, and First Boston Corporation. Each of these firms would become a significant market participant and outlast Childs.[43]

In 1917, Congress enacted the Second Liberty Bond Act, which gave the Treasury Secretary the authority to issue direct obligations.[44] Between 1917 and 1919, the Treasury issued debt totaling $21.5 billion, at that time the largest financing in U.S. history, to finance American involvement in World War I. These bonds were popular in part because the interest on them was not taxable.[45]

Until the 20th century, the Treasury Department generally auctioned its own debt. After the Federal Reserve System came into existence, the New York Fed distributed bonds to banks and brokers, which in turn sold them to customers, setting a lasting precedent for the Treasury's use of the Federal Reserve as its agent.[46] The Fed took over the function of handling original issuances of Treasury debt, leaving dealers to work in the secondary market and to bid on the Treasury's subscriptions.

The huge growth of the national debt after the United States entered World War I required a much broader market than had existed earlier.[47] Initially, this need substantially increased the trading of government securities on the New York Stock Exchange.[48] The Treasury Department supported this development by channeling its outright transactions through the exchange. However, by the mid-1920s, increased use of the telephone had led to a sizeable over-the-counter (OTC) Govie market.[49] Stocks started to dominate the NYSE, and the volume of trading in government securities in the OTC market came to far exceed that done on the exchange.[50]

In 1933, the Federal Open Market Committee was formed to oversee the Federal Reserve's open market operations, including the buying and selling of government securities.[51] In the 1930s, the New York Fed conducted open market operations on the floor of the NYSE.[52] Finally, in 1939, the Fed created a "Government Security Dealer Group" to build a closer relationship with the largest dealers, which it called "recognized dealers." It restricted its open market transactions to those dealers, and began informal surveillance of the Govie market (a practice that lasted into the 1990s).[53] By 1960, this had evolved into a "primary dealer" system, established by the New York Fed as a way to select counterparties for executing its market operations and to help it compile data on activity in the government securities market. Initially, there were 18 primary dealers, all of which were obligated to regularly buy and sell Treasuries.[54]

Before Franklin D. Roosevelt's presidency, the national debt tended to increase only during special circumstances, such as war or acquisition opportunities, and thereafter it would decline. But in response to the Great Depression, FDR fostered an expanded role for the federal government.[55] Roosevelt's domestic spending during the 1930s brought the debt to $49 billion by June 1940. The country's involvement in World War II raised the national debt exponentially to $259 billion by the end of the war.[56] In one year alone, 1944, federal government expenditures exceeded the total of those made during the *130 years* from the signing of the Constitution to the beginning of World War I.[57]

To allow for the cheapest debt financing of the war, the Treasury Department requested that the Federal Reserve commit to maintaining a low interest rate on government bonds. The Fed complied. But conflict between the Treasury and the Fed came to a head in 1950 when the Fed wanted to raise rates amid rising inflation, while the Treasury sought to ensure cheap financing for both the Korean War and the Truman Administration's domestic priorities.[58] The Fed prevailed in the "Accord" of 1951; since then, there has been continued questioning of the appropriate balance between the Treasury's fiscal policy objectives and the Fed's monetary policies.

The Govie market, vast in size but relatively small in number of players, has throughout history been overshadowed by its equities cousin, and the role of a Govie dealer or broker has been little documented. The day-to-day experiences of those active in the Govie market during the first two-thirds of the 20th century are largely lost.

The Govie market would evolve ever more radically beginning in the 1970s. Those involved in it then and later would shape the environment that existed on 9/11.

CHAPTER 5

HOW THE MODERN GOVIE MARKET DEVELOPED

"After a trade was done, it could take days to find out for sure what the profit or loss on it was. At E.F. Hutton, traders kept a hand record during the course of the day of trades done and money made. After trading ended, a 'wag sheet' would be passed out to all of the traders, on which they would estimate what they made or lost. That gave management an idea of what the floor did for the day. What did 'wag' stand for? 'Wild Ass Guess.'"

Jerry Rubin, long-time Govie bond trader[1]

Until the 1970s, the Govie world remained clubby and opaque. Trading was dominated by a select group of dealers. Many people, even those in the financial industry, didn't know that a professional Govie market existed. Or they misunderstood it; a common question asked of Govie traders was what they would pay on a client's savings bonds.

Dealers dealt directly with each other based on individual agreements, up to pre-set amounts that were miniscule by modern standards. If the New

York Fed were to designate a firm as a primary dealer, that firm was then allowed by convention also to trade through the inter-dealer brokers, which would preserve the anonymity of its activity. The federal budget deficit was low and there were a relatively small number of active securities. Many issues were illiquid and traded infrequently – "by appointment" was the phrase used. There was little price transparency, particularly for non-primary dealers. A firm would give out different prices to different customers, maximizing the spread obtained from each.

Traders were predominantly white men. In 1975, Chas. E. Quincey & Company, a small primary dealer, held a partners meeting solely to decide whether to promote a woman, who was a back-office star, onto the trading floor. One of the partners, Griff Clarke, argued against moving her and cast the lone dissenting vote. Years later, he married that woman. "She never let me forget that vote!" he recounted.[2]

A trader typically would be assigned two or three securities to make a market in. For each issue that he handled, a dealer or broker might call and ask him to quote an offer. The trader spent much of his day calling dealers with which his firm had trading lines (or one or more inter-dealer brokers), buying on the bid and selling on the offer. Spreads between bid and offer were large, which meant high profit potential for traders and fat commissions for their brokers.

To protect himself from being price-gouged, a trader needed information, which was normally obtained by frequent chats with other traders with whom he had built a relationship. Information was swapped on what was showing in an issue. Is there a bid? What's the latest offering? Where's the market? A good trader also studied the spreads in other, possibly more active issues to determine by correlation what made sense in the security that he was trading.

Technology was primitive; it hadn't changed much since the introduction of telephones in the early part of the century. The modern innovation was the desk console allowing for direct telephone connections to other firms through the punch of a button. Access to basic pricing and volume data was difficult; essential market information often had to be looked up in bound volumes of charts and statistics. Complicated bond computations were done with a hand calculator, as real-time analytics were not embraced until Bloomberg LLC introduced its terminals in the 1980s.[3]

Govie issues were listed on a sheet provided daily to traders by a number of firms, the most popular one being distributed by Discount Corporation of New York,[4] a primary dealer. Dealers used chalk boards to keep track of price changes; smaller brokers were known to project bids and offers from an overhead onto a bed sheet. Usually, the rookie on the desk marked price changes in an issue on a large board for the benefit of everyone in the trading room; those revisions would occur because of a transaction or simply because the trader wanted to change the market that he had.

After executing a trade, the trader would hand-write its key terms on a ticket, which he would put in a nearby box. Buys were written on black tickets, and sells on red tickets; a common quip was that, if trading was really slow, the tickets became yellow. Every half hour or so a position clerk, who sat in the trading room, would come by and collect them. The clerk would record each ticket by hand on a sheet, noting the type of security and its maturity, price and par amount. Afterwards, he would take the tickets to the back-office, where a confirmation would be created for each, also by hand. Then another clerk would check to make sure that the terms of the confirmation matched the ticket written by the trader. Operations staff also would compare the records of the position clerk with their records, and they couldn't go home until those records balanced. Finally, the tickets would be organized by dollar amount and delivery date, after which a messenger took them to the dealer's clearing bank.[5]

Settlement of trades was labor-intensive because government securities were represented by physical certificates. In 1966, the Treasury and the Fed began a process of converting all Treasuries to "book entry" (electronic) form, although it took two full decades before the last Treasury security was issued in paper form.[6] Into the 1970s, clearing banks kept stacks of paper securities, each normally representing

$100,000 or $500,000 in value, in huge metal containers resembling rolling vaults. A small-volume customer might have only a drawer, whereas a larger one could have a full "truck."

Each day, a clearing bank would send dozens of runners all over the Wall Street area, carrying certificates to and from its broker-dealer and bank clients to settle trades. Dave Gordon, who began his career at Chas. E. Quincey & Co., remembered: "You had to give the bank precise delivery instructions. It would be something like, 'Subbasement B at Irving Trust.' If you didn't get to the right window, you'd get 'DKed' ['DK' means 'don't know the trade,' which leads to it being rejected]." The bank would keep track of expected "receives" and anticipated deliveries on a large blotter that indicated each certificate involved. All certificates had to be examined to ensure that they were correct for the transaction, were not counterfeit, and had any necessary coupons attached.

As the bank's operations staff tried to match receives with deliveries, entries were penciled in and erased throughout the day. Naturally, reconcilement problems arose constantly. A significant challenge for operations staff was meeting a delivery requirement when its inventory didn't suffice. For example, if $50,000 was required to complete delivery and the bank had certificates only in $100,000 denominations, it might send a certificate to the New York Fed to get it "split," a process that could take a day or more. Alternatively, if the bank wanted to make a million dollar delivery and needed one more $100,000 certificate, the staff would have to wait for it. "You'd be hanging around for a runner, who might be in a nearby pub having a few," Gordon recalled. "So you'd go try to find him because you only had nine certificates."[7]

There was no regular process for offsetting deliveries against payments. On a particular day, to settle 250 trades, a bank might literally send its runners out to make 250 deliveries and get back 250 payments made by check.[8] Then the operations staff would have to determine which check completed which delivery. On top of all that, there was the constant risk of a runner losing certificates or having them taken from him.[9]

The method of establishing the terms of a trade and confirming that both parties accepted it as legitimate was particularly burdensome for the inter-dealer brokers, who normally had a large number of trades executed with various primary dealers on any given day. After the end of the trading session, around 4:30 p.m., a broker would begin to "check out" with his customers the trades done during the day, many of which had been executed in the early morning. Often, the broker would have to change the price or par amount to ensure that it matched what had been agreed to with the counterparty. Then he signed the trade ticket, which would be inputted by middle-office clerks into a master "trade log."[10]

There were no taping systems. If there was a dispute on the price or amount, traders negotiated with each other to resolve it. Usually, they'd compromise, likely leaving both sides irate. Sometimes, the trade would be canceled. Errors perceived to be "honest" and made in the heat of battle usually didn't cost the relationship, which was critical. As market veterans agreed, once a trader got a reputation for going back on trades, he was "done."[11]

Political correctness and modern business ethics hadn't yet arrived, and a locker room mentality prevailed. The language of the trading room was rough; few bothered to censor themselves. It was common to have strippers come in for office celebrations. College athletes were actively sought as traders by some firms, adding to the competitive, "boys' club" atmosphere. Jews and Italian-Americans, who had difficulty finding career opportunities at commercial banks, gravitated to the brokerage firms. And for women seeking a job on the trading floor, as one long time market participant observed, "In the sixties and early seventies, gals were generally hired based on the size of their chest."[12]

Dealers had much discretion over whom to trade with, making personal connections essential to getting business. Traders bonded constantly over dinners, drinks, and sports events. Some traders delved even further into strip clubs, drugs and hookers.[13]

It was particularly vital for the inter-dealer brokers to cultivate relationships, as they couldn't readily distinguish themselves to dealers based on how effectively they executed trades. Dealers had their favorite brokers; often this rapport was based on the broker making available all that New York City had to offer. Brokers prided themselves on their access to prime tickets to the hottest sports and entertainment events. One market veteran remembered, "It was all about how expensive the bottle of Bordeaux was, or sitting in the front row at Knicks games. For super duper customers, it was going to the Super Bowl." [14]

A representative story, dating back to 1975, was described years later by Ed Watts, then a young operations professional at Goldman Sachs:

"A Chorus Line" had opened to rave reviews. The show immediately was sold out for a year. You couldn't get tickets even from a ticket broker. And it was my parents' 35th wedding anniversary that weekend. I was leaving that Sunday on a business trip, so I had to do something by Saturday. I was telling this to one of our brokers. Next thing I knew, someone calls me up and offers to pick me up on Saturday in a limo, which would then go pick up my parents and drop us off in the theater district in Manhattan, where we would have dinner and then see the show in fourth row center seats. And then the limo would take us home. And I went. We had no restrictions then.[15]

Lavish gift-giving, at times including cars and jewelry, was common. The brokers' "entertainment" expenses came to be a major part of their budgets,[16] and even decades later, when regulatory limitations on gift-giving and entertainment had become much stricter, it was estimated that brokers spent as much as $500 million a year for this purpose.[17]

In general, entertainment knew few boundaries. Carroll McEntee & McGinley, a Govie firm, was renowned for the annual St. Patrick's Day party it hosted at the Midday Club at 60 Pine Street. One attendee reminisced: "People would fly in from all over the country to attend. The party got big enough in the later years that you needed a ticket to get in. The Irish music played so loud and people danced so hard, it seemed like the building vibrated." William E. Pollack, another Govie firm, for years threw a similarly lavish Christmas party for hundreds of clients at the Copacabana night club.[18]

In the summer, golf outings abounded, many of which were sponsored by brokers. Traders would work in the morning, then get picked up by limos that came with "hostesses." After a round of golf and a copious dinner, there would be a raffle of expensive gifts. "If there were 144 players, there were 144 prizes. And you weren't allowed to win twice," reminisced Watts.

Raucous humor ran rampant. When a 30-year Treasury bond issue was introduced in 1980 carrying a 10 percent rate, the securities were dubbed the "Bo Dereks" after the beautiful actress who had come to prominence the previous year in the Blake Edward's film "10." Others called them the "DC-10s," after the plane that crashed right after takeoff from Chicago's O'Hare airport in 1979, killing all 271 on board. Practical jokes were prevalent, often coming at the expense of rookie traders. A common one involved traders and their brokers conspiring to run up trades on a fake issue, creating hundreds of thousands of dollars in "losses" in a day. The novice would then have to explain the event to his boss, who was in on the ruse.[19]

Computer Trading Screens Arrive

In the 1970s, computer technology revolutionized the Govie market with the introduction of electronic screens for securities trading. The first screens widely used for Treasuries were produced by Telerate Systems, a firm founded in 1969 by Neil Hirsch with venture capital financing.[20] Hirsch was a 21-year old college dropout who worked as a clerk in a Merrill Lynch brokerage office. He observed that, although stock quotes were readily available on computerized terminals, information about the prices of other securities could be obtained only by calling around to various dealers. Hirsch recognized the need to expand the terminals to include the fixed-income markets.

Telerate began by making available commercial paper prices, which were gathered from dealers in that instrument.[21] Cantor Fitzgerald had just entered the Govie market as a broker, using

Telerate to offer price quotes on government securities. The other inter-dealer brokers refused to reveal their price information to non-primary dealers, but Telerate provided its screens to any company willing to pay, including non-dealers such as mutual funds, breaking the monopoly on Govie wholesale pricing information.[22]

Another pioneer in automation was Henry Watson, who left Cantor in 1973 to create his own version of an electronic Govie market screen. A Goliath at six-foot-six and weighing more than 300 pounds, wearing a scraggly beard and disheveled clothing, Watson walked from broker to broker with a shopping cart loaded with electronic equipment, asking each to invest $500,000 in his idea. Every broker threw him out except one, Garvin, Bantel & Company, which was run by Anita Seitz. Seitz knew Watson because he had worked for her as a funds broker years before. She provided the funding, and an automated arm of the company, called "Garban," was born.[23]

By the early 1980s, every broker offered its own screen to dealer customers. A trader at a primary dealer, who had access to every broker, often would sit with a set of six small screens, known as the "six-pack," piled up in front of him.[24] The screens didn't provide for automated trading; a trader still had to call a broker to put in a bid or lift an offer. His screen of choice was based not on how well a broker could advise on the markets (brokers were notorious for being the least knowledgeable people in the business) but, rather, on the strength of the personal relationship.

The screens crowded a trader's desk, throwing off a tremendous amount of heat. If the air conditioning system was inadequate, the trader was drenched in sweat by the end of the day. When one was removed, often because it had burned out, dust would fly up. Frequently a mouse or two, likely present because traders normally ate at their desks and always had food around, would scamper from the empty space.[25]

As screen trading became more dominant, increasing competition and transparency, the spreads between bid and offer narrowed, reducing dealers' profits. Some shifted to making money in the Govie market by taking on proprietary risk. They studied relationships between different issues and then sought to arbitrage them. But, gradually, those distortions on the yield curve disappeared.[26]

By the 1980s, many dealers also had developed an institutional business, speaking regularly to major clients and servicing their accounts. Such market making often was a loss leader, but it gave dealers insights as to when and to what extent large institutions were buying and selling issues. A dealer then would take its own position, just following the flow that it was aware of.

The competitive posture of the brokers changed as well. To force a reduction in commissions, many of the primary dealers got together to form their own broker, Liberty Brokerage, in 1986. The other inter-dealer brokers were compelled to make continuous commission reductions for years afterward.

But there were countervailing forces that favored the brokers. The dealer community became much larger, eventually including the sizable Japanese firms Nikko, Nomura, Yamaichi and Daiwa as primary dealers. With the dramatic growth of federal deficits by the early 1980s, the magnitude of the Govie market and the number of active issues exploded. Dealers broke apart the Treasury curve, fragmenting it into shorts, intermediates, longs, and other products such as zero coupons. No longer were there just bill, coupon, and agency traders; now there were specialists in Treasuries with specific yearly maturities, and a clear market for every issue. These factors, plus the fall in the cost of transacting, magnified the brokers' volumes. As Ron Purpora recalled, "From the mid-eighties to the mid-nineties, Garban had a string of great years, because even though we cut commissions three or four times, the volume doubled or tripled every time we did that."

Screen trading made the Govie market more professional. Time spent in phone conversations morphed into hours staring at a screen. As one long-time trader remembered, "When the screens came in, entertainment went down and the business became less fun. You didn't have the relationships you once had. Eventually, it became totally impersonal."[27]

Dealers opened offices in London to access the London mid-day prices – and indications of prices –

to get their New York morning started effectively. Then came Tokyo offices, to service the Asian trading hours. The brokers, of course, followed suit. This market globalization was made possible by its automation; the physical location of the business no longer mattered. Unfortunately, this didn't translate into most firms leaving lower Manhattan by 9/11.

A Simple Market Becomes Complex: Mortgage-Backed Securities and Financial Futures

Bond trading complexity increased dramatically in the 1970s. Govies became more than just straightforward debt instruments. In 1970, mortgage-backed securities (MBS) were introduced when Ginnie Mae first guaranteed a pool of mortgage loans. This new security represented a claim on the cash flows from mortgage loans purchased from banks, mortgage companies, and other originators and then pooled. This later evolved into a market in which banks and thrift institutions "securitized" their real estate loans by dividing pools of mortgages into slices and selling pieces of those to investors.[28] Securitization helped banks alleviate the maturity imbalance between long-term loans and the short-term deposits that financed them.[29] Significantly, it allowed mortgage originators to sell mortgages rather than retain them as an illiquid asset, a development that would lead to enormous negative consequences decades later.

In 1977, Salomon Brothers seized on this development, establishing the first separate MBS trading desk, led by Robert Dall and his deputy, Lewis Ranieri. Within a few years, it was the most profitable trading operation on Wall Street.[30] By 9/11, the MBS market had grown to more than $3 trillion in securities outstanding.[31]

The MBS market had a transformative effect on the Govie market. Mortgage traders hedged their long positions by selling cash Treasuries, driving up volume and affecting pricing in that market.[32] When rates came down, there was a prepayment increase that shortened a trader's mortgage portfolio; to maintain duration, traders would buy long-term notes, adding fuel to the fire of the falling yields. With the growth of this dealer market, the inter-dealer brokers soon got involved as well, to facilitate trading and provide anonymity.

Another new market was introduced in this decade: futures contracts based on financial commodities. Previously, the futures markets had been exclusively the domain of agricultural products, providing farmers with a price guarantee for their future deliveries. Forward contracts in wheat, soybean, and corn traded on the Chicago Board of Trade had dominated the futures markets for decades.

The intellectual foundation for financial futures was laid in 1971, when Milton Friedman published, "The Need for Futures Markets in Currencies."[33] The following year, the International Monetary Market opened in Chicago, listing seven foreign-currency futures contracts. By the mid-1970s, with inflation rising and interest rates more volatile, financial futures were extended to interest rate products such as Treasuries. The Chicago Mercantile Exchange (CME, or the "Merc"), which was founded in 1898 as the Chicago Butter and Egg Board, became the site for the short end of the yield curve and the Chicago Board of Trade became the home for the long end. [34] An entirely new arena for Govie trading had been created.

At first, financial futures were met with resistance. Established firms argued that they weren't a true hedging vehicle, just a speculative one. Many didn't know how to use them. Some futures had curious and confusing features such as being tied to an eight percent coupon bond and a range of deliverable issues, which itself created arbitrage opportunities. And there was concern from the Treasury Department and the Fed about the effect of these futures contracts on their operations.

Initially, the cash market led the futures market, which was viewed as a second-class citizen. But gradually, the tail began to wag the dog, and financial futures came to exhibit the type of liquidity previously found only in the cash market. More people could trade futures than cash because of leverage; they only had to put up initial margin (cash or other liquid collateral to support potential losses on outstanding trades) and then maintenance amounts. Govie and MBS firms heavily employed futures for hedging, introducing stability into the market because its use wasn't purely speculative. By the 1990s, the Fed would not auction securities if the Chicago Board of Trade was closed on that day. Dennis Dutterer, a long-time futures industry senior official, recalled, "It was a recognition that we weren't exactly someone selling beads on the street or a three-card Monte player. We were real."[35]

A symbiotic relationship between cash and futures developed. Because traders and customers knew there was an outlet in the futures market to lay off risk, they took larger cash positions, and vice versa. In later years, there would be attempts to directly link the cash and futures markets. Leading up to 9/11, Cantor Fitzgerald and the Chicago Merc were planning for cash Treasury bond trading by exchange members on the floor.[36]

All of the major developments in the Govie market in the 1960s and 1970s, amid rising inflation and interest rates, required traders to have increasingly sophisticated mathematical expertise to analyze bonds and their payment streams. As a result, mathematicians, particularly those with computer programming knowledge – known as "quants" – entered the world of bond trading. Perhaps the most famous quant was Martin Leibowitz, who joined the Salomon Brothers bond department in 1965 with the informal title of "house mathematician." Leibowitz was key to the development of MBS, fixed-income indexes, zero-coupon bonds, and bond portfolio measurement tools.[37] Decades later, there would be a backlash against the financial markets' dependence on quants, and a cry to inject more "common sense" into forecasting how markets will behave.[38]

Failures and Loss

While trading in the Govie market continued to grow during the 1980s, the market itself remained essentially unregulated, as it had been since its inception, because the Securities Act of 1934 specifically exempted U.S. government securities from its key provisions. The SEC, as overseer of the securities markets generally, had no authority in the Govie market except for cases that constituted fraud. Firms that dealt exclusively in government securities were free of formal government supervision,[39] which assisted the Treasury in selling debt at the lowest possible level.[40] "Why regulate a 'safe' market?" was the mantra.

Yet serious problems lurked beneath the surface in this market. The economy plunged into a deep recession in 1981-82, and the unemployment rate reached 11 percent. There also was a stunning rise in interest rates in the early 1980s, facilitated by the Fed policy of targeting monetary reserves instead of the federal funds rate.[41] Dealers had to finance their holdings at rates many basis points higher than the yields on the underlying securities, resulting in large losses. Even when rates started to drop, firms couldn't load up on securities because of the expense and difficulty of financing them. The asset-liability mismatch led to the failure during that decade of numerous thrift institutions, which were holding long-term fixed-rate mortgages and bonds.

Financial and accounting practices and controls were weak in the Govie market. Some Govie firms functioned with minimal, if any, true capital.[42] Nor did they have to take into account, in pricing securities, the value of the interest that had accrued to that point and that would be payable to the buyer on the next coupon date. Daily mark-to-marking of positions wasn't required; securities were booked at par when they were worth well less than that. Firms that engaged in repos on behalf of clients routinely held both the customer's money and securities pledged as collateral, readily allowing for game playing, if not outright fraud. Losses could be transferred through journal entries to an unaudited affiliate as a receivable. Many of the small broker-dealers, playing in a highly volatile interest rate market, became overleveraged.

There also was an inadequate legal framework for the market. [43] Significantly, the vast repo market operated without a fundamental understanding, much less clear guidance, as to whether a repo was a purchase and sale or a secured loan, a distinction that is critical in the event of a participant's bankruptcy. [44]

Not surprisingly, a number of government securities dealers suddenly went out of business during the first half of the decade. The first insolvency occurred in May 1982 with the collapse of Drysdale Government Securities Inc., which had been spun off from a 92-year-old brokerage house called Drysdale

Securities Corp. Drysdale Government Securities, which operated out of a fifth-floor attic above a clothing shop, was reputed to be using sophisticated trading strategies based on a secret computer program named "Arnold." Drysdale's main activity actually was taking advantage of the repo market's inadequate pricing convention. If a firm bought a Govie outright, its purchase price would include the interest that had built up to date. On the other hand, if the firm obtained a Govie through a reverse repo, as Drysdale did in bulk, it didn't pay for this accrued interest but, instead, gave the interest payment to the seller only when the coupon matured. Drysdale used this device to acquire a huge reverse repo book at a discount, though this game lasted only a few months.[45]

Many major dealers traded with Drysdale. But because of its small size and minimal capital, they booked Chase Manhattan Bank, which cleared for Drysdale, as their counterparty. When Drysdale went under, Chase initially denied responsibility for making good on Drysdale's trades.[46] After moral suasion from the New York Fed, Chase reversed its position, absorbing a $250 million loss.

The Drysdale matter was resolved without damage to the overall market. The event had a silver lining because, as a result of the weaknesses exposed, "full accrual pricing" eventually was adopted as standard market practice. This meant that accrued interest would be included in full in all purchase and resale prices.[47]

Yet the wave of government securities dealer insolvencies continued over the next three years, including Lombard-Wall,[48] Lion Capital,[49] E.S.M. Government Securities,[50] and Bevill, Bresler & Schulman.[51] These failures resulted in Congressional hearings on the safety of the government securities marketplace, held in 1985 and led by Tim Wirth, Chairman of the House Telecommunications Subcommittee. On the basis of those hearings, Wirth and another House Democrat, John Dingell, were planning to introduce a bill that would bring all government securities dealers under the supervision of a new panel called the Public Securities Rulemaking Board, which was modeled after the Municipal Securities Rulemaking Board.

During that time, Tom Russo ran into Wirth at a cocktail party. Days after the collapse of Drysdale in 1982, Russo had written an op-ed piece in *The New York Times* arguing that "unless Congress holds hearings regarding the ramifications of the Drysdale affair, and does something to prevent future defaults, we may not be so lucky the next time around."[52] At the party, Russo told Wirth that his proposed legislation wouldn't work, because the Govie market was quite different from the muni marketplace. Wirth responded, "If you're so smart, why don't you write the bill?"

Russo, who had worked at the SEC early in his career, agreed to write the bill *pro bono*. Soon after, he married and left with his bride for a honeymoon at the Villa d'Este in Italy. Sitting at a pool that floats on

Lake Como, Russo began to write the bill, faxing portions of it at a time to SEC and Congressional staff who helped craft it into legislative language. "Apparently, there's a rule that you should not write a bill while on your honeymoon," he recounted. "Because someone said to my new wife, 'Isn't it terrible that he's doing work now?' She replied, 'I'm reading a novel. He's reading something else. What difference does it make?' And I thought, this is a great woman."

Russo's original draft gave oversight of government securities dealers to the Fed, because of its independence. "The Treasury has its own interests to watch. It's hard to be objective in the seat that they're in," he observed. But the Senate changed the bill to give regulatory and rulemaking authority to the Treasury Department, on the theory that the Treasury would ensure the implementing regulations addressed the need to finance the federal debt at the lowest possible cost.[53] The following year, the bill evolved into the Government Securities Act (GSA), which was signed by President Reagan.

The GSA provided for the regulation and registration of government securities brokers and dealers for the first time. Surprisingly, this requirement actually pleased some firms, because they were losing customers to full-service broker-dealers that were regulated by the SEC and therefore perceived as safer.[54] Pursuant to its new authority, the Treasury Department also issued various rules for government securities broker-dealers relating to recordkeeping, examination, capital adequacy, and the protection of customer securities and funds.[55]

The 1986 legislation ended the "Wild West," unregulated days of the Govie market. It was followed by amendments in 1993 that granted authority for the establishment of sales practice rules for market participants, requiring them to furnish transaction records to the SEC on request.[56] Some urged that the 1993 revised legislation impose an obligation for real-time trade reporting, which in hindsight could have lessened the massive settlement and reconcilement problems caused by the events of 9/11, but that requirement was dropped.[57]

The timing of the GSA's enactment converged with the establishment of the Government Securities Clearing Corporation as the central utility for the Govie market.[58] Securities trading is intertwined with and dependent on the processes that occur after the trade is done. GSCC grew out of the great need for enhancement of the market's "back-end" practices.

In the 1980s, these procedures, still largely manual, were little changed from decades earlier. Firms' Govie trading volume had grown to the point where it overwhelmed operations staff. The large dealers traded all day and then, after hours, their clerks called each counterparty to confirm the trade. (Written confirmations followed only on the next day.)[59] That verbal confirmation process was supposed to catch any differences in price, CUSIP number, settlement date, or other key trade details.[60] But given the number of trades, sometimes discrepancies weren't caught until the following day, which was settlement day for most Govie trades. Any delay in finding errors would create further settlement headaches.

Firms attempted to minimize the processing of large trade volumes by offsetting buys and sells in the same instrument. If, for example, Dealer A bought $50 million in a security from Dealer B and, on the same day, Dealer A sold $40 million to Dealer B, the two firms would agree that those two trades could be considered a single buy by Dealer A of $10 million from Dealer B. This simple math process was known as "netting"; thus, the $10 million buy was considered a "net position."[61]

The netting systems employed by these firms were bilateral only, unlike the multilateral netting process across all market participants that the National Securities Clearing Corporation (NSCC) offered on the equities side.[62] For Govies, different net positions had to be established with every trading counterparty, limiting the process' value.

Nor was even bilateral netting done in the growing repo market, because of the larger size of trades. Every repo trade generated a hand-written ticket that was settled individually. As volume grew, firms just kept hiring more back-office staff, which became expensive and unwieldy. There was a limit to how much overhead a trading desk could support.

In 1984, Bill Tierney was running operations for Salomon Brothers, which had the largest Govie desk. Tierney pulled together a group of senior operations guys from the top firms and announced, "We can't continue this way." Tierney then arranged a series of meetings with Dave Kelly, who ran NSCC, and convinced the NSCC board and management to set up an equivalent clearing corporation for Govies.[63]

The formation of the Government Securities Clearing Corporation was actively supported by the Federal Reserve, for many reasons. One was the Fed's concern about the potential insolvency of a major firm and the consequences for the marketplace if that happened. For example, Drysdale's failure might have put a few dealers out of business if Chase hadn't stepped up and taken on Drysdale's positions. What was needed was a central guarantor. The Fed didn't want that role; rather, it asked the private sector to devise a solution, which would be a clearing corporation that risk-managed and guaranteed the settlement of Govie trading. The Fed's lawyers also felt that the bilateral netting done by firms didn't have a solid legal underpinning and might unravel if a firm went bust.

The New York Fed was further disturbed by the frequent delays in the closing of Fedwire, its large value payments network, because of the bunching of securities deliveries at the end of the day. For the most part, securities were released by firms over Fedwire just before it closed at 2:30 p.m., after their operations staff had spent the earlier part of the day building collateral to make their biggest delivery obligations. Operations guys prided themselves on how well they knew their system and being able to press the "deliver all" button at the last possible moment just before Fedwire closed. Wall Street wags on the operations side would joke that, in their building, "the elevators went down a lot faster than they came up," meaning that they would send securities out the door for payment more quickly than they would take in securities deliveries and pay for them.

Many of the last minute deliveries made by a firm would turn out to be unnecessary because the underlying trades had already been settled through the bilateral netting process. But often there would be no time for the receiving dealer or broker to determine the validity of the delivered securities and either reject them or send them on to another firm that had bought them. Firms frequently would return securities during the "reversal time" on the Fedwire that followed the 2:30 p.m. close, further muddying the waters.[64]

A market participant that got stuck with securities at the close of Fedwire had to finance them overnight. That was difficult for firms in the early 1980s, when interest rates were sky-high, particularly for the brokers, who worked on narrow spreads. Nor did the clearing banks want to lend a lot of money overnight to brokers, which had little capital.[65]

GSCC's operations began in August 1988 when its comparison system was introduced.[66] This new centralized and automated system, which handled the reporting, validating and matching of Govie transactions, eliminated the need for confirmation calls and paperwork.[67] The comparison system was a prelude to a more ambitious initiative: the netting system, which was implemented in July 1989. It provided for the offsetting of settlement obligations on a comprehensive scale (Figure 3). For each firm's trading in a security issue, the netting system would add up the obligations to buy securities and pay cash and, separately, the obligation to sell securities and right to receive cash, and take only the "net" (or difference) between the two sums.

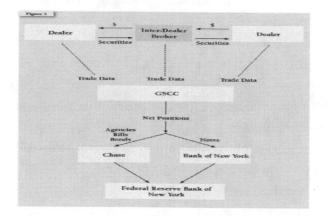

The introduction of GSCC initially was not welcomed by the large dealers, because the clearing corporation "leveled the playing field" from a counterparty credit perspective, taking away some of their inherent advantage. It also diminished a dealer's ability to play the "fails game," where it made money if another dealer did not timely deliver securities to it, by earning interest on securities while not having to pay for them.[68]

Separately, the three remaining clearing banks at the time – Bank of New York, Manufacturers Hanover Trust ("Manny Hanny", which was acquired by Chemical Bank in 1991 and by 9/11 had morphed into JP Morgan Chase Bank), and Security Pacific – feared that the new netting process would eliminate a large number of required deliveries, greatly diminishing their revenues. In 1985, when Chuck Moran, who was responsible for Manny Hanny's securities services operations including clearing and settlement, first heard that GSCC was a serious proposition, he thought, "We're not going to be in that business for much longer." Ironically, Moran would become the first president of the new company.

None of these fears proved well-founded, as everyone involved in the Govie market benefitted from the efficiencies created by the netting system and the consequent expansion of the market. GSCC members, particularly the brokers, realized tremendous operational savings as the number of settlements dropped markedly.

The clearing corporation also brought significant risk protections to the Govie market for the first time by guaranteeing settlement of all eligible trades and requiring daily margining and marking-to-market of positions.[69] This risk protection provided valuable comfort to the Govie market on various occasions. One example was in August 1992, when Fundamental Brokers Inc., an inter-dealer broker, fell below minimum regulatory capital standards and was on the verge of going out of business. GSCC issued a notice assuring members that it would guarantee settlement of trades between Fundamental Brokers and all other netting members, thereby calming market fears.[70] In 1995, the netting system was expanded to include repos, further revolutionizing and broadening the market by allowing many more firms to safely engage in long-term repo activity.[71]

The 90s: A More Egalitarian Govie Market Emerges
The 1990s was a decade of strong economic growth and a boom time for the financial markets. Scandal arose once again, this time triggered by the actions of a giant: Salomon Brothers. Salomon arguably was still the premier bond firm. As a long-time Salomon trader remembered, "Its trading volumes were extraordinary. If you wanted size in the fixed-income market, you went to Solly. If you joined Solly, it was for either fixed-income trading or sales. Until the 1980s, Solly owned the fixed-income markets."[72]

In August 1991, Salomon admitted that it had violated Treasury auction rules by systematically submitting billions of dollars in fraudulent bids from August 1989 to May 1991. In certain instances, those actions resulted in Salomon being awarded more than 35 percent of the auction amount, a violation of the Treasury's rules.[73] The crisis widened when Salomon admitted that three senior executives had been told of one illegal bid but none had informed the government. Salomon managed to avoid an indictment, but paid $290 million in fines and penalties. A number of senior executives resigned, including Chairman and CEO John Gutfreund. Warren Buffett, Salomon's largest shareholder, became CEO.[74]

The process for conducting Treasury auctions was archaic. Written bids were due at the New York Fed's window at 33 Liberty Street by 1 p.m. on the day of an auction. Some firms still sent runners to deliver their hand-written bids, while others had employees camped out by the telephones in the Fed's lobby. The scene was described by a former SEC Commissioner as being "right out of Dickens."[75]

Salomon Brothers' misconduct led to radical change in the Treasury auction process. Participation was broadened beyond primary dealers and large commercial banks. Better controls were put in place, including stronger enforcement of auction rules.[76] The auction structure changed from a multiple-price format, in which successful competitive bidders paid prices computed from their own bid yields, to a single-price format.[77] Meanwhile, the Treasury introduced electronic bid submission processing, which dramatically reduced the time between the close of bidding and the announcement of results, materially lowering bidder risk.[78] The scandal led to other, more unexpected changes, including allowing the inter-dealer brokers to expand their customer base beyond just the primary dealers.[79]

With the safety of the Govie market enhanced, federal regulators turned their attention to ensuring adequate "price transparency." Timely and accurate price information is critical to the operation of any market. It is particularly vital for Treasury securities, as Treasury yields are used daily to value a variety of fixed-income securities, futures, options, swaps, and other derivative instruments globally. But current market prices and yields on Treasuries weren't widely available beyond the inner circle of the market.

The situation in the Govie market stood in stark contrast to that in the equities market. Since 1960, equities market participants had available to them an automated price quotation system called "Quotron." The bond markets had lagged behind in automation, forcing traders to rely on data the New York Fed compiled by surveying five primary dealers each day.[80] Some transparency had arrived in Chicago during the 1980s thanks to the volume and liquidity growth in the Treasury futures market, where pit traders, often referred to as "cowboys," would knock down a million dollars or more in profit or loss a day.[81] Any investor going into the Chicago Board of Trade to hedge would be able to see market prices.[82]

In 1989, the General Accounting Office published a report recommending increased price transparency in the Govie market. That report was followed in 1990 with a proposal for Congress to require the inter-dealer brokers to make transaction prices available to the public.[83] The private sector was wise enough to get ahead of the government: the following year, the primary dealers and four inter-dealer brokers formed "GovPX" which provided 24-hour, worldwide distribution of real-time information on Treasury securities, such as price and size of best bid and offer. Over the years, GovPX expanded its coverage to include agencies, swaps, and repos.

GovPX information was made available on the Internet, and became distributed by all of the major vendors of securities information, including Bloomberg and Reuters.[84] Initially, some feared that this would sound the death knell for the Govie market by ruining spreads and liquidity. What it actually did was encourage small players to enter the market. Armed with wholesale price information, they no longer feared being taken advantage of by the large dealers. As Ed Watts recalled, "Governments became very attractive, because buyers felt they weren't overpaying any longer."

Before the late 1990s, bond-trading screens displayed quotes from dealers only for the purpose of helping to initiate voice communications.[85] Then the Govie market made a true shift to automated trading that would reveal active trading prices, allowing dealers to immediately hit live bids and lift offers.[86] In 1999, Cantor Fitzgerald introduced eSpeed, the first electronic bond trading platform, blurring the distinction between broker-dealers and exchanges. A consortium of dealers quickly launched a competitor, named BrokerTec.

A similar transition had already occurred in other markets. In the equities world, by the early 1990s, electronic communications networks (ECNs) such as Instinet had developed, enabling trading to be conducted around the clock and off exchange floors. Like the stock exchanges, the ECNs collected, displayed and executed customer orders, matching trades through algorithms.[87]

In the futures arena, "open outcry" trading made way for a variety of new electronic trading systems that matched trades virtually instantaneously. In 1998, Eurex, a German-Swiss all-electronic exchange opened for business; within two years, it had surpassed the Chicago Board of Trade as the world's largest futures exchange.[88] The large-scale pit traders who still controlled the Board of Trade fought the new trend, but eventually recognized that electronic trading was inevitable. They could stand in front of this train only so long.[89]

With electronic trading (which caused GovPX to lose some of its relevance), all pricing information is provided to the market at the same time; traders take positions based on their forecast of changes in the economic, regulatory or political environment.[90] Automated trading ensured that the smallest customers got the same opportunity as the largest ones. No longer was it a matter of getting called first or having the best relationship with the broker. For that reason, many large dealers weren't happy with the advent of eSpeed and BrokerTec; they were drawn into this new world kicking and screaming.

Electronic trading proved to be yet another development that drove transactional costs lower, leading to more volume.[91]

By 9/11, eSpeed and BrokerTec had begun to capture an increasing share of the Govie trading activity. Although voice brokerage systems remained popular, industry analysts were speculating on the eventual demise of the traditional inter-dealer broker firms.[92] On the institutional side, there was an explosion of on-line fixed-income trading systems that came and went, with names like BondUSA.com, BondLink, TruMarkets, Visible Markets, BondConnect and BondBook.[93] The most successful one was Tradeweb, launched in 1998 by several large dealers, with its offices in the North Tower. Tradeweb, which provided institutional customers with an on-line marketplace for U.S. Treasuries, quickly amassed a trading volume of $40 billion per day.[94]

Many large dealers began creating their own proprietary electronic trading platforms, providing their customers access to bids and offers. Each platform had a built-in analytics system; based on the client and the size and nature of the trade, it calculated how many basis points north or south of the spread the dealer would need to have a profitable trade.[95]

Electronic trading enabled firms to handle huge trade volumes with a small staff and to better manage risk and protect themselves by focusing just on the firm's net position.[96] It further removed the traditional "physical constraints" from the marketplace.[97] Someone participating in the Govie market in a totally automated way could do so anywhere in the world. The introduction of electronic trading in the 1990s was of enormous help in the recovery of trading after 9/11, when offices were abandoned, voice brokers lost, and telephone communications nearly impossible.

Further proving invaluable on 9/11 was the financial industry's preparation for Y2K, the threat posed to systems by changing the clocks from 1999 to the new millennium. At least for the larger firms, that preparation involved establishing enhanced contingency plans and backup facilities.[98] Businesses had to consider how they would operate in the event core systems and processes failed. As a result, by 9/11, the financial industry already had made improvements not only to backup systems but, also, to decision-making and communication channels, including developing lists of emergency contact numbers for financial institutions, regulators, and key infrastructure providers.[99]

Heading into the summer of 2001, the dot-com bubble had burst, the economy was softening, unemployment was rising, and recession loomed. Moreover, the Fed had cut interest rates seven times during the year to bolster the economy, which had been booming just a year earlier.[100] It was a unique time for the Govie market because by 2000, the U.S. had achieved three straight years of budget surplus, and Treasury debt was shrinking relative to the size of the economy and the capital markets. There was even talk of eliminating the national debt. Govie trading trailed off, leading primary dealers to shift activity to the corporate debt markets. Overall, the debt markets were having a banner year, with record issuances and profitability.[101] Then the world changed forever.

CHAPTER 6

DECISIONS: CLOSING THE MARKETS

"It was important to keep the system running as smoothly as possible, and continue to make sure that individuals throughout the country had access to banks. Or else there might have been a contagion effect on households across America, who were already traumatized by what they had seen on the TV screen."

Roger Ferguson, Vice Chairman, Board of Governors of the Federal Reserve System[1]

On 9/11, Alan Greenspan, Fed Chairman, and William McDonough, President of the Federal Reserve Bank of New York, were in Switzerland for an international bankers meeting.[2] Nonetheless, even before the first tower fell, the Fed began to communicate. Acting on Greenspan's behalf, Vice Chairman Roger Ferguson sent a message to banks over Fedwire assuring them that the system was "fully operational at this time and will remain open until an orderly closing can be achieved."[3]

A formal Fed announcement to the public was needed. Ferguson, the only one of the seven Federal

Reserve Governors in Washington that day, drafted a succinct statement: "The Federal Reserve System is open and operating. The discount window is available to meet liquidity needs." Before releasing it, Ferguson initiated a call with all of the 12 Reserve Bank Presidents or their senior staff to "take the temperature around the country."

During the call, held around 11 a.m., some participants argued that the Fed should close down and declare a bank holiday, to give banks and other financial market participants time to recover. Ferguson rejected that idea, wanting the Fed's key tools in a crisis – Fedwire, the discount window, and currency operations – to be available as needed. He also was concerned about creating a potential crisis of confidence.

Around noon, the Fed issued Ferguson's statement.[4] "I decided to keep it to two sentences and not talk about the broader economic system," Ferguson recalled. "The main message had to be clear." After the Fed's announcement, the FDIC, in reaction to numerous inquiries received regarding the effect of the 9/11 events on federal deposit insurance, issued a statement of its own: "The public can rest assured that deposit insurance is in full force - money is safe in an FDIC-insured account."[5]

In the afternoon, Jerry Hawke, the Comptroller of the Currency, released a proclamation giving national banks discretion to close offices that had been affected by the emergency situation. The statement contained the expectation that only those bank offices directly affected would close, and that even those offices "should make every effort to reopen as quickly as possible to address the banking and liquidity needs of their customers."[6]

On the morning of 9/11, Hawke was worried about his brother, who worked on the 54th floor of the North Tower (it turned out that he had escaped the building with just minutes to spare). Hawke was stuck in Dallas at an Office of the Comptroller of the Currency compliance conference with his senior staff. "We convened a war council at the hotel and spent the next two days communicating with our D.C. office and examiners in charge of the major banks, trying to find out what the problems were. Essentially running the office in exile," he recounted. By Thursday, realizing that they might not get a flight out for days, Hawke and three others rented a van and drove 24 hours to D.C.

In the late afternoon of 9/11, the Fed organized a phone call among the various senior market regulators. During the call, it was suggested that President Bush be advised to declare a banking holiday on Wednesday, in part to prevent a run on the banks. Ferguson dissented: "I felt that would take a very serious and challenging problem in Manhattan and maybe Washington and make it into a national problem. I could only imagine the challenges of closing and then restarting the banking system." Hawke was asked to gather more intelligence; then the group swiftly reconvened. Hawke's advice was to not declare a holiday, and the issue faded.[7]

In the following days, to prevent financial organizations from defaulting on their obligations and creating a widespread liquidity crisis, the Fed provided banks with more than $323 billion in funding.[8] And it greatly expanded its securities lending program to become a primary and ongoing source for dealers to cover their short (borrowing) positions. As lender of last resort, the Fed incurred after 9/11 what was, at the time, its largest balance sheet ever, well over a trillion dollars. Recollected Ferguson, "I fielded a number of phone calls from a variety of bankers asking if we would be willing to accept different types of collateral at the discount window. It didn't push us to do anything extraordinarily unusual. We made it quite clear that we were good to our word around discount window lending. And that proved to be critically important over the course of the next few days as the system started to right itself."[9]

The central bank's assurance was welcome and calming. The banking and payments systems remained open; their abrupt, unscheduled closure could have stalled the global economy. The U.S. stock exchanges, which had not yet opened when the attacks began, would remain closed. But what about the government securities market, which had already opened? There was no precedent for suddenly closing a market on a day when it had been actively trading for hours.

Closing the Markets

Many crucial decisions were made regarding the U.S. financial markets on 9/11. For the Govie market, the most fundamental one was whether, and how, to declare it closed. After the second plane hit in Manhattan and the nature of the events became obvious, volatility spiked, particularly in the active issues. But then volume faded quickly. Most firms were physically unable to operate or had evacuated their personnel. Of the inter-dealer brokers, only BrokerTec, which was based in Jersey City, continued to make a market for part of the day, until trading halted completely within a few hours.[10]

In Chicago, the two major Chicago futures exchanges – the Chicago Board of Trade and the Chicago Mercantile Exchange – had opened at 8:20 a.m. New York time, and pit trading in Eurodollars and Treasury bonds was underway. Soon after the events began, that trading experienced some dramatic price moves, then stopped, and both buildings were evacuated.[11] Closing the Treasury futures market had been an easier process, given their floor-based nature.

At the Chicago Mercantile Exchange, a small group of senior executives – Scott Gordon, the Chairman, Jim McNulty, the CEO, Craig Donohue, the General Counsel, and Phupinder Gill, head of the Merc's Clearing House Division – had conferred immediately after the second plane struck, deciding to shut down the floor and the exchange. Gill had already heard from many exchange members and staff. "With the exchange being a prime target for terrorists, people were afraid for their lives and wanted to leave," Gill recalled. "I had gotten calls from many other traders with the exact same message. 'This isn't like a pipe burst in the building and you evacuate until the pipe's fixed. It's not the time to be heroes, the exchange better stop trading.'" The building emptied swiftly, except for Gill and a few staff members who stayed to allow the exchange to finish processing and to distribute reports for the day.[12]

A similar mass departure occurred at the Chicago Board of Trade, which was shut down by late morning. U.S. stock index futures were trading when the attacks began. They immediately plunged in value, even though the crash initially was understood to be an accident.[13] As the equity floor traders started to evacuate the building, Tom Hammond, the Chief Operating Officer of the Board of Trade Clearing Corporation, which handled the settlement of the CBOT's activity, rushed over to the pit. He implored a few key traders to stay a bit longer to provide closing prices, in order to ensure an orderly market settlement.[14]

Bernie Dan, soon to become President of the CBOT, was an executive vice president at the time: "We got 6,000 people out of the building because of rumors of bombs. Me and a couple of other guys locked the doors and left in the late afternoon. It was my shortest drive home ever. There was no one around." While managing the evacuation of the CBOT's landmark skyscraper building in the Loop, the commercial center of downtown Chicago, Dan received a frantic call from his brother and sister-in-law. Their son had graduated from college in May and had just completed a training program at Goldman Sachs. His first day of work was on 9/11, in the Trade Center. Dan reached out to every Goldman official he could find. By the afternoon, he had located his nephew, who was safe.[15]

That morning, the New York Stock Exchange had announced it would remain closed through Wednesday, as would the American Stock Exchange and the NASDAQ Stock Market. All three exchanges, after consultation with the SEC, had made this decision "in light of the heinous attack on America." The release also disclosed that there would be a notice the next day regarding the reopening of U.S. equities markets. SEC Chairman Harvey Pitt followed with a statement emphasizing that the Commission "strongly supported this decision."[16]

The Govie Market

At that point, there needed to be an equivalent declaration for the fixed-income markets based in New York. However obvious the need to "close" them, that determination had to be made definitively and communicated broadly. Some market participants might have felt pressure to maintain operations in the face of unsafe conditions; they needed assurance that continued trading was not expected, on both 9/11 and the following day. [17]

On what would otherwise be a regular business day, the Govie market would close completely (or early, such as on the Friday before a three-day weekend) only on a recommendation by the Bond Market Association. The BMA in turn would rely on its "Calendar Committee," an executive group of the organization's most senior representatives from member firms, representing the Govie, muni, repo, MBS and corporate bond markets.[18] Although technically voluntary, compliance with BMA recommendations was the norm.

The calendar for 2001 had been set in December 2000 by the committee. It would tussle with issues such as whether to recommend the bond markets close on Good Friday, which was not a bank holiday and, therefore, the Fed would be open while the fixed-income markets were closed. Two weeks before each holiday close, the BMA would issue a reminder announcement. The Calendar Committee wouldn't need to meet during the year except for unexpected events, such as whether to delay the markets' opening because of severe weather conditions (leading some to dub the group as the "Snowstorm Committee").[19] The last time the Committee had recommended an unscheduled close of the Govie market for a full day was in April 1994, when Richard Nixon died.

The Secretary of the Calendar Committee was Eric Foster, who had come to the BMA from the legal department of the New York Fed a year earlier. Foster was in the BMA's office at 40 Broad Street on the morning of 9/11. "Calls kept coming in from members wanting to know if the market was closed," he recollected. "They asked me if I had the authority to close it and I said no, I needed to get approval from the Calendar Committee or from someone senior in the BMA." By 10 a.m. Foster was forced to evacuate the building and the area.

Foster and other BMA staffers found refuge elsewhere. They spent much of the remainder of the day trying to reach and consult with as many members as possible, using contingency phone lists they found and contacting "friends of friends." Virtually every firm reported that it had stopped trading. In effect, the market had closed itself on 9/11.[20] It became evident that there was no need to issue a close recommendation for Tuesday, nor an ability to do so in a timely manner. But what about Wednesday?

Many people, both in the government and within the industry, would weigh in on this decision. Most of the Calendar Committee members reached by BMA staff endorsed a closing recommendation for the following day. Of great concern was potential lack of liquidity, which would likely lead to violent price swings and an inability to properly hedge risk.[21] As Micah Green, President of the BMA, would later observe, "You could have done trading on Wednesday, but it would have been really spotty at best, and we knew that we could be putting some firms at a severe and maybe irreparable disadvantage."[22] And there was recognition of the stress inflicted on financial industry workers. SEC Chairman Harvey Pitt made clear on 9/11 his regard for "the mental state of people exposed to this kind of tragedy up close. We need a period to calm down. It would be unwise to force people back to work."[23]

Not everyone agreed with the wisdom of closing on Wednesday. Gary Gensler, former Under Secretary of the Treasury for Domestic Finance, opined on 9/11 that, "keeping the markets closed shows that terrorists brought you to bay, and it creates more uncertainty."[24] Tom Wipf and his Morgan Stanley colleagues felt that, "the government wanted us to be open. And we wanted to do everything in our power to do that." Senior market regulators and many others throughout the financial community shared a concern about establishing an undesirable precedent in the aftermath of violence.

Typifying the attitude of many Govie traders, Joe Blauvelt remembered: "We all were saying that there's no fucking way that these guys are gonna close our financial system." Late in the day, the Fed called Blauvelt to ask if Chase would be ready to execute a tri-party open market operation the next morning to send a vote of confidence to the market. Blauvelt responded that Chase would be ready even if they had to walk over to the Fed with the collateral. Blauvelt followed that up with an e-mail to staff declaring, "NO WAY ARE WE GOING TO ALLOW THE REPO MARKETS TO BE CLOSED TOMORROW!"[25]

The consensus was to close the buy-sell market on Wednesday. Of great importance was that the message faith in the stability and health of the financial system, and that the terms of the closing be limited and precise as to scope and impact.

The announcement of the Govie market closing was crafted by Paul Saltzman, the BMA's General Counsel. Saltzman, who that morning had been trapped in a subway near Trinity Church when the North Tower fell, eventually made his way home by train to Westchester, still covered in soot. Upon arriving home, he created a "command center" in his library with two cell phones and two land lines. Saltzman's wife soon handed him a message from the White House, asking him to call Peter Fisher, Under Secretary of the Treasury for Domestic Finance.

Fisher, after a long confirmation process, had been in his position only a month. He was a logical choice for the position because of his many years of running the New York Fed's open market and foreign exchange operations. In 1998, Fisher was instrumental in coordinating the handling of the collapse of a major hedge fund, Long-Term Capital Management, including facilitating a $3.6 billion creditor rescue that avoided market panic.[26]

Fisher had started his day in the main Treasury building next to the White House. When American Airlines flight 77 flew into the Pentagon, the 19th century windows in the Treasury building began to rattle. "Then pretty quickly alarms went off, and the Treasury and White House evacuation was underway," Fisher recalled. "We poured out onto 15th Street, and really didn't know where to go." Someone thought to isolate Fisher and a few others. They traveled to the Secret Service's headquarters, where they took up residence in a control room with dozens of monitors showing TV coverage from around the world.[27]

Fisher settled into a windowless conference room, "feeling very secure but somewhat lost. Then the phone rang, and several of the heads of the major dealers, including Phil Purcell and David Komansky [the CEOs of Morgan Stanley and Merrill Lynch respectively] had already found me. Which I thought was interesting since I didn't really know where I was."

Fisher spent much of the day speaking to senior industry and government officials. He was concerned, among other things, whether the Presidents' Working Group on Financial Markets would both bless the closing of the Treasury market on Wednesday and put out a statement to that effect. The Working Group, comprised of the Treasury Secretary and the Chairmen of the Fed, the SEC and the Commodity Futures Trading Commission (CFTC), had been created in response to the 1987 Black Monday stock market crash, and became known colloquially as the "Plunge Protection Team." The Group's mission was to coordinate policy making and the exchange of information among the leading federal regulators.[28] But it was so early in the new

Bush administration that many White House officials didn't even know that the Working Group existed.[29]

Fisher's boss, Treasury Secretary Paul O'Neill, was at an engagement in Tokyo. Aside from Fed Chairman Greenspan, the other two Working Group members, Jim Newsome, the CFTC Chairman, and Harvey Pitt, the SEC Chairman, were in D.C. Because both the CFTC and SEC had staffed offices in the World Trade Center complex, Newsome and Pitt had to deal with a myriad of personnel issues, paramount of which was determining the safety of their employees. They asked Fisher to put together a Working Group conference call for the afternoon.

As the four group members discussed the morning's events, the call was interrupted by a White House operator, who asked them to accept a tie-in from President Bush. The President spoke briefly, characterizing the attacks as an assault on capitalism and imploring them to get the markets back up and running as fast as possible. As Newsome recalled, "It was a direct mandate from the President, and that's what we focused on."[30]

Fisher spoke frequently with his former colleagues at the New York Fed. One conversation was with Sandy Krieger, a good friend who had worked for Fisher in the Markets Group. Fisher was telling Krieger about the need to ensure price discovery in the market. After a pause, Krieger responded, "Peter, I really don't think it's about price discovery. There are dead bodies all around here." As Fisher admitted later, "That was a fair comeuppance.

It was helpful for me to get in touch with the tragedy in that way."

Many Govie industry executives increasingly looked toward the looming deadline of 6:00 p.m., when fixed-income trading in Tokyo was scheduled to open. They would need to announce the market's Wednesday closing before then. It was clear that if buy-sell trading were to take place in Tokyo, Asian investors would come in strong and buy Treasuries heavily. The dealers would need to make a market for those investors, but liquidity likely would be insufficient to offset the dealers' risk.[31]

Fisher spent much of Tuesday coordinating a round-robin of conversations among staff from the White House, the Fed, the SEC, the Treasury, the major dealers, and the BMA. No one liked the idea of the bond markets being closed, but everyone understood the reality. The question became, how quickly can the fixed-income markets restart? With the inevitable heavy buying interest in safe assets like Treasuries, there needed to be an outlet for investors. "You don't want the global anxiety to have to express itself by driving up the price of gold. You'd rather it express itself through the normal base asset, which is U.S. Treasuries," Fisher noted.

Saltzman asked for Fisher's advice. Fisher made clear that the government wasn't dictating what the private sector should do, telling Saltzman twice that the Treasury would understand if the BMA closed the market.[32] Recalled Saltzman, "That was clearly a code, because when Peter was running the

Open Market Desk at the New York Fed, he had hated the BMA closing recommendations, especially the ones for an early close, and tried constantly to get us to stop them." But Fisher also emphasized that, while he didn't mean to "exact a pound of flesh," he was planning to press Saltzman by the next day to consider how fast the market would be reopening.[33]

Working Out the Press Release

Saltzman's eight-year-old son had been told in school that morning that "Wall Street had been attacked." Knowing that his father worked there, he was distraught. While trying to simultaneously reassure his son, isolate himself from three of his wife's friends who couldn't get back into Manhattan and had camped out in his house, and take innumerable calls, he contacted his boss, Micah Green, and Warren Spector, President and Co-Chief Operating Officer of Bear Stearns and that year's BMA Chairman. Saltzman needed their confirmation to release a press statement that would announce the following day's market closing.

Once that consent was acquired, Saltzman worked on the wording of the press release. He conferred with Brian Roseboro, Assistant Treasury Secretary for Financial Markets. Roseboro had joined the Treasury Department at the end of July 2001, after a confirmation process that had been as difficult as Fisher's was. Roseboro felt he had been confirmed only because someone was needed to conduct the quarterly refunding in August and the related press conferences. "My first week, I sat in on meetings involving the Bonneville Power Administration in the Pacific Northwest and fish credits, as well as an employee issue involving rats in the basement and where we were gonna relocate employees. One day, I called my wife and told her that I was dealing with fish and rats." Just before 9/11, Roseboro had been consumed with helping the Treasury's international staff resolve Argentina's continuing economic woes.[34]

Roseboro had been in Fisher's office that morning, in the southeast corner of the main Treasury building, when the Pentagon was struck. "The building shook, and we could see this giant plume of white smoke. Then the building alarm went off," Roseboro recalled. Treasury Department staff were forced to exit the building. Don Hammond, the Treasury's Fiscal Assistant Secretary, later admitted: "By the time I finished my call and opened my door, the hallways were packed with people running and Secret Service officers yelling, 'Let's go. Let's move!' Made me realize that the situation was worse than I thought."[35]

Roseboro walked five blocks to the Bureau of the Public Debt, a small agency within the Treasury Department responsible for borrowing the money needed to operate the federal government through sales of Treasuries and Savings Bonds. Its offices were across from the FBI's building, which building had been quickly vacated. That day, a quarter of a million federal employees in D.C. had been told to go home, and they evacuated around the same time.[36] A massive traffic gridlock soon ensnarled downtown Washington. The Metro was overwhelmed and, as in Manhattan, many people had to walk miles just to get to a car or bus.[37]

A typical story involved Yvette Hollingsworth, who worked in the Fed's bank supervision and regulation area. Around 10 a.m., she exited the garage onto C Street, next to the State Department: "By then, I was only able to drive a little past the Board of Governors building. Security was out and they were stopping cars to let the military vehicles pass. In the meantime, there was a rumor of a bomb at the State Department. People started getting out of their cars and running." To avoid the abandoned autos in front of her, Hollingsworth drove over the sidewalk. She recalled, "And plenty of people were right behind me."[38]

Roseboro and other staff from the Treasury and the Bureau of the Public Debt ignored the order to leave their building, remaining the entire day. They hastily took over a fifth floor conference room at the back of the building, selected because the front faced the FBI's building, which might be a target. Technology workers were summoned to hook up TVs in what became a "war room," where senior Treasury staff watched the CNN coverage.[39] In mid-afternoon, when everyone started to get hungry, some senior people, including the Commissioner of the Bureau of the Public Debt, Van Zeck, volunteered to pick up pizzas from around the corner. "We figured that, if anyone, they'd let the Commissioner back in," explained Lori Santamorena, executive director of the Government Securities Regulation Staff.[40]

Roseboro and Fisher spoke in the morning, discussing the need to hold the four-week Treasury bill auction, conducted every Tuesday at 1p.m. They consulted with career staff from the Bureau of the Public Debt, who performed an immediate analysis of the Treasury's cash position. The Bureau staff determined that the Treasury had compensating balances with commercial banks that would allow it to cover its immediate cash needs.[41] Fisher and Roseboro subsequently agreed to postpone that day's auction (which was later cancelled outright), concluding that "we really didn't need the money, so why force the market to go through this exercise."[42] That deliberation led Santamorena to consider whether there might be a problem with the scheduled Thursday settlement of the 13-week and 26-week Treasury bill auctions that had taken place on September 10. Over $20 billion had been awarded competitively, a majority of which would need to be delivered to GSCC for redistribution to the Street.[43] She called Dave Buckmaster, who assured her that GSCC would be ready to accept delivery of the auctioned securities.[44]

Roseboro and Saltzman barely knew each other before 9/11, yet by the early afternoon they had spoken at length and crafted the statement that the BMA would release.[45] Understanding the potential harm to market participants from pent-up but unfulfilled trading demand, unmet funding and risk management needs, and the demoralizing effect of a lengthy market shutdown inflicted by terrorism, they emphasized that the recommendation to close the Govie market would apply to Wednesday only. Given the global nature of the market, the proposal would affect only New York trading hours. It would not include the repo market, whose operation was essential for the liquidity of market participants and the banking system.[46]

Because BMA staff had been displaced and their office inaccessible, publicizing the recommendation became a challenge. Saltzman used word of mouth, calling senior officials at several of the larger firms. Later in the week, interest in the nuances of the BMA's deliberations would be so high that on one call, to Credit Suisse First Boston, Saltzman was piped into hundreds of people on the trading floor.

Ultimately, the Association's Washington press officer managed to inform media contacts of the recommendation to close the market, and the organization's website, which was being maintained by its Washington office, posted a brief notice. At 5 p.m., an official announcement from the BMA was made via CNN. The President's Working Group on Financial Markets also put out a statement supporting the decision to close the market, expressing "confidence that trading will resume as soon as it is both appropriate and practical."

Coordinating with the Futures Market

There remained one more piece of unfinished business on the trading side: coordinating with the futures market. On October 20, 1987, the day after Black Monday, the stock market had continued to decline in the late morning, leading many to believe that the New York Stock Exchange would close by mid-day. In reaction, the Chicago Mercantile Exchange closed its stock index derivatives market, not wanting the selling hysteria to spill over to the futures side. The NYSE never did close, creating dysfunction in the pricing of futures and cash trades. That episode highlighted the necessity of coordinating the closings of the two markets.[47]

By 9/11, market participants could readily trade Treasuries through futures as effectively as they did in the buy-sell and repo markets. If the Govie market was closed for policy considerations, nothing would be gained if the Chicago exchanges allowed Treasury futures trading to go on. New York traders, who hadn't had time to unwind their open positions, were exposed in what was a highly volatile environment, and could see the value of their positions and collateral decline markedly. Conversely, Treasury futures trading might not be properly hedged against cash Treasury activity.

Many members at the Chicago Board of Trade and the Merc called Eric Foster, some repeatedly. "I knew why they had reached out to me," Foster noted. "They wanted industry consent to open the futures markets on Wednesday, but they didn't want to piss off all of the primary dealers, and they didn't have time to call all of them."

Foster had been told by Saltzman to do whatever it took, and to speak to whomever he needed, including the White House, to get the futures exchanges to remain closed. He could use his relationships and the imperatives of the situation, or he could just try to "beat the shit" out of them. "I was prepared to scream at them as I had been screamed at by my members," Foster admitted. "'We got a crisis! We got a lot of dead people here! Are you gonna help us?'"

No coercion of the futures exchanges was necessary. At the Board of Trade, Bernie Dan was being pressured by some members to open on Wednesday. "We dismissed that right away," Dan recounted. "The markets were too integrated. If all sources weren't available to manage the anticipated volatility, it would make the situation worse."

Meanwhile, the Merc was facing similar member resistance to a Wednesday closing. Recalled Gill, "We got a lot of flak from a small but vocal minority, but we stuck to our guns." For those members looking to hedge their positions to manage risk, the Merc triggered a pre-existing arrangement with the Singapore International Monetary Exchange (SIMEX) that had been established in 1984. This arrangement allowed trades to be opened on the SIMEX in the evening and closed on the Merc the next day.[48] Merc members offset their risk at the SIMEX, which resulted in a huge spike in that exchange's volume.[49]

Following the decision to close the Govie market, focus shifted to the large amount of trading, mostly in repos, that had been done in the early morning, before the devastation to market participants and communications links. Could those lost trades be reconstructed? No major market had ever faced this issue.

CHAPTER 7

LOST ACTIVITY: RECONSTRUCTING TRADES DONE ON 9/11

"Most of the big brokers were in the towers. The brokers are the heart of the business. Virtually everything is brokered. And they had disappeared."

Dave Buckmaster, managing director, GSCC[1]

The Government Securities Clearing Corporation's most fundamental mission was trade comparison – the recording and matching of transaction data submitted by both parties.[2] Sometimes, the terms of Govie trades don't match up in one or more important respects, such as security, price, or settlement date. Dealers' and brokers' operations staff were responsible for recognizing and resolving discrepancies so that each trade could be compared by the clearing corporation. GSCC's comparison role was necessary because there's no centralized exchange for Govie activity. No single entity holds all of the data on key trade terms.

Any trades from the early morning of 9/11 that hadn't been compared would remain unsettled, as if the trades had never happened. An unthinkable result.[3] At that time, it was standard to submit data on Govie trades at the end of the day.[4] But that would have been impossible for many firms on 9/11, particularly the major inter-dealer brokers.

For the initial group of GSCC employees who went back into the building, there was, for about an hour, essentially no visibility. A rumor spread that the New York Stock Exchange building had collapsed. Marc Golin assumed that, "the catastrophe was working its way east. That it inevitably would reach us."

Roughly 20 of the staff remained at 55 Water Street, distant enough away from the Trade Center not to have lost power or any systems. They began making calls to determine which member firms were still functional and likely to submit trade data that day. But the sporadic phone service made that task difficult.[5]

GSCC managers reviewed the list of member firms, checking off which ones had been contacted. The staff also searched for their own relatives, including Bob Trapani: "I could reach no one from Cantor, so I kept calling my wife," Trapani recounted. "At last, I found out that my brother-in-law was in transit to Houston. He was in the air when the events happened, and ended up in Atlanta. Otherwise, he would have been gone."[6]

With phone and email communication ability intermittent, Rob Palatnick took advantage of getting an outside line to open up a dial-up connection with

AT&T Global Services, using his personal credit card. That connection was later used to exchange files with Cantor's London office and other members.[7]

Staff analyzed the trade information that came in during the course of the day, some of it obtained by member firms via unusual methods. Morgan Stanley, which had lost its World Trade Center offices, subsequently evacuated its main building at 1585 Broadway in Midtown. Tom Wipf and other Morgan Stanley executives negotiated with security to allow a few people back into the midtown building to process trade tickets. "Two men and a woman volunteered to go back in," Wipf remembered. "That allowed us to get a jump and not lose that day."

Critical Issues for Chase

Meanwhile, Chase staff in lower Manhattan were having difficulty finding a home. Those from the credit area had started their day at One Chase Plaza, across from the New York Fed building. That group had been evacuated in the morning to Chase's operations offices at Four New York Plaza, on the southeastern tip of downtown Manhattan. There they joined the investor trust services team responsible for processing dealer and broker customers' Govie trades, headed by Al Clark.

Hours later, Four New York Plaza also was ordered evacuated, and the staff was asked to shift to a contingency site on 45th Street in Midtown. Jon Ciciola recalled, "A dozen or so of us were the last ones left in the building. Just us and our data center people. But they wanted everyone to leave. We were continually getting calls. Security was on the floor, asking us what we were still doing there and when we were getting out and telling us we were crazy."[8]

In the late afternoon, Four New York Plaza lost power and connectivity. The emergency backup generators were functional, but they were needed to run the data centers, compromising other power needs. The lights flickered on and off, and the internet and cable TV became inoperable.

With nighttime approaching, the Chase group considered walking over the Brooklyn Bridge to backup offices in MetroTech in downtown Brooklyn. Looking north toward 55 Water Street, they noticed that there were lights on. Someone remembered that Chase's corporate trust function had space on the fifth floor.

Around eight p.m., the group left their building, using the freight elevator, the only one still working. They walked through a thick layer of dust that looked to Al Clark "like a yellow-whitish bad case of dandruff across all of lower Manhattan. You could see it glowing off the sidewalks." One woman in the group was a diabetic. "She started not to feel well, because she needed food," recounted Ciciola. One of Clark's staffer's, Ray Stancil, crossed the street to the Water Street Gourmet Deli and bought all the food he could carry – mostly Crackerjacks, pretzels, cake, and soda. [9]

They set up a command center in a large conference room, before realizing there was only one phone that had only one line. Ciciola could foresee the aggravation to come, "as everyone wanted to talk to us." Ciciola, a relationship manager with contacts throughout the Street, was tasked with calming callers and screening them, to determine who would get through to Clark, a well-respected Wall Street veteran whom every client was trying to reach.[10]

Chase's settlement system had continued running throughout the day; as a result, tens of billions of dollars worth of securities had come into its client accounts from the selling dealers. Because most brokers and dealers couldn't be reached, either no instructions had been transmitted to Chase indentifying which deliveries were valid or, if they were available, Chase didn't have complimentary instructions as to whom the securities should be redelivered. Ordinarily, if securities came into Chase's account without proper instructions for redelivery, Chase would label the transactions as a "don't know," or "DK," and return them to the delivering dealer. That dealer would then re-deliver the securities to Chase with proper instructions. But that wasn't happening on 9/11. Consequently, the securities positions just sat in Chase's book-entry account at the Fed.

Al Clark became concerned about Chase's exposure. "It was in the back of our minds that we might never get those delivery instructions," he admitted. "Our immediate reaction was to refuse the transactions to protect the bank, and return them to the guys who sent them."

If Chase had DK'ed the deliveries, it could have triggered an endless chain reaction of banks and firms rejecting securities movements. Clark and Doug Anderson, who headed the credit group, were advised by senior management that the Fed had asked Chase to do everything possible to maintain normal business function. The Fed had indicated that it would "support" Chase. Clark recalled, "We interpreted that to mean that we should take in transactions and do our best to settle them. And we thought that our individual clients would be best served by this, that it was the outcome that they wanted, and that it was the most appropriate thing to do." (Years later, reflecting on 9/11, Clark offered that, "In hindsight, it might have been better for us to have taken the view that we didn't really know firsthand what our customers wanted us to do with their transactions, which weren't complete. Had we pushed some transactions back, we and GSCC and the rest of the industry probably would have avoided much of the subsequent problematic two-year reconcilement process. And avoided much confusion.")

By borrowing at the New York Fed's discount window, Chase was able to finance all of the $63 billion in securities that had come in to its account. While this helped ensure market stability and prevent systemic risk, it was a huge financial commitment, well above the couple of billion dollars that Chase might borrow on occasion.[11] The mechanics of recording the details of the loan were exacting.

Normally, loans were logged into an automated system, but on the night of 9/11 they were recorded on paper. The Chase bookkeepers didn't get the proof until 3 a.m., and then they reviewed it by flashlight.[12]

Chase's financial commitment was a precarious one. It couldn't be sure that some of its clients, particularly the brokers that had been in the Trade Center, would survive to take delivery of the securities and pay for them. Clark and his colleagues brainstormed about forcing the top dealers to decide who would get those brokers' securities, but then held off doing so. In the end, the risk Chase accepted was mitigated by the rising value of the Govie securities that it held, predictable given the rush of investors seeking the safety of those securities. However, the reconciliation issues created by taking in securities that it didn't have proper information for would linger at Chase for close to two years. And later, when Chase sought to charge its customers for the significant overnight financing costs of holding those securities in its account, those charges were fiercely resisted by many firms.

The imbalance in Govie securities positions was mirrored in the funds arena. Cash payments flowing among the major banks, made largely through Fedwire, grease the wheels of the financial system. But on 9/11, Bank of New York lost its capability to communicate with the Fed and with other banks. Many banks sent money to BONY's account at the New York Fed, but no payments came out of it. Funds accumulated in BONY's account, growing to around $100 billion.[13] The payments process gridlocked.

By the late afternoon, Chase estimated that it needed about $50 billion more than it had in cash to make all the necessary payments on behalf of its customers. There was only one recourse. Chase's senior management team called the New York Fed's Jamie Stewart, who had his own senior management team on the phone with him. The Chase execs told Stewart that, for Chase to keep making payments, they wanted assurance that the Fed would lend them whatever amount they required, because Chase couldn't count on BoNY's ability to pass through funds and it faced the risk of running out of money.

As a regulator of banks as well as a lender to them, the New York Fed knew that the banks remained financially sound and should be capable of repaying any amounts loaned to them. The Fed management team agreed to meet all of Chase's funding needs, to ensure that payments would keep flowing and prevent a liquidity crunch. Stewart considered first consulting with the Board of Governors staff (an open line had been set up with them), but time was of the essence. Chase immediately released payments, and all the rest of the system, aside from BoNY, kicked into gear. As Stewart explained, "The same money recirculates around several times a day and, because the flow got started again, it turned out in the end that Chase needed to borrow only a small amount from the Fed."

The Brokers had "Disappeared"

By day's end, it appeared that most GSCC members had the capacity to submit their trade data for comparison, though this was not true of the most crucial firms – the major inter-dealer brokers. Given the loss of life, offices, and records, and the communications and connectivity issues that prevailed, the only inter-dealer broker that GSCC could establish as being fully functional was BrokerTec. On 9/11, however, BrokerTec had been in business for little more than a year and was still a fairly minor player in the market.

Nor was BrokerTec left unscathed. Although its offices were in Jersey City, its trading system was located at 140 Broadway, which was inaccessible. In the evening, the firm's management arranged to shift that platform to Jersey City, a risky move because, if unsuccessful, BrokerTec would have been out of business. Operations staff copied the trading system and re-ran it, then waited until 3:30 a.m., when they received output from the clearing corporation confirming that the cutover worked.[14]

GSCC staff spoke of the morbidity of "processing dead people's trades." After hashing out all the alternatives, management determined as the overriding consideration that failure to settle the thousands of brokered trades executed that morning would disrupt the entire market and cause harm to many firms. Inaction also had the potential to create huge financing costs for the brokers, which might be stuck with securities delivered to their clearing bank accounts by dealers that could not then be re-delivered to others.

Because the brokers wouldn't be sending in any trade data, Tom Costa concluded that the clearing corporation itself would need to artificially create comparisons, by presuming that the information on the early morning trading that had been sent to GSCC by the dealers was accurate. But this "force comparison" process had never been done, and it wasn't clear how to implement it.

Among those at 55 Water Street that day was Neal Arbon, who was the main architect of the code that ran GSCC's systems. "One of the first things I did when I got back to my office, after I called home and told my wife I was okay, was to phone the data center in Brooklyn," Arbon remembered. "The guy told me that they were evacuating. I said, 'Just do this one thing before you go. Get the account enabled.'" That gave Arbon special privileges on the system. "Looking back, I don't know why I did that. Subconsciously, I must have known that the situation was worse than it looked." [15]

Arbon identified a utility that had been built for quality assurance purposes to simulate emergency events. On the fly, he changed code to trigger the force-compare process: "I typed in a command and ran the utility. It had two phases – create for and create against. We used both. The function looks at the trades, for example, that Garban did, and then the trades submitted against Garban. And it can generate a comparison either way."

Based solely on dealer data, GSCC established more than 2,000 compared trades that could then be settled.[16] However, some of the trade data received from the dealers was inaccurate, giving GSCC reconciliation headaches at a time when it could least afford them. Forcing the comparison of thousands of trades also was risky because the clearing corporation, by its own rules, was immediately guaranteeing their settlement. GSCC had no clue at the time whether the brokers, particularly those in the Trade Center, would ever reconstruct their books, or even survive, yet it was now on the hook for all of the trades that the dealers claimed they had done with those brokers.[17] One dealer, while appreciative of the settlement risk that had been eliminated, noted that night, "We could be making up phony trades right now and submitting them."[18] This proved to be just a theoretical risk; there was never the specter of fraudulent data.

The following day, many firms weren't prepared to process any of the force-compared trades on their books, and they made unnecessary securities deliveries based on other trades that had already netted against administratively compared ones. This would contribute to the Street's snowballing books and records discrepancies. Some would argue that the comparison and settlement processes should have been allowed to recover by having the market and Fedwire remain closed through Wednesday. That would have created a 36-hour window for market participants to review their records, balance out, and attempt to send to, receive from, and compare with their clearing bank and GSCC all relevant records.

As the events of the week later revealed, many key market participants didn't return to business as usual until Thursday morning or later. It would have been disruptive in many ways for the market to have closed for more than one day. Beyond that, there was one consideration paramount for Jamie Stewart and the Fed. "Keeping the Fedwire open and business as usual would fuel confidence in the entire financial system," stressed Stewart. "We would not let the bastards close it down!"

Although he had decided to move ahead with the force-comparison concept, Costa wanted reassurance that this would be acceptable to his members. He reached Ron Purpora, one of GSCC's directors and the person who on 9/11 was effectively heading Garban from his home. Costa asked Purpora for permission to match up any trade where someone was either looking to deliver to Garban or to get a delivery from Garban, disregarding for the moment price and other discrepancies. Purpora, who had no records of his own, told Costa to go ahead. (Dave Buckmaster years later would observe, "To get through what was going on, we relaxed our normal rules substantially. For example, regarding money differences. We didn't worry about them. But it's exactly in this type of crisis that you need those rules the most. If we had insisted on that, we would have prevented a lot of other problems from happening later on. But it's very easy to see this in hindsight.")

Purpora had spent most of the day on the phone trying to determine the status of more than 700 Garban employees who worked in the Trade Center. By mid-afternoon, he had learned that most had made it out of the buildings, although it would take several days and innumerable phone calls to verify that all but one person had survived. Purpora remembered, "There was this runner. Typical Wall Street one, a guy about 75 years old. He had left the office at about 8:30 that morning to make his deliveries. No one saw him leave, and he went straight home after the events occurred and didn't call in. For four days, no one was sure what happened to him. We couldn't find the guy. He was home resting, but didn't bother to tell anyone."

Once he had established a process for finding his staff, Purpora turned his attention to the Garban business. He realized that he had no idea what to tell his employees about the company's status, or even where they should report to the next morning. Then he received a call from a friend at Prebon, a competitor, offering Garban space, rent free, in Jersey City.

Purpora immediately called the home of Steve McDermott, another top Garban executive, who had worked in the North Tower. Animatedly, Purpora spoke with McDermott's wife: "When Steve gets home, tell him that we're gonna meet tomorrow morning at 7:30 at Prebon's offices!" In his excitement, Purpora forgot to consider one basic fact. McDermott's wife still hadn't heard from her husband, and didn't yet know whether he was alive. Purpora found out later that she was "really pissed off" at him.

After 9 p.m., GSCC started to assess the roughly $18 billion in trades in which a dealer had named Garban as the counterparty. Purpora received updates. Around midnight, GSCC had whittled Garban's positions down to $6 billion by finding the second dealer counterparty to each trade. And that was it; nothing further could be done. Garban had relatively little capital and, as a broker, it should have had no positions in its account at Chase, its clearing bank. Instead, it was holding $6 billion in securities, which it would need to finance.

Purpora and Costa got on the phone with Al Clark of Chase. As Purpora later explained, "I had no idea what the market's done, or what issues my $6 billion position are in, whether Notes, Bonds or Bills. I just had a par amount. And I had no idea how I'm going to get that much money at midnight." Purpora asked Costa, "What do we do now?" Purpora worried that he might be out of business.

After a long pause, Clark jumped in. "Ron, you have the securities, don't you?" Purpora turned the question to Costa, who confirmed that the securities were in Garban's "box" at Chase. Clark then reassured Purpora that Chase would lend Garban the money. Purpora had never financed an amount remotely close to ten figures. "Really, you'll lend me the money?"

Clark responded, "Well, you'll give me the securities, won't you?"

"Sure," Purpora replied, and hung up the phone, still grappling with the implications of having borrowed $6 billion, and what the funding cost of that would be.[19]

$96 Billion in Repo Fails

Most of the Govie transactions conducted early on 9/11, measured in dollar value, were in repos. A repo, for settlement purposes, can be thought of as two ordinary "buy-sell" transactions rolled into one. In the first transaction, one party buys securities from a dealer or institution that wants to borrow money. Later, the seller buys back those securities for a specified price plus interest. All of the repos executed in the morning of 9/11 had to be "started" on that same day by two dealers moving cash against securities through their clearing banks. Normally, this was done right after the trade was entered into, and GSCC wasn't involved because it didn't handle same-day transactions.

Settlement of a repo often wasn't a problem on 9/11 if the repo had been executed directly between two dealers. But most of the repos entered into that morning were "blind brokered," meaning that the dealer on each side had done the trade with a broker and didn't know who the counterparty dealer was. Only the broker in the middle of the transaction knew the identities of both dealer parties.

In many cases, the movement of money against securities to start brokered repos had already been completed early on 9/11. But no instructions would be coming to GSCC from the brokers later in the day providing information on the return of the securities (in the closing leg of the repo, which GSCC did handle). Since the two dealers involved were "blind" to each other, those broker records were essential.[20]

When a brokered repo wasn't able to fully settle (both start and then close), the repo was known as a "broker fail." On a typical day, there might be a couple of hundred broker fails at most. That night, there were *more than 2,000 such fails, worth in excess of $96 billion.*[21]

Although the clearing corporation was able to obtain some information from the two clearing banks on those broker fails,[22] it was impossible to confirm with all parties to the transactions the validity of that data. Absent that critical failsafe measure, GSCC had no responsibility under its rules for settling those fails, and ordinarily wouldn't do so.

Nonetheless, Costa and his management team decided to "take in" (or assume as good) the brokered repos and include them in the end of day net.[23] "It was our role to absorb all that mess in house. That's what the central clearing corporation was there for," said Costa later. "Otherwise the Street would have been left with the need to unravel hundreds of billions of dollars in transactions." Assuming responsibility for the broker fails also saved the Street significant financing costs by preventing dealers from delivering back to the brokers the next day securities that would have sat in their clearing bank accounts.[24]

Inputting the broker fails information into the GSCC system required an enormous manual effort. Much of that work was done late into the night in Brooklyn by Dave Cosgrove and his small crew. The company's remaining employees in Manhattan also were called into action. Adrien Vanderlinden, who had arrived in the States from Belgium only weeks earlier, was getting ready to leave around 6:30 p.m. He remembered: "I was lacing up a pair of hiking boots when Dave Buckmaster came over and said, 'Where are you going?' I told him I was going home and he said, 'No you're not.'"

Buckmaster rounded up almost everyone left. Most had no operations background, requiring Buckmaster to give them a crash course in entering the information contained on tickets into a terminal. This called for handling stacks of sheets, each with a couple of hundred trades, which were divided among the staff. Given the fungibility of Govie securities, the task was to find two like sides and match them. As time went by, Vanderlinden got the hang of it. "They were all $50M trades that hadn't entered the system," he explained. "Because a lot of participants hadn't come in, we needed to match them up with another side that had. I tried to be as accurate and fast as possible. I inputted for over six hours."

Taking in all of the broker fails added to GSCC's reconciliation problem, because many of the fails were unbalanced or had invalid information.

And in some cases, because GSCC didn't have connectivity with BoNY, it assumed that settlement of the transaction had failed when it hadn't. Hundreds of money differences resulted.

As GSCC staff completed its processing cycle at close to 3:30 a.m. on Wednesday, they repeatedly heard on the radio that "the Financial District has been completely evacuated." Vanderlinden, along with many others, worried, "What might they do if they think that no one is in our building?"

In Brooklyn, someone had obtained a hotel room for the one woman left among the company employees at SIAC. At about 4 a.m., Dave Cosgrove and Carlos Cardenty were given cots, which they had to carry to their small disaster recovery room and assemble. "They were heavy, like army surplus equipment," recalled Cosgrove. "I had been up for about 24 hours straight, hadn't eaten except for a bagel I had early that morning, and we're standing there fumbling with these things. You needed dexterity and we didn't have any at that point."[25]

A group of GSCC execs in lower Manhattan also stayed in their offices overnight, as they would for the rest of the week. Late at night, someone mentioned that Danny Corrigan, a colleague and repo market veteran from Australia, had brought them two bottles of Shiraz days before. Buckmaster had a corkscrew-like tool received from an industry conference. They split the wine, then figured out where to go to catch some sleep.[26]

Some lay down on the floor of their office; others went into the board room. Many created makeshift pillows out of jackets or books, or in one case a combination of napkins and interoffice envelopes. With no ventilation or air conditioning, the floor was stifling hot. A few who regularly worked out changed into gym wear, but most had no other clothes. No one slept more than two or three hours.

Over in Brooklyn, near dawn, unable to sleep, Cosgrove went for a smoke. Foregoing a hellish smoking room in the building (there was "tar running down the wall"), he walked outside of the MetroTech complex, close by a mustering point for police. Earlier in the day, Cosgrove had gone there to ask if anyone knew the whereabouts of his brother, a Police Department captain, whom Cosgrove later located and spoke with. Now the area was roped off. Every car was being stopped; only emergency vehicles were allowed to continue on towards the Brooklyn Bridge. "There was a parade of 18-wheelers with generators and lights and heavy cranes. And dump trucks," Cosgrove said later. "The incident hadn't taken place that much earlier, and all of these vehicles had already shown up."

Jon Ciciola left his Chase colleagues around midnight. Soon after exiting the building, he was stopped by police on South Street: "I said to one of them, 'I'm parked up there somewhere. Any chance I can get out?' He said, 'You can leave, but you can't return.'" Walking to his car, Ciciola saw "about a dozen fire trucks, as many ambulances, and 20 or so police cars under the FDR. They had thought there were tens of thousands of dead people and there would be a need for lots of triage and body bags."

Ciciola drove north on the FDR Drive, his black car covered in white dust. "Lower Manhattan was pitch dark," he continued. "Just some auxiliary lights, through which I could see smoke rising out of the pit of the Trade Center. I barely saw another car until I reached Westchester. The roads in Manhattan and the Bronx were barren."

On the ride home, while making calls, Ciciola found out that one of his friends from Chase, Joe Howard, had died of a heart attack while walking uptown to catch a train home. Ciciola pulled over on the shoulder of the Saw Mill River Parkway and wept. After getting home, he spoke with his wife at length, trying to account for all of their family and friends, including Ciciola's sister's husband, Mike, a fireman in Ladder Company 22 headquartered on West 100th Street. That morning, Ladder Company 22 had rushed down the West Side Highway to get to the Trade Center. Nine crew members had died. Ciciola's wife conveyed the news that his brother-in-law had the good fortune to have had off that day.

The human and physical devastation wrought by 9/11 had left the back-end of the U.S. financial markets crippled. Their rehabilitation, an effort unprecedented in scope and difficulty, would soon begin.

CHAPTER 8

WEDNESDAY: THE MESSAGE

"They delivered their message. Now we were going to deliver ours..."

Suzanne Cutler, Executive Vice President, Federal Reserve Bank of New York[1]

Wednesday dawned, all too quickly, as bright and clear as the previous day. President Bush had declared New York City a disaster area. The stench from Ground Zero permeated through Midtown and into upper Manhattan. At St. Vincent's Hospital on 12th Street, medical staff waited outside for ambulances that never arrived.[2] On the south side of the hospital, a bulletin board was set up with pictures of the missing, along with notes about whom to contact. That board would eventually become a repository for thousands of photos.[3] Along Second Avenue, from 30th to 32nd Streets, near the Medical Examiner's office, a convoy of ten refrigerated tractor-trailers was parked, ready to provide space for about 1,000 bodies.[4] American flags were hung in front of apartment and office buildings.

Public access to bridges and tunnels into Manhattan was barred. City schools were closed. It was matinee day on Broadway, but the theaters were dark.[5] The Fresh Kills landfill in Staten Island, which had been the city's main garbage dump until it was shut down earlier in the year, reopened to receive the debris from the towers. FBI agents would use small front-end loaders to drag through the rubble and sort it by hand, looking for body parts.[6] In the evening, candlelight vigils were held in Washington Square, Union Square, and Central Park. As one Union Square participant observed, "The park was packed. Most were bawling their eyes out. Everywhere you looked there was a picture of a missing person."[7]

A "frozen zone" was established in lower Manhattan south of 14th Street. In that area, most stores were closed and subway trains didn't stop. Huge dump trucks and heavy construction equipment lined the streets.[8] Police barricades were at every major intersection, and only "essential personnel" were allowed in. Individuals who could prove they lived in the area also were permitted to enter; however, thousands of residents would have to wait weeks or months before returning to their damaged apartments.[9]

National Guard troops were deployed to patrol lower Manhattan and to protect transportation links such as Penn Station and Grand Central Terminal. Inspectors and engineering consultants began a building-by-building assessment of damage around Ground Zero. In the late afternoon, New York City Transit halted service on the Lexington Avenue subway line in that vicinity because of fears that vibrations from the trains might impact the structural integrity of the buildings.[10] The Brooks Brothers store in One Liberty Plaza, across from the World Trade Center, was serving as a morgue.

At the American Stock Exchange, just south of the Trade Center, CEO Sal Sodano and his staff walked from the basement to the roof in the early morning, assessing the damage. The previous afternoon, with fires continuing to burn, the same group had searched the building to be sure no one remained. Around 3:30 p.m., his driver, accompanied by New York City firefighters, found Sodano and told him that they needed to get out of the building. The firefighters directed the men to the back exit. "The street was covered with debris and melted cars," Sodano remembered. "One of the firemen told us, 'Everything is unstable. There's fire out there. Just go to the middle of the street, turn left, and run. And don't look the other way.' Of course, all of us did look. If you could paint a picture of Hell, that's what it looked like."

On September 12, Sodano returned to the AMEX building. "Windows had burst and a huge amount of debris, some of which were like projectiles, had flown in," he recalled. "We found papers, files, business cards, and photographs from offices that had been in the Trade Center." On the roof, a fire still burned. Sodano and the others found some extinguishers and doused it. Sodano explained, "I think that if we hadn't gone up to the roof, the fire would have continued and the building might have burned down."

Sodano began the task of reviving his exchange: "There were so many issues to consider. How to account for all our people? What was the extent of the physical damage? There was no power, no water, no way to cool the computers down, no telephone lines, no access, nothing. And we had no backup trading site."

Officials of the New York Mercantile Exchange likewise were struggling to resume business. Around midnight of 9/11, National Guard, police, and some senior NYMEX officers had been allowed to enter the NYMEX building, located at the north end of the World Financial Center. There was little physical damage, but the city had cut off the water supply, causing the air conditioning to shut down. By the time the building was first re-entered, the temperature had reached near 105 degrees, raising fears of permanent damage to computers. A decision was made to dock a barge next to the building, which borders the Hudson River, and use it to pump water in. Fortunately, the city soon turned the water back on, and the barge wasn't needed. NYMEX officials then shifted their attention to a laundry list of other issues, including getting diesel fuel to the building and testing the air quality.[11]

Having returned to Washington on a U.S. Air Force tanker, Bill McDonough, the President of the New York Fed, flew up to New York with that state's two U.S. Senators, Hillary Clinton and Chuck Schumer, and other officials, including Joe Albaugh, Director of the Federal Emergency Management

Agency.[12] Fedwire remained open, to the dismay of many front-office and operations professionals who had expected the declaration of a bank holiday, particularly given the closing of all the other major markets. Whatever problems a market participant had, it would need to address them while also handling new trading and settlements.

Wall Street staff who had gone home the day before weren't supposed to return to lower Manhattan. Nor did that appear possible. Bill Langan of GSCC reached the foot of the Brooklyn Bridge, intending to walk the two miles to his office, but was confronted by police who told him to "get lost." Langan instead walked over to the backup site in MetroTech. Joining him there was Bart Schiavo, who brought with him a small transistor radio with an antenna: "One of the young guys said to me, 'What's that?' We were kidding around about it, but it served its purpose. We were able to hear what was going on outside."

Many, like Bob Trapani, found a way into lower Manhattan. He took a New Jersey transit train to Hoboken and then boarded the PATH. Trapani was pleasantly surprised when the subway train stopped and allowed passengers to exit at the Christopher Street station, which is a block south of 10th Street in the West Village, well into the evacuated zone.

He walked south to Houston Street, where a line of police cars blocked pedestrian access. Then he turned east. Every corner or so, Trapani presented his

ID card to police, pleading his case that the clearing corporation was crucial to the financial industry. After many attempts, he found a sympathetic cop who let him pass. Yet as he walked through Chinatown, Trapani was stopped every few blocks and had to repeat the same spiel.

Arriving at the Brooklyn Bridge area, he could see his footprints as he walked. "Business cards all over, many from Cantor," he recounted. "Dozens of crushed cars that had been dragged out of Ground Zero and dumped by the FDR Drive. National Guardsmen on almost every corner. It reminded me of when I was a kid in the 1950s. This is the kind of disaster you were practicing for, hiding under your desk."

Steve Greenberg was another who managed to make it to the Water Street office. He walked from his Manhattan apartment down Broadway and got as far as Canal Street before being denied further access. Greenberg then headed east, pulling out his Government Securities Clearing Corporation business card at each corner and emphasizing the word "Government" (GSCC was a private company). At the FDR Drive, when he could go no further, Greenberg was allowed through, although he continued to be questioned frequently by National Guard troops during his walk.

The world had been informed of the Govie market's Wednesday close. Despite that, a small amount of buy-sell trading was being done by a few dealers.[13] Some inadvertently was facilitated by BrokerTec.

The President of BrokerTec, Lee Olesky, was in New York on a visit from London. Olesky, along with Jim Toffey, had been instrumental in establishing Tradeweb in the late 1990s, and he would later become its CEO. On 9/11, Olesky spent hours in his midtown hotel room making calls in search of information about the 85 Tradeweb staffers who worked in the North Tower (all made it out safely). "It was hard to get a phone line," he later explained. "When I got one, I kept it open for two and a half days. That was quite an expensive phone bill."

Early in the morning New York time, per its standard routine, BrokerTec in London started brokering buy-sell trading in Treasuries. On his Blackberry, Olesky soon began to see nasty e-mails pointing out that the BMA had recommended a stop in such trading: "So I made a unilateral decision to immediately shut that trading down."[14]

Significantly, and consistent with the BMA's recommendation, the repo market remained open in order to allow financial institutions access to critical funding. Except for BrokerTec, none of the brokers participated in this trading, nor did many major dealers, including Citibank, Daiwa, Dean Witter, Fuji and Mizuho Capital. Nevertheless, by day's end, close to 3,000 repo transactions, worth more than $111 billion, had been submitted to GSCC for comparison.

With the normal market-pricing mechanism for the funding market now gone, it was unclear what the rate on repo trades should be. Joe Blauvelt was Chairman of the Bond Market Association's Funding Division: "We needed to open the market, but we couldn't go into a real bid-and-offer mode yet because many desks weren't up and running." With the knowledge of the BMA staff and regulators, albeit in a manner that might have raised distinct anti-trust questions in ordinary times, Blauvelt and the heads of several larger repo desks entered into a gentlemen's agreement to set the general collateral repo rate at 3.5 percent, based on the target federal funds rate. They limited trading only to transactions done for funding purposes, and to not take on matched book or risk-taking positions. With the exception of one uncooperative trader (who was ostracized by the others), the agreement held for the rest of the week, although the agreed-upon repo rate swiftly dropped to one percent as the Fed poured money into the financial system.[15]

With the financing market open, operations staff were needed, and Jersey City was the destination for many of them. Known as "Wall Street West" since the development of its financial district beginning in the 1980s, the space along the Jersey City waterfront had become home to various large financial institutions. Geography had been unkind to the Govie market on 9/11, and lower Manhattan and Jersey City are close enough to each other that their skylines meld when viewed from afar. Nonetheless, the separation of the two areas by the Hudson River, and their different power and communications grids, proved crucial to the healing of the market.

Nick Gialanella went to Jersey City, where Refco had offices, for the first time. By mid-morning, around 300 Refco staffers had shown up, assembling in a space designed to hold 60. Many were assigned to establish a working communications structure, requiring some to go shopping at the nearby Newport Mall for laptops, printers, cables and related equipment.

Work progressed until about 1:30 p.m., when a bomb threat was called in and the building was evacuated. Gialanella and his colleagues, working on the top floor of what was then the tallest building in Jersey City, trudged down 36 flights along with displaced staff from Merrill Lynch and other financial companies using that building as their disaster recovery site. Given the building's swollen population, it took Gialanella almost an hour to walk down. As he waited on the street for the "all clear" announcement, his wife called. Hearing about the bomb scare, she pleaded with him to come home, but he stayed, along with most of his colleagues.

After only a couple of hours of sleep, Ron Purpora also was bound for Jersey City, heading to Prebon's offices, which Garban would be using as a backup location. On the drive there, and throughout the morning, Purpora received calls from customers concerned about their transactions in Treasuries that had been executed with Garban. One Chicago customer, who was owed $5 million of five-year

Treasury notes, called solely to ask Purpora if Garban would fail to deliver on those securities. Purpora had no clue at that point. He considered telling the guy "go fuck yourself," but opted for a benign "don't know yet."

After Purpora located Prebon's offices, he and his Garban management team settled into a conference room. With their London office on the phone, Purpora asked the group, "How do we put the company back together again?" The most immediate issue was deciding what to tell their people. Purpora was particularly worried about retaining his brokers, who might get job offers from functioning firms. And, if he could keep them, where would he tell them to work?

The group reviewed the role of every employee, and how each one would be best used over the coming days. Then they discussed the bare infrastructure they required. "Our IT guy tells me that we needed at least 200 PCs. I screamed, 'Where are we gonna get them? Everyone else is looking for them!' I thought we'd literally have to go to California to get that amount," Purpora recalled.

Recapping their financial position led to the stark realization that the $6 billion borrowed from Chase represented an interest cost that could bring down the firm. Reducing that obligation to zero became a priority. To accomplish that, Garban would have to reassemble its operations department as quickly as possible, even before re-establishing its trading function.

Garban's management had called in SunGard, a large business-continuity vendor, to assist. One of SunGard's clients, Buy and Hold Securities Corp., a small broker-dealer, had a large disaster recovery site in Edison, New Jersey. Buy and Hold quickly agreed to sub-let space there to SunGard for Garban's benefit. Garban shifted most of its operations staff to Edison; that site came to be known as the "Bunker."[16] As SunGard's John Schipano emphasized, "Not only did Buy and Hold immediately give up space, but they also installed over a hundred phone lines for Garban. And shared their connectivity pipe."[17]

Many of the large dealers grappled with their September 12 priorities. Tom Russo, by then Vice Chairman and chief legal officer of Lehman Brothers, had been asked by his boss, Dick Fuld, to write up the agenda for the Wednesday morning meeting of the top brass, who were assembling in cramped backup space in Jersey City. Russo, who had no access to a PC, wrote out the agenda in long hand, thinking that he hadn't been taught in law school how to bring a major firm back to life. Lehman's focus that morning was similar to Garban's. "We discussed where we were and what capabilities we had," Russo recounted. "It turned out that one of our first tasks was to buy a massive amount of equipment."

At Nomura, late at night on 9/11, Murray Pozmanter had gotten in touch with a portion of his operations staff, instructing them to report the next day to their backup location in Piscataway, located in central New Jersey. Around 5 a.m., Pozmanter drove down the New Jersey Turnpike, which was virtually empty: "At the point on the turnpike where you could see all the way to New York, you saw the smoke coming up. The signs simply said, 'New York City closed.' There seemed to be such finality to it."

The Piscataway backup site originally had been set up for only a limited number of traders. It had minimal equipment and systems.[18] Fortunately during 1999, as part of its Y2K preparations, Nomura had invested in improvements to that facility. Pozmanter, joined by about a third of his staff, found the site in decent shape, although with some connectivity and systems problems. Turning his attention to the business, Pozmanter recalled, "We were concerned about what happened to all the activity that had been done the morning of 9/11. Did it count? Were those trades going to be voided?"

The Regulators Weigh In

Peter Fisher had left the Secret Service office in D.C. in the middle of the night of 9/11, traveling in a downtown Washington laden with armored vehicles and policemen at key intersections. He'd been given a large, solid silver briefcase containing a secure phone that made him feel like Maxwell Smart. Fisher had come home to discover that his eight-year old daughter had been extremely upset by the day's events, because she knew that when they lived in New York, her father had walked between the "Twin Towers" on his way to work at the Fed.

On Wednesday morning, Fisher assured his family that he was just going to the office, and would stay in D.C. But within the hour, he had called his wife to tell her that he'd be traveling to New York on Amtrak with Harvey Pitt and several SEC staffers. Pitt had become SEC Chairman just a month earlier. His swearing-in ceremony, which is traditional but not officially required, had been set for September 17 with Vice President Dick Cheney. It never happened.[19]

Pitt had issued a statement on 9/11 supporting the exchanges' decision not to open for trading, but indicating that "the disruption to normal trading patterns is a temporary phenomenon; trading will resume as soon as it is practicable to do so."[20] On Wednesday, September 12, Pitt made an appearance on ABC's "Good Morning America" to update the public. Pitt startled the program's hosts when, towards the end of the interview, he opined that when the markets reopened, "there would be some nifty values to be realized by buyers." Pitt later admitted, "I'm not sure Congress intended an SEC Chairman to advocate stock purchases. But we were already focused on avoiding an imbalance of supply and demand."[21]

Pitt wanted to meet with the major New York firms to discuss how to resume the markets. Fisher agreed to join him. Fisher already had been in touch with the White House, mainly through his conversations with Larry Lindsey, Director of the National Economic Council and Assistant to the

President for Economic Policy, and Lindsey's deputy, Marc Sumerlin. On the ride up, he conferred with the large dealers and BMA staff on multiple conference calls. Fisher lectured them on the importance of returning to a fully functioning Treasury market, and he spoke concretely about reopening the next day. "There was a lot of anxiety about that," he recalled. "People felt strongly that we weren't ready, because of all that had been lost."

Fisher's Treasury colleagues faced many issues. One was the impact of the 9/11 events on expected tax receipts. Would a tax holiday need to be declared? What specific extensions to filing deadlines would be available? What would be the effect on the federal government's cash flow of any waivers of due dates? Don Hammond of the Bureau of the Public Debt was worried that certain tax processors based in New York might not make payments. He spent the afternoon at the IRS.

Fisher focused on the Treasury market's overall health. In talks on 9/11 with his boss, Treasury Secretary O'Neill, they had agreed that key for the Treasury market, beyond rebuilding infrastructure, was the restoration of trust in the financial system. During his calls, Fisher was candid about the intangible factors at play: "Certainly there's a hardware and systems component. But underneath, markets are about the faith that people have in one another. The belief that, if I say, 'Done,' you can deliver your side of the deal to me. And when you shatter that trust, it takes something more than just blowing a whistle and saying 'Okay' to build it up again."

A major step towards building confidence in all of the markets would be to reopen the most critical one. Fisher realized that the de-centralized nature of the Govie market was an advantage. There was no single building that needed to be restored in order to resume trading; the Govie market is a global network and adaptable. Fisher asked the large dealers: since they were quoting prices and making markets in Treasury securities out of their London and Tokyo offices to non-U.S. clients, why not make the same markets for U.S.-based clients from whatever locations they might have available, including New Jersey. No one disagreed.

As their train left Newark's Penn Station on its final leg into Manhattan, Fisher and Pitt could see the pillars of smoke that had replaced the Trade Center. They arrived in New York in the late morning, assisted in traveling through Manhattan by Governor George Pataki's office, which had arranged for them to have cars at their disposal as well as police escort.[22] By the time Fisher and Pitt arrived, the Bond Market Association was finishing an extraordinary conference call.

How and When to Reopen the Fixed-Income Markets

It was a call that might have been impossible to arrange if Eric Foster, the secretary of the BMA's Calendar Committee, hadn't found in his apartment a list of the home phone numbers of the organization's key officials. Soon after Foster arrived home on 9/11, he spoke with his boss, Paul Saltzman, about the need to convene the Calendar Committee first thing the next morning, both to clarify that the market wouldn't open on that Wednesday and to decide whether it would reopen on Thursday.

Saltzman had gotten little sleep. Up before dawn and stuck in his house in Westchester, he began a flood of phone calls, many with officials from the Federal Reserve and the Treasury. "I don't want to say that the government ran the show, but I made sure that there was nothing we did of importance in those early days that wasn't first discussed at length with them," Saltzman explained. It was a symbiotic relationship because the Treasury and Fed officials were sensitive about mandating private-sector decisions, and they looked to the BMA to create an industry consensus. Saltzman also provided the regulators with critical information on the status of the players in the operational crisis, including reporting later in the day that he had just come off a Primary Dealers Committee call where "we polled every BoNY client as to whether or not they were connected to BoNY, and every one said no."

Saltzman wanted every significant action ratified by his members: "There was a tremendous sense of civic and collective interest and goal," he later noted. "Everyone was trying to do the right thing." He and Foster decided to schedule a 10 a.m. call for members of the Association's board of directors and the Calendar Committee. Earlier in the year, Saltzman had asked Foster to compile a list of board and Calendar Committee members' home phone numbers. Foster spent much of the afternoon and evening of 9/11 trying to reach each one. He also posted a notice of the meeting on the BMA's website. That website had rapidly become the market's central forum for communication, receiving more than 382,000 hits on September 12, more than three times the historical high.[23]

Saltzman and Foster knew that, despite the agreeability of members during individual calls, the collective discussion of when and how to reopen the market could be a difficult one. There were many valid arguments for keeping it closed on Thursday. Resuming activity would make sense only if the trades could be timely and accurately confirmed and settled; yet this was unlikely given the damage to the operations infrastructure. A respite to give the market's "plumbing" time to recover, and for the gathering of records, was desirable. In addition, given the absence of the inter-dealer brokers (who helped promote liquidity), and the dislocation of several major dealers, the overall viability of the market was suspect. It was uncertain whether trades could be adequately priced or if risk could be properly hedged.

The most sensitive issues related to those brokers whose offices in the Trade Center had been destroyed: Cantor, Euro Brokers, Garban and Tradeweb. It was reasonable to assume that it could take weeks for them to get back into business. Would the prompt resumption of trading sound the death knell for those firms? Some dealers appeared unsympathetic towards the brokers' plight. When Omer Oztan of the BMA called the global head of repo for one primary dealer to get some market color, he was treated to a tirade about the brokers not being there to make a market. "He tells me that if they weren't brokers, they'd be out on the street boosting cars," Oztan remembered. "I just hung up the phone."

Also, the President's Working Group on Financial Markets had issued a press release on Wednesday supporting the decision of the equities, options and futures markets to remain closed. That release emphasized that the decision to close "reflects respect for the terrible loss of life."[24] Given that, was it appropriate to reopen a market in which hundreds of colleagues had been killed and their remains awaited identification, memorial services and burials? Would restarting the Govie market be perceived as grossly insensitive?

Fisher had weighed in with Saltzman that morning, deliberately playing the bad cop by making clear that a reopening of the Govie market should not depend on everyone's participation. All that was needed was a sufficient core group. "That was an unpleasant thing to have to say, but I worried that if it were left unsaid, we would never get there," Fisher recounted. Saltzman understood that the government would press for this, even at the price of some market players' demise.

From a public policy perspective, the closing of any segment of the market was unpalatable. On Wednesday morning, a small group of the senior management of the New York State Banking Department, driven out of their offices at Two Rector Street a few blocks south of the Trade Center, had convened in Midtown. They made use of makeshift space across from the New York Public Library that had been donated to them by HSBC Bank. The group debated the merits of declaring a formal bank holiday. (In the afternoon of 9/11, Governor Pataki had issued a proclamation allowing banks to close at their discretion.) Sara Kelsey, the General Counsel, argued in favor of it, out of concern for the potential liability the banks might incur from the numerous branch closings and operational disruptions. "If there were ever grounds for a bank holiday, it was during that first week," Kelsey said. But Banking Superintendent Elizabeth McCaul, weighing in from Japan where she had been fulfilling a speaking engagement, nixed the idea, fearing the message such an action would convey to the world.[25]

A delay in the resumption of the Govie market presented tangible negative impact. The federal government needed to fund itself. Investors sought the market's safety. Traders relied on the market to hedge risk. Other markets depended on its pricing mechanism. And perhaps the greatest imperative – that acts of terrorism must not be allowed to impair the markets.

The BMA roll call alone took almost a half hour. Although the meeting was intended exclusively for the Calendar Committee and the board of directors, hundreds of people dialed in, including representatives of every major market regulator.[26] Saltzman, who was moderating the call, quickly realized that he would be unable to control who was participating. He allowed it to proceed as a "general information" meeting. Micah Green, President of the BMA, had dialed in from California, where he was stuck. "Paul had to constantly remind people to put their phones on mute if they weren't speaking," remembered Green. "People weren't as teleconference savvy then. So the initial speakers were somewhat unintelligible at first. But it worked out."

During the roll call, many participants learned for the first time that Howard Lutnick, the head of Cantor Fitzgerald, and Steve Merkel, his General Counsel, were alive. As the meeting began, Saltzman, on behalf of the industry, expressed deep sympathy for the loss suffered by Cantor and Euro Brokers, and asked for a moment of silence. Lutnick then assured those on the call that Cantor would remain in business. Tom Wipf of Morgan Stanley was listening in from London: "That set a big tone. If Cantor would continue, then there was no sense anymore that any market participants would cease to exist."

Saltzman told the group that he had just been contacted by a senior Treasury Department official, who had expressed strong support for reopening the bond market the next day. The Fed and SEC representatives on the call followed this comment by asking that the market reopen as soon as possible. Only then did GSCC, BoNY, and Chase, the three branches of the "golden triangle" of settlement, report on their status. Tom Costa stated that the clearing corporation was up and running and that output was available, but he noted that most members had not been receiving that output. Tom Perna assured that BoNY, despite having lost both its primary and backup locations, was still operating from a tertiary site that was processing the trading activity of September 11 and 12. And Al Clark reported that Chase had maintained its operations throughout 9/11 at a backup facility.

A question and answer session followed. Though initially orderly, it deteriorated as speakers shouted commentary into the phone, drowning out others. Saltzman, after pleading with the operator to mute the lines, and telling various participants to "shut up," attempted to close the call in order to start another one on the crisis in the commercial paper market, where a massive failure to settle had occurred.[27] As he tried to end the session, participants screamed out questions about where and how they could contact each other. Saltzman reminded the audience of the Association's web site availability for posting the location of people and sites.[28]

An Unpleasant Reality

On 9/11, Tom Perna had walked up to BoNY's backup management post in its Fifth Avenue branch in Midtown, where he spent most of the day trying to obtain information on BoNY's positions and communicate with clients. Around 11 p.m., Perna and his staff decided they could be more productive at BoNY's contingency facility in Pleasantville, a village in Westchester County about 40 miles north of lower Manhattan. They took a midnight train from Grand Central Terminal, stopping to shower at the home of one of them.

When Perna reached the Pleasantville site, he was faced with an unpleasant reality. "We had plenty of desktops, but they were all sitting on the floor, covered in dust," he recalled. "Many weren't even connected. It was a huge, beautiful building, but it wasn't properly set up for contingency." That assessment became more apparent on Wednesday morning, when over 2,000 staff showed up, but many were unable to be productive.

Perna's Plan B was to get over to BoNY's designated government securities backup center in Maywood, New Jersey, a small town not far from the George Washington Bridge. "There was a kid working for me who also lived in my town," he remembered. "I found him and told him that he was my driver. We stopped at my house, where I grabbed about a week's worth of clothes, and off we went to Maywood."

When Perna arrived in Maywood, he found his top staffers huddled in front of the building. "What the fuck is going on?" he demanded. They showed him one terminal and one phone that together constituted the backup center for government securities clearance. Maywood was a large, new facility, full of PCs, desks, plants and art, but it had been set up as a retail call center. It had little that would accommodate the requirements of the government securities operations staff.

Perna screamed at the manager running the facility, who was focused on retail activity and unhelpful. Perna then called Tom Renyi, BONY's Chairman, and vented. The facility manager was given his marching orders to cooperate with Perna. (That manager and his staff were soon relocated.)[29]

Across the Hudson, Al Clark's Chase team, who had slept overnight in their offices, focused on communicating with clients to assess their positions. They helped other Chase operations staff, who couldn't get to the bank's offices in Manhattan, find alternate space with customers. "That proved useful as those guys were able to represent the bank and give in-office help to clients," said Clark.

In both Manhattan and Brooklyn, GSCC staff were attempting to figure out which of their members were still functioning. Bart Schiavo kept the list of member contacts. "One by one, by phone, e-mail, whatever communication means was available, we determined who we had talked to and who we hadn't and, if we hadn't talked to them, why," Schiavo recounted. Others worked the phones to locate members' disaster recovery sites, although in many cases that information was of little use given the telecommunications hurdles throughout the area.[30]

Meanwhile, conditions at 55 Water Street remained challenging. To the dismay of many, a handful of those working on the floor smoked in their offices, in defiance of company policy and building code, compounding the poor air quality. The vending machines were bare, as were the local stores. The TV stopped working, while rumors ran rampant, including one of the potential for additional building collapses nearby.

Allison Mansfield was assigned to call the homes of those employees not yet accounted for. "Each time I dialed the phone I thought, 'Please let this person have made it home.' Luckily, everyone had," she recalled.

Around noon, Tom Costa was on the phone with Joe Blauvelt of Chase, discussing how repo trading was going. Blauvelt, who was at 40 Wall Street, only a few blocks away, mentioned a cafeteria. Costa cut him off: "Does it have food? We're starving!" Blauvelt offered him their extra food, including enough roast beef sandwiches to feed 30 people. He told Costa that his guys would bring it over within the hour, but nothing arrived. "As it turned out, there were National Guard units on Water Street, with machine guns," Costa explained. "The unit on the east side of the street was different from the one on the west side, and they didn't communicate with each other. So they wouldn't permit the Chase guys, who were wheeling huge platters of food on carts, to cross the street."

Costa asked Marc Golin and Murray Targownik, one of the GSCC attorneys, to meet the Chase staff at a halfway point. Wearing paper masks, they walked to the corner of Water and Wall streets, but were prevented from going further. Golin used his cell phone to get the number of someone on Blauvelt's staff. "I didn't have a pen or paper in my hand, so I relayed the number to Murray, who wrote the number with his fingers on a mailbox covered in a gray film," Golin remembered. "That was effective but not so smart because we thought it contained asbestos." Blauvelt vouched for the carts, but even after getting the food, Golin and his coworkers had to negotiate with their building's security staff before they were allowed to bring the metallic trays into the building.

When Could the Stock Markets Reopen?

Regardless of the importance of the bond markets, the most recognizable segment of the financial markets was the stock exchanges. Their status would send the most visible public message to the world about the health of the U.S. financial system.

With that in mind, Peter Fisher spent the afternoon with Harvey Pitt in the board room at Bear Stearns' midtown offices, at a meeting attended by all of the senior market regulators, the heads of most of the major financial firms, and representatives from the Federal Emergency Management Agency, and the offices of the Governor and the Mayor. Because the main topic of conversation was the viability of infrastructure in the city's Financial District, senior officials from Con Edison and Verizon were in attendance as well. Sal Sodano of the American Stock Exchange made it to the meeting from lower Manhattan. "Everyone was in their suits and ties," he remembered. "I came in wearing jeans covered in dust, with a mask on my head."

The summit had been requested by Pitt and arranged by Dick Grasso and James Cayne, the Chairman and CEO of Bear Stearns.[31] The meeting focused on the equities and options markets. Pitt made it clear that the senior market regulators were there not to dictate the decision as to when to reopen the markets but, rather, to facilitate a solution.

Fisher sensed the "prisoner's dilemma" that had arisen. The firms wanted sufficient certainty that the physical environment and communications network would be restored. Reinforcing the point, several executives left the meeting repeatedly to assess the damage to their operations.[32] On the other hand, the representatives on the infrastructure side needed to understand what the exchanges and firms required to recommence trading. Verizon's capacity to restore connectivity in lower Manhattan was discussed at length.

Fisher challenged the group to reopen the markets the next day. "If you all tell me that you want the 82d Airborne here, and that will help, I bet I can make that happen. And if you tell me that there's some generator that you need flown in here by helicopter, I bet that I can make that happen too," he assured. But he knew that the problem was greater than that. What everyone really feared was a premature opening of the equities markets without sufficient infrastructure or liquidity to handle large trading volumes. On September 11 and 12, global equities markets had uniformly plunged in a high-volume environment.[33]

Other considerations argued strongly against a Thursday reopening. The crippled American Stock Exchange building could not support any activity. It wasn't safe to send employees back into a Financial District that was still being cleaned and wired up. Moreover, the representatives from the Mayor's and Governor's offices were concerned that any return of people to Ground Zero might disrupt the rescue efforts.[34] The group also weighed the morality of resuming normal activity when the AMEX and many firms still had employees unaccounted for.[35]

Should the Govie Market Reopen on Thursday?
BMA's second call of the day on the Govie market started at 2 p.m. In the hours leading up to that call, Eric Foster, Omer Oztan, and other BMA staffers had spoken with dozens of members to gauge industry support for a reopening the following day. The response was almost universally positive.

Fortunately, the trading side of the fixed-income markets didn't have the same physical limitations as the equities markets had. But the members debated among themselves and with BMA staff as to whether the settlement process could handle a full day of trading. Brian Roseboro, listening in for the Treasury Department, had begun his career at the New York Fed and knew that the true risk was on the operational side. "We didn't want the trading to get too far ahead of the settlement process," he recounted.

One proposal was to open the market on Thursday but for abbreviated hours only. Opening later and closing earlier would help ease the trading side into a steady state. There was ample precedent for that. Normally before a major holiday, the market would close at 2 p.m. It was a comfortable proposition for firms to accept.

Fisher had argued against the idea with Saltzman. "Trying to be a hard ass, I said that we should just reopen the market and not get into a lot of fine print about what it means," Fisher admitted. "Clearly, there was a certain volume of pent up demand that was anticipated and which we wanted to see expressed in the markets. And that was the economically important thing to happen."

But the logic of an early closing was compelling. A briefer trading day would give operations staff more time to devote to settlement issues, and would signal to market participants that a day of light trading was expected.

Even with shortened trading hours and an absence of brokers, no one could predict the trading volume. There would likely be significant selling activity in the initial hours. The Kennedy assassination in November 1963 was perhaps the closest precedent, because many people at first believed that it was part of a broader attack on the U.S. government. The equity market was open at the time of the assassination and quickly fell four percent before trading was halted.[36]

If Govie volume on September 13 were considerable, it could overwhelm the capacity of an already overtaxed settlement process. Given the major reconciliation challenges for trades that had occurred on the morning of 9/11 and previously, which already had placed a tremendous strain on personnel and operations systems, a measure was needed to alleviate that burden.

Saltzman is a lawyer; he needed insight on this issue from operations professionals. He called, among others, Larry Lemmon of HSBC, a Wall Street veteran. Saltzman knew him well from when Lemmon was Chairman of the BMA's Operations Committee.

Lemmon had slept in his office on West 39th Street, in the shadow of the Empire State Building and within range of the burning Ground Zero stench. He ended up staying in Midtown until Saturday. Twice, the entire area around his building was evacuated because of bomb threats, and security told Lemmon to leave. "At times, it became a pain, because you needed pass keys and security codes to get through certain doors and hallways," Lemmon recalled. "One time, I got stuck in the hallway between doors and had to kick one open. Actually broke the door. Security came rushing in."

Unlike the equities markets, which settle trades on a fixed schedule three days later, those who trade Govies decide themselves, on a trade-by-trade basis, when settlement occurs. As a practical matter, the vast majority of buy-sell trades settle the next day, and are referred to as "T+1" trades (or, "trade date plus one"). If the market were to reopen on Thursday with a high volume of trading, the operational processes would be burdened with settling all of the trades by the very next day.[37]

During a brainstorming phone session, Lemmon asked Saltzman, "What if we extend the time for settlement? Make it T+3 settlement like it is on the equities side, and give two extra days to confirm and settle trades. That'll give opportunity for the operations guys to pick up the pieces." Saltzman and Foster floated the idea to others, and then planned to present it during the 2 p.m. call.

Extending the settlement cycle to help buy the Street time to resolve back-office problems was not novel. It was one of the measures used during the Paperwork Crisis that had occurred over three decades earlier, when the manual processes for executing and recording equities transactions, and moving paper in settlement of them, had needed time to catch up.[38] Now, this same measure could help the Govie market resume trading.

Extending the Settlement Cycle

Lengthening the settlement cycle had its advantages but created its own problems as well. The longer it takes for a trade to settle, the greater the attendant market and credit risks.[39] Although it turned out that no firm failed as a result of 9/11, that was a realistic prospect on September 12. Also, to switch to a T+3 schedule would require programming changes by dealer shops that in many cases were running at backup locations with minimal staff. And it would lead, down the road, to days of double settlements, which inevitably would cause other burdens.

Extended settlement further presented the danger of building a huge backlog of information for GSCC and the clearing banks. Increasing their trade files could overwhelm their systems.[40] If GSCC couldn't receive a market participant's trade data within three days for comparison and settlement, the clearing corporation might be forced to either extend its netting period, which had never been done, or again artificially compare trades, which could compound the ongoing reconciliation effort. From a risk perspective, GSCC would be guaranteeing those trades over a longer time period. Because it was essentially an industry cooperative, this would put the entire Street at risk if a firm were to actively trade and then fail.

Saltzman was concerned that the BMA had no precedent for issuing settlement recommendations in Govies. With the 2 p.m. call looming, Saltzman and his staff reached out to members to gauge their reaction to the early close of trading and extended settlement recommendations. Their responses were generally positive.

Again, the call was meant for specific groups – the board of directors, the Calendar Committee, and the Primary Dealers Committee. But more than 150 persons dialed in, including all the market regulators and the White House. After technical difficulties forced a termination, the call was reconvened at 2:30 p.m. as a general conference call of members, regulators, and other interested parties.

The clearing banks were asked for their status. Chase reported that its system was operating at 100 percent capacity. BoNY also indicated that it had full processing ability, although it needed to clear up trades from the day before. But callers openly challenged that representation, noting that trades they had attempted to clear through BoNY had not yet been resolved.[41]

Participants complained that their back-offices were already facing two days of trade reconciliations, and that operations personnel would be inundated unless there was light and orderly trading activity over the next two days. BMA staff then vetted with the group the ideas of a short day and an extended settlement cycle for Thursday and Friday trading. Both were readily approved.

At 3:15 p.m., Saltzman finally had a true Calendar Committee meeting, held together with the board and members of the Primary Dealers Committee. He again proposed a shortened trading day on Thursday. The group welcomed the idea, then considered whether the market should reopen on Wednesday night in Tokyo or Thursday morning in New York. It was decided that opening in Tokyo would be problematic; for one thing, it meant that the market would reopen in less than three hours with a small group of traders who usually handled a limited trading volume. In response to points raised by meeting participants, Saltzman reported that the Chicago Board of Trade had agreed to coordinate the opening and closing of its open outcry pits and electronic trading platform with the BMA's schedule.

The settlement recommendation for Govie buy-sell trades was then considered and fairly quickly adopted, given the human resources constraints and extensive operational difficulties. But the group rejected changing the settlement period for the funding (repo) market, in light of the broad span of that market and the individualized nature of business arrangements. They also decided to keep their alternatives open by limiting the Govie market's extended settlement change to Thursday and Friday.

The draft press release, which would be sent to media outlets and posted on the BMA website, was read by Saltzman. Regarding the resumption of trading, to blunt any criticism, the group asked that the press release include the language "taking into consideration health and safety concerns and the current logistical environment." To further shield against second-guessing of their decision, they asked that the statement include wording that the Association had consulted with the SEC, the Treasury

Department, and the Fed. Additional language was inserted noting that the BMA's proposals were just "recommendations," and market participants must decide for themselves whether to follow them.[42]

Saltzman informed the callers that any member firms that needed help gaining building access should contact the BMA's D.C. office. That office was preparing a list of "essential employees" to be delivered to the White House, which had pledged to assist. Soon thereafter, firms sent their lists to the BMA. Most provided a half-dozen or so names, but Goldman Sachs, lacking a backup site large enough to accommodate all of its staff and intent on returning downtown as soon as possible, faxed over about 1,500.[43] Seeing this, a fuming Saltzman instructed Foster not to accept any Goldman names at all, prompting a call to Saltzman from a senior Goldman official. "He starts screaming at me, telling me that everyone on that list was essential," Saltzman remembered. "I hung up on him. Later that day he called to apologize."

Critical decisions had been made by Wednesday afternoon that would alleviate some of the issues on the settlement side. But the operational crisis would continue to grow.

CHAPTER 9

THE SETTLEMENT CRISIS BUILDS

"BoNY couldn't send us any money or accept money or tell us what money had come in or gone out of our account. I was worried about whether we were going to survive as a functioning company."

Tom Costa, Chief Operating Officer, GSCC[1]

At Bear Stearns' midtown offices, the discussions regarding the exchanges were progressing. The extent of damage to lower Manhattan infrastructure had stunned those at the meeting. They addressed which telecommunications were working and, if internal systems were functioning, whether they could effectively connect with those of other banks and brokerage houses.[2]

Peter Fisher was in attendance, despite his even greater concern for the status of the bond markets. He was relieved to discover in the late afternoon that the BMA would support the reopening of Govie trading on September 13: "That was desperately important to me, because the consensus at the meeting I was sitting in on was that equity trading was not coming up on the 13th, nor could they say when it would be returning. And that was not what the White House wanted to hear, or what any of us wanted to say."

The assemblage at Bear Stearns weighed the desire to become operational as quickly as possible against two critical considerations. One was whether reopening would interfere with the efforts to rescue those who might remain trapped in the rubble.[3] The other was fear of market collapse and loss of investor confidence in the face of what likely would be record trading volume and possible panic selling when the equities exchanges reopened.[4] The consensus judgment, for a multitude of reasons including the uncertain viability of infrastructure and telecommunications as well as the safety of those returning to lower Manhattan, was to wait until at least Friday to reopen.

After the meeting, Harvey Pitt, Peter Fisher, and Dick Grasso, together with Hardwick Simmons, Chairman of the NASDAQ, held a press conference in the Bear Stearns auditorium. They put a best face on the circumstances: The banking system had remained open, the repo market was still functioning, trading in the Treasury market would be reestablished on September 13, and the industry was working on the reopening of the equity markets. Fisher later learned that the White House was surprised by and disappointed in the decision to postpone restoring the equities markets. "I made a boo boo by not phoning the White House before the press conference," he admitted.

At the New York Fed's building, a skeleton crew remained, including top management. Fedwire was being managed by staff at a backup facility in New Jersey. The Fed's Markets Group had managed to conduct its business on that day, albeit via the telephone and using manual records instead of the usual automated channels. Despite the difficulties, the Fed, wanting to show as much resilience as possible, continued to collect the standard statistical data from the primary dealers.

On 9/11, New Yorkers in droves had withdrawn a great deal of cash from their automated teller machines and bank branches. By the following day, local banks raised with the Fed their concern about cash shortages. With all bridges and tunnels into and out of New York City essentially closed, how would these institutions replenish their supply? If the public couldn't readily access their money, there might be panic and a potential run on the banks.

The New York Fed's Jamie Stewart asked his Cash and Protection functions to make special arrangements to deliver more than $425 million to local banks.[5] A convoy of 18-wheelers was dispatched from the Fed's operations center in New Jersey, driven by uniformed Fed staff accompanied by New Jersey state troopers. On the New York side of the Lincoln Tunnel, National Guard troops and New York City police were waiting to continue the escort. The ATMs in the city were restocked.[6]

Around 4:30 p.m. on Wednesday, New York City engineers in lower Manhattan were assessing the damage to One Liberty Plaza. They judged the building's structure suspect, fearing it had the potential to collapse or, worse, fall over. Upon hearing this, Stewart ordered an immediate evacuation of the Fed's building.[7] Suzanne Cutler was among those who left, walking east to William Street, past a National Guardsman who yelled to her, "I'd run!" She did. At 14th Street, Cutler managed to hail a taxi. The driver, wearing a turban, turned to her and announced that he was a Sikh, not an Arab, then drove off. "As we traveled north, people were sitting in cafes having food and drinks," Cutler recollected. "It was as if I had entered another country."

Running down Liberty Street, Jamie Stewart looked west over his shoulder: "I guess your mind can play tricks on you because I thought I could see the building twisting and getting ready to fall over. But of course it didn't." Back home in Cobble Hill, Brooklyn, he spent time comforting his four-year-old granddaughter, who kept asking about the burning buildings.

Tom Baxter, the New York Fed's General Counsel, was the last person to leave. Closing the massive black iron doors, he realized that there was no key to lock them. The building had never before been evacuated nor left unmanned. Those employees who were not relocated to the Fed's New Jersey backup site were asked to stay home, to the dismay of some who interpreted that to mean they weren't "essential."[8]

In the afternoon on Wednesday, Jon Volpe of GSCC operations started his trip to the MetroTech center in Brooklyn by catching a train out of Morristown, New Jersey. "There weren't a lot of cars parked at the station, but those that were there were scattered all over," he recalled. "They had been parked by people who I assume stayed at work. Or were gone."

Inability to Communicate

For GSCC, the day had opened with a huge amount of securities – $266 billion – that had failed to be delivered to buyers on the scheduled date ("fails").[9] It was likely that some of the deliveries actually had been made, but the data communications disruptions with BoNY prevented GSCC from determining, for a good chunk of the market, what had settled. Convention required it to assume that nothing had, resulting in many inaccurate delivery instructions for participants.[10]

The clearing corporation's systems were functioning; it conducted netting and created settlement obligations in the early morning. GSCC had regained voice contact with all of the brokers to varying degrees, and received approval from those who had lost connectivity with Chase to access their accounts through GSCC's interface with Chase. Also, using the standard file transfer protocol and email, GSCC and SIAC staff established the means to receive and transmit participants' data files. Development personnel then worked with Chase staff to write and test the code to load receive and deliver orders.

Ordinarily, GSCC sent electronic transmissions and a backup tape every morning to Chase and BoNY with instructions about which members it should receive securities from and deliver securities to. Those dealers and brokers that cleared through Chase were able to receive and deliver securities.[11] But what about the other half of the market that settled through BoNY?

On Wednesday, settlement instructions for securities handled by BoNY were generated and distributed to members, but they would be useless unless GSCC also could load them with BoNY itself. When Seven World Trade Center collapsed in the late afternoon of 9/11, GSCC's link to BoNY had gone down. On Wednesday morning, GSCC staff couldn't communicate with BoNY, or even be sure that BoNY was operational.

This lack of communication with BoNY put GSCC in crisis. The clearing corporation was essentially a middleman between its numerous members; its role was to facilitate the movement through it of securities and funds, not to retain them. On that Wednesday, GSCC was in the dark as to which securities had either come into its BoNY account or been delivered out, and BoNY was unable to receive instructions from GSCC. This meant that the clearing corporation couldn't accurately inform its members which securities to deliver to it or receive from it. Proper settlement was impossible.

In addition to settling securities movements, GSCC used BoNY to collect and pay out money, primarily mark-to-market and margin amounts that were crucial to ensuring appropriate risk management for the market. If members had sent money to GSCC on 9/11 or on the day after, it wasn't aware of that. As a result, GSCC might ask for the funds again. Conversely, if GSCC had paid members, it might repeat payment. The funds settlement process needed to be suspended.

BoNY also provided prices for securities posted as collateral to GSCC's margin pool, known as the Clearing Fund, which protected the entire industry. Because the clearing corporation couldn't receive BoNY pricing files, securities collateral on deposit from members in the Clearing Fund was priced at the same value all week instead of being marked-to-market.[12] The combination of lack of pricing capability and suspension of the funds settlement process eliminated GSCC's capacity to properly risk manage its positions, including the enormous fails that had been created. If a market participant went out of business as a result of 9/11, the industry as a whole would be at risk.

Reinstating communication with BoNY became the main priority. Late in the day, GSCC managed to reach BoNY operations staff at a home in Staten Island. A connection with BoNY was finally established, enabling the clearing corporation to obtain information on its account, revealing what had cleared late on that second day.

But that data flow came at a cost. Dave Buckmaster drafted almost everyone at 55 Water Street into manually punching in the information. "This compounded the problems that were being created, as we were bypassing our normal controls," Buckmaster recounted. "At one in the morning, people were inputting data instead of sleeping. Not the safest or most secure way to do things. But we were trying to get through the day."

By early Thursday morning, operations staff could see that GSCC had about $31 billion in securities sitting in its account at BoNY. A staggering amount for a not-for-profit company with minimal working capital that was expected to be "flat" at all times. BONY's automated systems had accepted delivery of and made payment for securities on behalf of GSCC without receiving settlement instructions from it as to where the securities should be redelivered to.[13] Reducing its box would be an issue GSCC would deal with later in the day.

No senior operations official on the Street got much respite that night. BoNY's Tom Perna was still working feverishly to get the Maywood site up to snuff. Because of the lack of connectivity, firms that cleared through BoNY had not received the transaction journals (TJs) that detail which securities had moved against money. Those firms were uncertain about which of their trades had actually settled.[14]

One key BoNY client was Goldman Sachs. Ed Watts headed Goldman's global operations. He tracked Perna down in Maywood: "I told him that BoNY should have had real backup, and that he was responsible for all the securities in my BoNY box. That I wasn't paying any financing cost on them!" Watts earlier had been screamed at by Goldman's eager-to-resume-business Govie traders after he told them, "Listen, our bank can't move anything. We gotta roll everything over today."

The securities portion of Fedwire had closed at 10:45 p.m., which was more than seven hours after its normal closing time. The funds Fedwire had remained open until 11:30 p.m., five hours past its usual closing time. Fed staff had considered carefully how late Fedwire could remain open, determining they couldn't let it extend beyond midnight in order to preserve the integrity of the business day.[15]

The extension of Fedwire was a double-edged sword. Although it provided more time for firms having operational difficulties to settle trades and clean up errors, their operational staff had to monitor the ongoing Fedwire activity. They were simultaneously trying to square their books and records while reconciling *new* activity, delaying preparation for the following day's opening.

As the Fedwire's close time continued to be extended, Tom Costa grew angry: "The same staff who were actually handling government securities clearances were the same and only ones responsible for reconciling differences. But they were exhausted and had no time to do this." Costa called Fed officials and argued that they shouldn't extend Fedwire in the coming days, and that it should be opened only at noon and closed by 2 p.m. "They probably thought I was insane," he admitted. "But I felt that all we needed was a short window to move securities, not a day-long one that was draining staff energy and taking focus away from unraveling the mess of the prior two days." That night, GSCC operations personnel in Manhattan and at MetroTech worked around the clock to complete the day's work and to prepare for the market's opening on September 13.[16]

Some staff were allowed to go home and sleep so that they could relieve others the following day. Adrian Vanderlinden left work at about 10:30 p.m., ignoring advice from colleagues to stay and sleep there, given the rumors that people who were out late near Ground Zero would be arrested. "I figured that, since I lived within the frozen zone, I could go home and be able to come back," he said. "Outside our building, there was no electricity. Everything was still smoldering. There was a terrible smell and a layer of powder about an inch-and-a-half thick. By the time I got to the end of Wall Street by Broadway, it was literally four inches thick. There were abandoned cars in the middle of the street with their doors open. ATM machines covered with dust. Shoes strewn all over and phones off the hook. The only people around were emergency personnel."

That night, Joe Grima, head of operations for BrokerTec, stayed in Weehawken, New Jersey, at a business complex right off the water. After arriving there at 1 a.m., he couldn't sleep. "So I went out back to look at the city," he recalled. "It was aglow, with smoke still rising. There must have been 25 other people out there, also quietly watching."

While lower Manhattan remained devastated, and the search for Trade Center survivors continued, the Govie market would reopen in full within a few hours. No one could predict with any certainty how it would function. Those with even a modicum of responsibility in that market had to be on the verge of physical and mental exhaustion. The next 24 hours would be critical.

CHAPTER 10

THURSDAY: RESURRECTION

*"Secretary O'Neil and Chairman
Greenspan, soon after they stepped onto
American soil, were able to make the
announcement that the bond markets were
back. It was so important that the leaders of
our economy be able to say these markets
were up and running 48 hours after the
attack. Particularly given that the stock
markets wouldn't open until Monday."*

Paul Saltzman, General Counsel, Bond
Market Association[1]

On Thursday, September 13, U.S. air traffic
resumed, but only a limited number of flights took
off. The Federal Aviation Administration gave
couriers, critical to the check-clearing system,
approval to recommence their chartered flights.[2] On
Tuesday and Wednesday, in order to keep that
system operational during the flight ban, the Fed had
guaranteed deposit settlement to collecting banks,
even though checks couldn't be timely presented.[3]

While the rest of the world tried to make sense
of what had occurred, New York City strained to
return to normal. Telephone service in lower
Manhattan was being restored, although at least

200,000 of the roughly half-million phone lines south of 14th Street remained out.[4] The mayoral primary, halted in mid-vote after the attacks, was rescheduled for September 25. The Mayor's Office of Emergency Management established a "compassion center" where thousands of New Yorkers lined up to find or identify loved ones. It was located in the Armory, a windowless brick fortress at 26th Street and Lexington Avenue that had been a former weapons warehouse. As one observer described: "The distressed and distracted filled out long forms, provided dental records, recited wedding band inscriptions, tried to describe scars and tattoos – all of it more clues for the coroners. Some needed counseling; others simply needed an ear. All had to wait for hours."[5]

For firms that had been based in lower Manhattan, the scramble to locate new office space continued. Lehman Brothers moved staff to a cramped space in Jersey City. It also took over a good part of the Sheraton Hotel on Seventh Avenue in Midtown, discarding beds, turning rooms into offices, and recasting a ballroom as an IT hub.[6] Merrill Lynch relocated workers to crowded offices in four separate towns in New Jersey.[7] The Securities Industry Association's displaced New York legal staff worked out of the midtown offices of Bernard L. Madoff Investment Securities.[8] The SEC's Northeast Regional Office took space in an auditorium at Fordham Law School, near Lincoln Center.[9]

Salomon Brothers, now a part of Citigroup,[10] had its trading floors less than a mile north of the

World Trade Center. Salomon relocated to a makeshift facility in Jersey City. Paper taped to cubicle dividers identified the various trading desks, jammed with staff. As one Citi executive put it, "People feel an obligation to each other to be here."[11]

Refco found a unique solution. Two years earlier, a Refco trader had given money to Baruch College, his alma mater, to help build a mock trading floor for educational purposes. Located at Lexington Avenue and 23rd Street, the Baruch classroom was fully stocked with T1 lines, Reuters terminals, and an electronic wall display with real-time market prices. On Thursday, Baruch agreed to install additional phone lines. Soon thereafter, 25 Refco futures traders took over the facility for a month.[12]

In a U.S. crisis, individuals and institutions impulsively hoard dollars. As much as two-thirds of dollars in circulation are held abroad,[13] worrying the Fed about the availability of dollars worldwide. It promptly entered into a currency swap agreement with the European Central Bank (ECB) that allowed the ECB to draw up to $50 billion in exchange for euro deposits.[14] The ECB made those dollar deposits available to European central banks, which helped European commercial banks meet any dollar liquidity needs.[15] Along with his Fed colleagues, Jamie Stewart saw that "once we made money available in Europe, the dollar started recirculating, and people weren't holding on to everything out of fear that they couldn't get new dollars." Similar arrangements were made with the Bank of England and the Bank of Canada.[16]

The Treasury Department took further measures to reassure the public, including announcing a tax relief program for individual and business taxpayers unable to meet their Federal tax obligations, due on September 15, because of the disruption caused by the 9/11 attacks.[17] Treasury Secretary O'Neill stood before TV cameras to reject the concerns, voiced by many private economists, that 9/11 would destroy consumer confidence and tip the slowing U.S. economy into a recession.[18]

The Stock Exchanges Remain Closed

The business world's attention was on the U.S. equities markets, which remained closed. Peter Quick, President of the American Stock Exchange, with help from Governor Pataki and Ron Shindel, who ran the Ground Zero operations for the New York Police Department, received permission for about 200 workers from Turner Construction Company to repair the AMEX's severely damaged building. Escorted through the cordons by police, they began restoration work that Thursday morning, while the search and rescue efforts continued nearby.[19]

Harvey Pitt and Peter Fisher traveled to lower Manhattan in the morning.[20] To Pitt, it was a scene "straight out of some science fiction movie depicting an invasion from outer space."[21] They met at the New York Stock Exchange with Verizon officials, only to learn that 80 percent of the Exchange's communication network was out of operation.[22]

Later in the day, the group that had met at Bear Stearn's offices reconvened at the offices of Credit Suisse First Boston to resume discussion about reopening the exchanges on Friday. That idea was quickly rejected. The target date would be Monday.[23]

A host of concerns, similar to those that had been put forth the day before, lay behind the decision to delay. Securities firms and mutual funds worried that a Friday reopening would be piecemeal at best and might further damage investor trust. Don Kittell of the Securities Industry Association helped to give voice to that view: "We understood the policy and symbolic reasons for a quick reopening, but the last thing we wanted was to open the market and not have it be sustainable."[24]

The physical condition of downtown Manhattan remained an overwhelming consideration. The small and congested Financial District was filled with rescue workers, emergency vehicles, and debris. Flooding that area with tens of thousands of people from the financial industry would challenge not only the transit system but, also the salvage efforts, which took top priority.[25]

Through the efforts of Verizon, MCI WorldCom, and the affected firms and markets, the area's telecommunications capability had improved in the past two days.[26] But significant issues remained. Notably, the intermarket trading system that allowed the NASDAQ and the popular electronic communication networks, such as Island, Archipelago and Instinet, to trade NYSE-listed stocks had an unresolved connectivity point of failure.[27]

While government officials were increasingly anxious for the equities markets to resume, they recognized the inevitability of the decision to delay. Bill McDonough, the New York Fed's President, had a paramount concern: "The additional volume of clearing that would have been needed on the first day would have tested a system that was still being repaired."[28]

The weekend lay ahead and, with it, further time to assess and recover. Would the two days provide enough cushion to risk announcing a Monday reopening? It was believed that access and infrastructure were sufficient for personnel to conduct a widespread test on Saturday of systems' operability and connectivity. If problems were uncovered, there would be Sunday to resolve them. Dick Grasso pushed for this, arguing fiercely that another day couldn't go by without a public pronouncement of when the equities markets would reopen. Some firms grumbled that if the test proved unsuccessful, they might not be there on Monday. Peter Fisher responded that not every market participant would be needed on Monday, just "a critical mass."

On Thursday afternoon, Grasso announced at a press conference that the New York Stock Exchange and the NASDAQ would resume trading at 9:30 a.m. on Monday. Grasso emphasized the importance of ensuring that the reopening not interfere with rescuers still endeavoring to save victims and recover bodies. Hardwick Simmons, NASDAQ Chairman, then revealed that the NYSE and NASDAQ would run a full-scale test on Saturday. Steve Randich, chief technology officer for the NASDAQ, remembered: "There was a big sigh of relief because we knew that we weren't going to enter Monday blind, without having tested the production environment."

Resumption of Fixed-Income Trading

As for the U.S. fixed-income markets, trading resumed at 8 a.m. on Thursday and proceeded smoothly, albeit lightly.[29] Govie prices rose as investors fled to the quality of Treasury securities and anticipated further cuts in the federal funds rate. The yield on the Two-Year Treasury note fell below three percent, the lowest rate for that security since it was first issued in the late 1970s.[30]

Atypically, the Govie trading done on September 13 was largely dealer-to-dealer. BrokerTec did a modest amount of trading, but with many dealers at contingency sites, connectivity to BrokerTec was an issue.[31] The large dealers all were back in business, although J.P. Morgan evacuated its trading floor in Midtown at noon after a "word-of-mouth alarm" that proved false.[32] Joe Blauvelt was among those forced to leave. He recounted: "As we walked down the stairs, you thought about the people in the Trade Center. By the time we got out, there was complete paranoia. People began saying that there were vans that were gonna blow up. I called my [financing] desk together. We huddled up on 48th

Street and I told them, 'Anyone who wants to go home should go home. I won't hold this against you.' Most stayed."

The greatest speculation regarded the status of the inter-dealer brokers that had been located in the Trade Center. One of them, Euro Brokers, sent a volunteer to the Armory to check its hospital lists against the firm's list of missing employees. There were no matches. There was, however, already one match against the medical examiner's list of bodies.[33]

At 10 p.m., Euro Brokers posted a notice on its website: "We believe that one of the best therapies for this cowardly and evil attack is to get our business back up and running as soon as possible. To this end, we are negotiating over several alternative new locations and will update you as soon as possible as soon as we have something more definitive to report."[34] Euro Brokers' CEO, Gil Scharf, had been at the firm's London office on 9/11. Returning by the weekend, he gathered his surviving managers to rebuild. An empty office space in One New York Plaza in lower Manhattan became the company's temporary home.[35]

Garban wouldn't resume trading until September 24. Its operations staff had moved to "the Bunker" in Edison, New Jersey, where it worked on reducing the $6 billion that it owed Chase down to zero. By Thursday's end, as further trade information became available, they had whittled that amount down to $1.5 billion. The remainder would take a month to resolve, by reviewing trades one at a time to determine their legitimacy and whether securities had been delivered to or from Garban in settlement of the trade.[36] Garban's operations staff would spend days interviewing each of the brokers about specific trades. What were the terms? Who was your counterparty? Many had little or no recollection of the trades, having been traumatized.[37]

Cantor Fitzgerald was back in business for U.S. trading by the time the markets opened on Thursday morning.[38] With its voice brokerage operation decimated, it had resumed U.S. trading through eSpeed, its electronic trading platform, facilitated by operations staff located in London and a backup facility in Rochelle Park, a New Jersey suburb.[39] On 9/11, few imagined how quickly Cantor would recommence trading. One repo trader had speculated on that day that BrokerTec "would have a virtual monopoly in the days/weeks ahead."[40]

Several factors aided that swift reestablishment of trading. Foremost was an enormous resolve in the face of unspeakable loss.[41] Market trends that had developed in recent years also assisted – particularly globalization of the Govie market and the shift to electronic trading. Some crucial technology executives had survived, thanks to a planned fishing trip for that day.[42] In addition, Cantor had the foresight to have built eSpeed's systems on a dual architecture platform, which replicated all connections and functionality at the Trade Center and the Rochelle Park site with a third facility in London.[43] Meanwhile, on the settlement side, a competitor electronic trading company, ICI/ADP, helped eSpeed send its transactions to Chase, its clearing bank.[44]

Of considerable concern on Thursday was not whether the market could effectively trade but whether it was capable of moving money and securities in settlement of transactions done on that day and prior. GSCC had completed its processing cycle for Wednesday at about 4 a.m. on Thursday. Two hours later, its systems were up and running for the new day. But it opened with a staggering $444 billion in transactions that had failed to settle on their scheduled settlement date, well more than the record level of the previous day.[45] It also had a huge overdraft at BoNY. In many cases, firms had delivered securities to GSCC's account at BoNY. Based on the new instructions, they duplicated deliveries to GSCC on Thursday, to be later unraveled.[46]

Connectivity Efforts

GSCC and BoNY continued their attempts to establish connectivity. Working with BoNY engineers, GSCC verified that the primary "frame relay" data transmission network from both 55 Water Street and MetroTech to Maywood was inoperable. There was a secondary digital phone system connection, known as the Integrated Services Digital Network, or ISDN. After considerable testing, those backup lines to Maywood proved useless because all of the circuits had been routed through the same damaged Verizon office. A more primitive dial-up connection was attempted, but that too was unsuccessful.[47]

As GSCC staff worked on the connectivity issue, their isolation began to lessen. Steve Greenberg again walked to work, this time with an assortment of bagels, spreads, and fruit. With him was his boss, Ron Stewart, President of the company, who had crashed at Greenberg's apartment the previous night. The food was welcome, but those who hadn't left the building remained in the same clothes. Some relief finally came, provided by Neal Arbon, who had gone home to New Jersey late the previous night with Pat Gordon, another technology staffer: "When Pat and I got on the train at Penn Station, we must have stunk to high heaven because people moved away. I got a lot of space on the train." Arbon returned early on Thursday morning, walking the two and a half miles from the 14th Street subway station. He lugged a huge bag bulging with clothes that he had asked his wife to buy the previous day from their local Macy's: "I said to get one size fits all – elastic is best. She came back with underwear, shorts, socks, T-shirts, and even stuff I wouldn't have thought of, like towels."

Relationship management staff continued to compile a list of each member's location and primary contact, though they were hindered by a phone service that was sporadic at best. One techie made a helpful suggestion - to shift to old-fashioned analog models, although no one could easily explain why they received better service. But it took days to find those phones along with the adapters required in the new digital environment. In the interim, GSCC staff made do, at times asking family members living outside of Manhattan to make calls on their behalf.[48]

Across the East River in MetroTech Center, Dave Cosgrove and a small crew of operations staff were coping with bare resources. Dina Deluca of the marketing department had made her way from Tribeca to Brooklyn that morning on an R Train that skipped all of the lower Manhattan stops. Exiting the train at the DeKalb Avenue station, she met police officers on the subway stairs announcing a bomb threat at the MetroTech office building. After the threat was determined to be a hoax, Deluca took a few extra minutes to calm herself, then joined Cosgrove's group in a small room equipped with only a few phones and PCs. "I ran around MetroTech trying to find a fax and a printer to print reports," Deluca remembered. "We had a hard time trying to do the simplest of things."

Sal Matera, who headed GSCC's applications development, also made it to MetroTech by subway: "On the ride, I got claustrophobic, and was nervous as we got to lower Manhattan. I knew that the train was going close to the World Trade Center. There were concerns at that point about vibrations and what you could knock loose." Once at MetroTech, Matera helped set up the PCs and track down applications like Microsoft Access®, critical to maintaining the margining process central to the industry's management of risk. "Being somewhat of a chauvinist, I told a number of women that they needn't come in but could work from home," he admitted. "But they showed up anyway, including a woman who had served in the Israeli army. She told me I was out of my mind."[49]

Dave Cosgrove set his sights on getting settlement instructions to BoNY. Electronic transmission was still unavailable. Cosgrove had told SIAC, which ran his data center, to cut two magnetic tapes: primary and secondary. Clutching the tapes, he paced back and forth muttering, "Where the fuck is Mayfair?" Jon Volpe heard him and asked, "Do you mean Maywood?" Volpe had grown up nearby there. Cosgrove barked, "We've gotta get this to BoNY!" Volpe told him that he knew the exact location of the BoNY building: right behind the Hess station on Route 17.

The night before, Cosgrove had called Steve Jukofsky, managing director in charge of administration, after hearing that Jukofsky intended to drive to Brooklyn that morning to lend a hand. Cosgrove asked Jukofsky if he could do him a favor; bring two packs of cigarettes. When Jukofsky offered to pick up new clothes, Cosgrove insisted that all he needed were cigarettes.

Later that day, after being teased by colleagues that his clothes reeked, Cosgrove walked over to Dr. Jay's on Atlantic Avenue and bought a new outfit. He recalled: "I remember finding a pair of jeans and underwear, socks, and tee shirts. But I also wanted new shoes. All they had were basketball sneakers. So I walk up to the guy and ask, 'You got any

Docksiders?' He says, 'What's Docksiders?' I explain that they're boating shoes. He says, 'Hey buddy. Look around this place. We don't have a lot of boaters.' So I bought a cheap pair of sneakers. They didn't even fit. But they were better than what I was wearing."

Jukofsky showed up at dawn, cigarettes in hand. A couple of hours later, he, Volpe and the tapes were on the road to Maywood. Unable to cut through Manhattan, they took the Gowanus Expressway to the Verrazano Bridge, which crosses into Staten Island. But as they were about to get on the Verrazano, the entrance was blocked, as streams of police cars chased suspected terrorists over the bridge. After an hour's wait, they crossed over the bridge and made it to Maywood.

BMA Recommendations

Throughout Thursday morning, Bond Market Association staff were canvassing their available market contacts to learn how trading and settlements were proceeding. The feedback was positive on the trading side, but the back-office response was brutal. The logjam caused by inaccurate information and lack of connectivity continued to impair settlements.

At 1 p.m., the BMA's Calendar Committee held a conference call, again widely participated in, which highlighted trading hours and settlement procedures in light of the large backlog of unsettled trades. The participants promptly agreed to maintain the 2 p.m. close of the U.S. fixed-income markets on Friday.

After a lengthy discussion, however, a consensus built within the large group that it was important to return to normalcy. Friday's cash trading would again begin in Tokyo on Thursday evening New York time, and the Chicago Board of Trade would be encouraged to open its ACE electronic platform on an overnight basis to facilitate a full trading day in the cash markets in both Tokyo and London.[50] The ACE platform, while small in volume, offered traders the flexibility to execute transactions from a terminal anywhere, regardless of pit trading availability.[51] Saltzman and his BMA staff were asked to speak with the Chicago Board of Trade and Chicago Merc to ensure coordination of trading hours on Friday.

With respect to the back-office side of the market, the discussion became contentious. Participants complained about the large number of transactions that remained to be addressed and reconciled, and also about the lack of connectivity between BoNY and its customers, between BoNY and GSCC, and between GSCC and its clearing members. Some argued for a move from T+3 to T+4 (settlement would occur four days after the trade), to give the firms' operations staffs even more relief. Others felt that changing the settlement period again by one additional day was not worth the increased burden and the risk of having to adjust internal systems.

Underlying the discussion were dramatically different philosophies. Should the market encourage trading to the extent possible, and then take measures such as extending the settlement period to facilitate clearing and settling all those trades? Or should the Street bite the bullet and limit trading until the settlement process was sufficiently healed? The group was polled, and although some supported moving to T+4 and some even to T+5, the majority voted to stay with T+3 settlement for transactions done on Friday.[52]

Peter Fisher listened in on the call while on Amtrak heading back to D.C. He was scheduled to meet with Treasury Secretary O'Neill, who had returned from Tokyo. Fisher sat next to Harvey Pitt, with whom he had traveled to New York two days earlier. Fisher was in the same clothes that he had worn on Tuesday. During a quiet moment, Pitt looked at him and said, "That's a really wonderful shirt."

Communication Between GSCC and BoNY

Over at Maywood, Steve Jukofsky and Jon Volpe planned simply to deliver the tapes, then head back to Brooklyn. They ended up staying, and became the conduit for communication between GSCC and BoNY. Volpe was provided a BoNY terminal to manage and monitor the settlement process, but could not access GSCC's system or records. "There were a ton of people in a small facility, and not enough computers for everyone," Volpe remembered. "I'd have a computer for an hour or so, then have to give it up."

Volpe didn't know the BoNY clearance system or staff but Jukofsky did, having worked at BoNY for many years. With land lines still not functional, Jukofsky, Volpe, Cosgrove, and others used cell phones, speaking for hours with their BoNY counterparts trying to work through the $31 billion in positions. When Cosgrove's phone died, he sent someone from SIAC into downtown Brooklyn in search of a phone charger, meanwhile commandeering that person's phone.

GSCC staff came from varying operational backgrounds, creating confusion with verbal shorthand communication. At one point, Jukofsky told them to "kill this item," which the others translated as an item that should be cancelled because it didn't exist. They realized later that he meant the item had already cleared.[53]

Volpe had joined the clearing corporation just a month earlier. He recalled "dealing with billions of dollars in transactions on our unmatched report screen. Dave was walking me through what to do on the phone, as I'm reading to him what's on my screen. It was a lot of money and I was worried about getting fired, because I didn't know BoNY that well. I would DK a transaction and a person sitting two computers down would yell at me, 'Why are you fucking DK-ing me!'"

In the early afternoon, Jukofsky went outside for a smoke. Volpe kept him company. As they stood in front of the building, two CompUSA trucks pulled up, each loaded with PCs. BONY's backup plan had prearranged to obtain PCs and tables in bulk. When the trucks arrived, Perna said to his staff: "Guys, have you ever heard of a bucket brigade?" Perna took his shirt off, and lined everyone up from the trucks to inside. We got the stuff in. Tom Renyi sent techies to hook them up, and to work on communication."

Back at 55 Water Street, TV reception returned in the board room. Staff alternated in and out of the room to keep current on events. One of them was Steve Kling, managing director in charge of systems, whose wife had delivered their baby on the morning of 9/11. Kling had planned to take some time off, but he was in the office by Thursday. In the late afternoon, Marc Golin watched a report, which later proved unfounded, on a number of people detained at JFK and LaGuardia airports on suspicion of attempting to infiltrate planes. "That was scarier than maybe any other time," he confessed. "When was this nightmare gonna end?"

Early in the day, Rich Visco had gone into the bathroom, taken off his underwear, washed it in the sink with bathroom soap, and hung it up under his desk with paper clips, using a fan to dry it. By nighttime, Visco and five others who had been living on the 31st floor since Tuesday had enough of their own uncleanliness. Someone remembered that the 22nd floor had a shower reserved for NSCC executives. After 10 p.m., they marched to that floor but found the shower room locked. They rummaged through every nearby desk, trying dozens of keys until they unlocked it.

After opening the outer door, they encountered yet another one, thick and heavy, requiring a different key. Visco, noticing that the door's hinges were on the outside, went back to the 31st floor to retrieve a tool kit from his desk, then returned and removed the pins. ("I was very proud of myself when I announced that the door was open," recalled Visco.) Before them was a classy bathing room, filled with soaps and towels. They let the sole woman take the first shower; the men followed in turn. Tom Quaranta later said: "To go three days without a shower and then take one, it's the greatest feeling."

Height of the Crisis

After the close of the securities Fedwire at 8:30 p.m., BoNY sent an email, via a new WorldNet account, attaching a flat text file detailing securities settlements for September 12, including those occurring after BoNY closed on 9/11. BoNY informed GSCC that a second file containing settlements for that same day, September 13, would also be arriving shortly. But there would not be enough time to process both files.

GSCC management decided to first process the settlements of September 13. They would wait until the next day, Friday, to process the settlements that had been created on September 12, even though this would lead to sequencing problems. The only other option was to reject all of the settlements in the second file, effectively returning $31 billion in securities transactions to the Street. But that would create systemic risk and immense additional reconcilement challenges for members, making it an untenable choice.

Near midnight, BoNY's flat text file of securities settlements for September 13 arrived. GSCC staff attempted to read the file into the netting system in an automated manner, but were unsuccessful because it was in a format where the usual "binds" had been broken. Binds were what the clearing corporation used to inform its bank which firm was to deliver securities to its account and which other firm the securities should be redelivered to.

GSCC staff faced two basic choices for handling the thousands of items on the file received. One was to instruct the master netting system to assume that all delivery instructions originally generated by the system had settled, then manually recognize those that actually hadn't. The alternative was to identify by hand and then input into the system each item that appeared on BoNY's file as having cleared.[54] Dave Cosgrove offered that his staff would undertake either manual task, but admitted that the process would take until after the opening of business on Friday to complete.

Tom Costa sat with his senior team, considering their options. When the idea of GSCC arose in the mid-1980s, it was Costa, fairly new to the settlement side of the industry, who had volunteered to lead the effort to create the new company. By 2001, GSCC was, measured by dollar volume of activity handled, the largest clearing corporation in the world. Costa felt as proprietary about the company as if he personally owned it. "I'm thinking that if we can't straighten this thing out tonight and clear those trades and generate our receive/deliver output tomorrow, we're dead as a clearing corporation. I almost lost it at that point," he admitted. "But I couldn't do that in front of all those people, who were drained and exhausted."

Costa walked to the bathroom, stuck his head in the sink, and cleared it with cold water. He returned to the room, and the management team methodically reviewed potential solutions. Neal Arbon offered to write software to interpret the old program and convert it into something usable. Two hours later, the BoNY file was run through the rewritten software. "It wasn't completely accurate, but it was good enough that we could recognize and clean up 95 percent of the securities that had gone through the bank," Arbon recalled. "Everything else we considered a fail."

For a third straight night, staff members worked around the clock to complete the day's work and prepare for the next processing day. Shortly after 5 a.m., GSCC completed its processing cycle, generating output to the Street.

Govie trading would begin again in a couple of hours, with the prospect of record volume. Yet the viability of clearance and settlement remained suspect. Would it be capable of catching up to an accelerated pace of trading? The success of the Street's back-end processes would depend critically on one factor: computer network connectivity.

CHAPTER 11

FRIDAY: CONNECTIVITY

"Verizon had made a good point, that they couldn't really give everyone dial tone everywhere. So, do you need dial tone for ten thousand people in lower Manhattan, or do you want it in New Jersey? There was a bit of a chicken and egg issue."

Peter Fisher, Treasury Under Secretary for Domestic Finance

Friday was declared a national day of prayer and remembrance for 9/11 victims. At noon, a service was held at the Washington National Cathedral, led by the Reverend Billy Graham and attended by President Bush and many senior government officials. Hours later, the President arrived at the Pier 11 Heliport, in sight of many Wall Street staff. He was shuttled to Ground Zero, where he delivered his historic address by bullhorn. Elsewhere, the New York City Office of Emergency Management completed the setup of an operations center at Pier 92, on the West Side at 51st Street, to replace its office that had been in Seven World Trade Center.

In the afternoon, urged by New York locals who wanted to avoid a physical shift of their activity to Chicago,[1] the NYMEX resumed trading, not on its floor but electronically over the Internet through its after-hours ACCESS system.[2] NYMEX's return to business was significant. Its West Texas intermediate crude oil contract (known as "Texas Light Sweet") was the world's most actively traded physical commodity and was relied upon globally as a price benchmark.[3] The NYMEX had come under pressure from large energy traders to reopen as soon as possible because of anticipation of military action in the Middle East.[4]

The trading session crashed initially. Unable to log on to the NYMEX's platform, some members required assistance from other firms.[5] Although the session was brief, volume was higher than expected, providing yet another indication of the promise of electronic trading.[6]

Preparing for a Monday Reopening

With the reopening of the New York Stock Exchange and NASDAQ looming, there was widespread concern that the equities markets would go into free fall on Monday.[7] Early in the day, the SEC announced that it had taken steps to facilitate the planned resumption of the U.S. equities exchanges. After characterizing those markets as "the world's strongest and most vibrant, in spite of the heinous acts of last Tuesday," the Commission revealed that it had used, for the first time, its emergency powers granted after Black Monday to ease certain regulatory restrictions. The SEC prepared a series of investor questions and answers for the public's benefit. One answer simply urged investors to "remain calm."

Many companies had earlier emphasized to the SEC that they needed maximum flexibility to prop up their stock prices. Those firms wanted the SEC's permission to repurchase their shares without having to adhere to the usual restrictions on timing, price and volume designed to prevent market manipulation. [8] The Commission responded by granting public companies greater latitude to buy their own shares, without suffering adverse legal or accounting consequence, on Monday and for the rest of that week. [9] That regulatory relief led to announcements by large companies of significant buy-back programs.[10]

The major securities firms also lobbied the SEC, warning that normal capital requirements would constrain their liquidity.[11] Of particular concern were those mandated for "aged" fails caused by the Govie market's clearance and settlement problems. Annette Nazareth, head of the Commission's Division of Market Regulation, understood that those requirements "would have caused gigantic capital charges to firms that were really not representative of the actual financial conditions at the time."[12]

The SEC reacted by authorizing firms to disregard the days when the markets were closed in calculating their net capital.[13] This development would be significant for broker-dealers that had accounting imbalances in addition to fails.[14] The Commission eased other burdens as well, including allowing mutual funds to borrow from and lend to related parties, permitting accounting firms to provide bookkeeping services to clients with offices in and around the Trade Center without violating auditor independence rules, and relaxing in-person meeting requirements for mutual funds' board meetings.[15]

On the banking side, relief short of declaring a bank holiday was provided by the New York State Banking Department, an effort led by Sara Kelsey: "There are different actions you can take under the banking law to ease the strain of deadlines being missed or requirements being impossible to meet. One example was, for those foreign banks who had been in the World Trade Center, normally you have to put in for prior approval to change your headquarters. That wasn't feasible. So we created workarounds." The Banking Department, with help from volunteers from the Sullivan & Cromwell law firm, also temporarily changed the state's trusts and estates law to enable the dependents of those who had died to withdraw sums of money while the search for the bodies continued.[16]

To maintain an orderly Treasury auction process in the near term, temporary respite was needed from the Treasury Department; specifically, a relaxation of the rule that had triggered the Salomon Brothers scandal back in 1991. That rule had limited auction awards for any one bidder to 35 percent of the total amount offered to the public less the bidder's own "net long" position. By the end of the day, the

Treasury had placed a notice on its website that, for purposes of bid limits on Monday's Treasury auctions, firms with books and records problems could use a best estimate of their own holdings. Paul Saltzman, whose BMA lawyers were in the thick of the discussions with the SEC and Treasury Department, was struck by the regulatory responsiveness: "They came together quickly and shed their natural inclination to be green-eye-shade accountants. The support that they gave the private sector to work itself out of this situation was enormous. And a testament to the trust and confidence that they had in the people in the industry to do the job."

The Govie market again opened with short trading hours. Liquidity in the repo market had improved dramatically, leading to re-establishment of the "specials" market in which the lender of funds wants a specific security delivered to it, often because that security is needed to redeliver against a short sale.[17] This measure allowed for clearer identification of supply and demand imbalances.[18]

BMA Conference Calls Continue

The BMA phone conferences continued, each requiring long roll calls and maddening coordination. Saltzman continued to moderate these calls from his home: "In the mornings, I would be very emotional. Drained and crying. I spent my early mornings watching CNN. One of the most emotional moments for me was watching Queen Elizabeth and the English

Parliament singing our national anthem.[19] And then it was back to business. At times, my daughter and son would bang on the door wanting to talk to me. My wife would pull them away, telling them to leave daddy alone."

At 10:30 that morning, during a Funding Division call, GSCC requested that two temporary adjustments to trading practices be implemented to ease operational burdens. The first was a moratorium on collateral substitutions for repos, meaning that firms could not request that the collateral underlying a long-term repo be sent to them and replaced by other securities, as was customary. The second was for counterparties to reveal or "give up" their names to each other when submitting repo trades to GSCC through brokers.[20] The dealers effectively would be submitting trades against each other, leaving the brokers out of the picture.[21] Both requests were unanimously approved.

At 11 a.m., the BMA's board of directors, the Calendar Committee, and Primary Dealers Committee again met jointly. Tom Perna and his second-in-command, Art Certosimo, noted that BoNY's Govie clearance system was fully functional and that it had established incoming and outgoing capabilities with the Fed. Perna indicated that BoNY continued to have connectivity issues with clients that used ISDN links. For GSCC, whose frame relay link with BoNY wasn't functioning either, it was a double whammy. This news led the Calendar Committee to recommend yet another early market close on Monday.

Hearing that a $31 billion difference between BoNY and GSCC remained, the group was stunned. Recalled Saltzman, "The call got quite heated, including some bashing of GSCC and BoNY. It got so bad that we actually had to have a moment of silence. The civic mindedness had started to wear off, and people began to focus on their situations."

Perna reassured them that BoNY had three people dedicated to narrowing the difference, who already had identified $10 billion of the problem.[22] But the general concern about the settlement process ratcheted up further. Many argued that additional breathing room was needed to allow back-office staff to reconcile outstanding and failed transactions. After long debate, consensus was reached to stretch the settlement period two more days to T+5, starting with Monday trading.[23] This move would soon cause confusion and consternation on the Street, as firms would need to once again adjust their internal systems, frustrating operations professionals who speculated on when the increasing settlement cycles would end.

One BMA board member raised the issue of whether the T+5 recommendation should apply to muni and corporate securities as well (by industry convention, MBS only settled four times a month). Fortunately, the same operational predicament didn't exist in those sectors, in part because trading in these markets had been light over the past several days and the level of failed settlements was comparatively small.[24] No further change was made.

Left unaddressed in the BMA calls was the emergency looming on the equally critical funds settlement side of the Govie market. As a normal part of the settlement process, dealers owe each other cash amounts due to changes in securities values, margin requirements, accrued interest, billing, and the like. For all of the large market participants, these funds payments ran through GSCC, which would establish a single daily cash amount for each member - debit or credit. The clearing corporation's goal was to end each day totally flat except for margin that it held. Often the amounts of these debits and credits were huge. For the time being, again because this information from BoNY was inaccessible, those critical money movements had been suspended.

Root of the Problem

GSCC opened with $509 billion in securities to be settled, four-fifths of that being fails from prior days.[25] Steve Jukofsky repeated his drive from central Jersey to MetroTech in Brooklyn and then on to Maywood to deliver a magnetic tape to BoNY containing settlement instructions. GSCC operations staff began the intensive process of clearing the activity of September 12 based on information in the flat file delivered the night before. This entailed researching each item on the file to ensure it was valid and then matching it against an outstanding settlement. Once more, these manual functions would be carried out by a limited number of exhausted staff members, some of whom had no background in operations.

It became obvious that the Govie market settlement process, broken on both the funds and the securities settlement sides, would not heal until connectivity was restored. But like many in the financial community, GSCC was in a long queue, in this case awaiting WorldCom to connect it with BoNY in Maywood.

Late on Thursday, Rob Palatnick, frustrated by the delay, called his WorldCom contact, who confirmed only that GSCC was "on the list." Palatnick then reached out to a contact at SIAC, who provided him the number of a senior person in the Defense Department. Palatnick immediately called him. After listening to his explanation, the Defense official "paused, and all of a sudden I had a senior official of WorldCom on the phone who tells me they would get people right on it." On Friday morning, a WorldCom crew determined that only Verizon circuits were servicing the Maywood facility. To work on the lines, Verizon would have to subcontract WorldCom, after obtaining evidence of this effort's priority.[26]

Meanwhile, BoNY's Perna had explained the connectivity problem to Una Neary, a New York Fed examiner present on the Maywood site. Neary, working with the Board of Governors staff in D.C., requested use of the Department of Defense's high-priority phone access.[27] This access, together with the coordination between WorldCom and Verizon, finally unblocked connectivity between the Street and BoNY after the close of Fedwire on Friday.[28]

"Hundreds of Issues, Trade by Trade, Item by Item"

In the late afternoon on Friday, while sitting outside on a garbage can smoking a cigar, Perna remembered the broker-dealer tapes stuck at 101 Barclay Street. The information in those tapes would help unravel the settlement jam. He discussed this with Neary, who assured Perna that she could gain entry to that building.

They drove to lower Manhattan, using Neary's credentials to pass through barricades. "When we got to the Fed, they took us in an SUV to about a block from the building," Perna remembered. "All around us, the telephone and Con Ed guys were quietly going on about their business. I was amazed that they knew what to do given all the debris and destruction."

With connectivity between BoNY and the Street restored, Cosgrove and his staff in Brooklyn were inundated with calls from members. "Everyone now could see how fucked up things were," Cosgrove recounted. "'Why are you delivering this stuff to me? You owe me this! You didn't deliver that!' And firms were DK-ing us right and left, which just made things worse."

Once more, Cosgrove's operations group was forced to clear an entire day's activity manually. "In hindsight, I should have turned around and told Costa that everyone's going to the hotel to rest and would come back at 10 a.m. tomorrow. Instead, we opted to stay there and go through hundreds of issues trade by trade and item by item. We did a good job, but we could have done a lot better if we had some sleep."

By 6 a.m., the team was close to proving out, but not quite. The netting system, known as IONS (Industry Operating Netting System), was built to remain open until every trade was pegged against a delivery or receive position and until those positions equaled each other so that GSCC was flat. "I knew that we had to create bogus obligations just to balance the system," said Cosgrove looking back. "But we couldn't do anymore at that point. We had a dozen people there who collectively couldn't count to a hundred." Cosgrove called Dave Buckmaster, waking him, and asked him to come to Brooklyn to provide some relief.

Just a few hours earlier, Buckmaster and three others had left lower Manhattan. Buckmaster had called for a car to meet them in the Village: "By that point, I had gone three nights plus with only two hours sleep at most a night. My fuse was short, and when I called to arrange the car, the guy referred to me as 'Fuckmaster.' So I went off on him." Initially, the group had to walk in the middle of a deserted Water Street, because the water trucks were cleaning the sidewalks. Soon after the four reached the FDR Drive, they came upon an area covered with high-intensity lights and military tents, the identification point for body parts and remains.

On the call to Buckmaster, Cosgrove vented: "We're fucked up and not balanced. We haven't generated output. The Street's going to hang me from a lamppost!" Then Cosgrove walked outside. An hour later, Buckmaster popped out of a cab down the block. Both men knew that all of the communications problems and manual effort had created erroneous positions within the system. They agreed that they had to create "adjustment trades" to balance them out. This was the only option that would allow them to generate output for the Street that day.

The two got coffee and went back upstairs. Cosgrove teamed up with Brian Klembella, a techie who had gone to MetroTech to help. "I'd be typing and just fall asleep. And Brian would poke me in the ribs," Cosgrove remembered. By late Saturday morning, they had closed out the system.

That Friday night, many in the financial industry finally went home. Murray Pozmanter of Nomura Securities made the long drive from Piscataway, New Jersey to Long Island: "Just around sundown, as we were cutting through Staten Island, streets were full of people standing in front of their houses holding candles. Coming over the Verrazano, it struck me that you couldn't now differentiate between the lower Manhattan and Jersey City skylines from that distance, because you'd lost your point of reference."

Joe Blauvelt drove to Nutley, New Jersey. "On my block there were all these American flags. I was blown away. When I walked into my house, my son, who was eleven, grabbed me and hugged me and said, 'Daddy, I thought you were hurt.' He started crying. And so did I."

The Street's long workweek on and after 9/11 was a prelude to a critical weekend of preparation. And a true beginning of the return to normalcy.

CHAPTER 12

MONDAY: ALL MARKETS REOPEN

"Even though we were running normally by the following Monday, you could say that we were doing so on faith."

Tom Perna, Executive Vice President, Bank of New York[1]

Over the weekend, sermons in houses of worship across the nation would speak to the horrors of 9/11 and its meaning. One common theme was tolerance.[2] The National Football League canceled the games scheduled for Sunday, delaying the playoffs and Super Bowl XXXVI.[3]

Relatives and friends of the missing continued to pour into the family assistance center in the Lexington Avenue Armory. At a Saturday news conference, the city's Chief Medical Examiner announced that New York had contracted with several private DNA-analysis companies to assist in identifying remains.[4]

The "frozen zone" in lower Manhattan kept shrinking. On Sunday, lower Manhattan east of William Street reopened to pedestrians, its boundaries marked by metal barricades, yellow police tape, or a rifle-carrying National Guardsman. Near

Ground Zero, repair crews continued working around the clock to restore phone and data services; a TV reporter found Verizon employees sleeping on the streets and in tents.[5] Across the Hudson, in a Jersey City parking lot that would later become the site of a Trump Plaza condominium, Joe Grima could see that "Verizon and other utilities had set up generators and all kinds of other equipment."

Larry Lemmon of HSBC, who still lived on the same block in Bay Ridge, Brooklyn that he had been born on 50 years earlier (and who had literally married the girl next door), got home early on Saturday. Sitting with his wife, he filled her in on the events of the past few days, while she told him of the soot that rained down at times when the wind shifted. Saturday night was to have been the annual block party. "Instead, the whole block got together and we held a candlelight vigil and sang patriotic songs," described Lemmon. "There was a lot of hugging." Joe Grima took a cab to his Long Island home. "It was another beautiful day. When we got onto Oyster Bay Road heading north, every tree was lined with a yellow ribbon."

By 3 p.m. on Saturday, the New York Stock Exchange had successfully tested its systems for the reopening on Monday morning. As for the NASDAQ, which had telecommunications issues but not physical floor problems, it had built during the week a temporary operational center in one of its buildings in Connecticut. All sales and customer support personnel relocated there; they worked into the weekend contacting the entire broker-dealer community for up-to-date information on each one's operational status and ability to trade. Do you have connectivity to NASDAQ? Do you have access to your facility? Where's your backup located? The NASDAQ tested with firms continuously to ensure that they could connect and be ready to trade on Monday.[6]

On Sunday afternoon, a joint NYSE-NASDAQ press conference was held to announce the success of the tests. By that day, with the reopening of the stock exchanges imminent, a campaign was mounted to bolster investor confidence. President Bush told the country, "The markets open tomorrow, people go back to work, and we'll show the world." On NBC's "Meet the Press," Vice President Cheney asked the American people to "stick their thumb in the eye of the terrorists and say that they've got great confidence in the country, great confidence in our economy, and not let what's happened here in any way throw off their normal level of economic activity." Warren Buffett, the renowned investor and Chairman of Berkshire Hathaway, Robert Rubin, the former Treasury Secretary who had run Goldman Sachs, and Jack Welch, the recently retired chairman of General Electric, appeared on CBS's "60 Minutes," where Buffett announced that he "won't be selling anything" when the market opens and that, if prices fell enough, "there's something I might buy."[7]

The public pitched in as well. An e-mail circulated calling for people to invest in America:

"Many of those in the World Trade Center made their living financing the American dream… If you buy stock when the markets reopen, you will show the terrorists that their attack failed to destroy America, you will help our economy spring back to life, and you will honor the profession of many who died."[8] In a letter to the *New York Times* that Saturday, one reader characterized the 9/11 attack as "a calculated assault on our economic system" and urged that, when the exchanges reopened on Monday, "we should buy American stocks."[9]

That Sunday afternoon, Jim McLaughlin and others from the New York Fed brought buckets over to the Trade Center site to help the workers clear debris. "We saw the police searching for survivors," recollected McLaughlin. "Firemen climbing on the wreckage. Fires still raging." McLaughlin also went to flag store in Midtown and bought about $1,500 worth of bunting and American flags, which were hung on the Fed building.

At 5 p.m. on Sunday, the Bond Market Association held an update call.[10] The first issue raised was the ongoing settlement reconciliation. Tom Perna reported that, on the previous day, BoNY's system had run in production and was operating effectively. Its connection with GSCC was up and running with real-time connectivity, the Maywood center was fully staffed, and the reconciliations backlog was declining steadily.[11] He assured the group that BoNY would be ready for the early opening of the securities Fedwire planned for the next day at 6:30 a.m.

GSCC described similar successes on the connectivity front. It was now sending data to and receiving data from most of its members,[12] including Cantor Fitzgerald, from whom it had now received information on all of Cantor's Thursday and Friday trades.[13] Chase reported that its systems were fully operational; it had experienced no significant outages in the prior week.[14] Now that GSCC and BoNY had reestablished communication with each other, standard conditions at last could be expected on Monday for securities settlement.

At the end of the meeting, the conversation shifted. Paul Saltzman announced that the BMA would use its website to provide information on wakes, shivahs and funerals for industry members, and that Cantor's website already contained a list of services for its staff. Memorial services for the Wall Street victims would last well into October, causing guilt for many, who felt the conflicting compulsions to both attend those services and stay focused on their jobs.

Return to Normal

By Monday morning, most of the streets in the Financial District had been cleaned of inches of residue. In the dust that clung to windows of stores and cars were written aphorisms such as "We'll never forget" and "Rest in peace."[15] Con Edison, which had lost two substations and much of its lower Manhattan infrastructure, had engaged more than 2,000 workers to run miles of electric cable above ground or in trenches, and had deployed more than 80 temporary generators, many for the benefit of the NYSE.[16]

Mayor Giuliani and his staff returned to City Hall and held their regular 8 a.m. meeting.[17] Staten Island Ferry service to the Whitehall Terminal at the tip of lower Manhattan resumed operation. On 9/11, those ferries had carried tens of thousands out of lower Manhattan, often in zero visibility. During the following days, the ferry fleet transported emergency personnel and equipment to and from lower Manhattan, including U.S. Army tanks to Governors Island.[18]

At 7:30 a.m., the Federal Open Market Committee met by conference call, voting to lower the target for the federal funds rate (the rate at which banks lend overnight to other banks) by 50 basis points to three percent. The Committee assured that "the Federal Reserve will continue to supply unusually large volumes of liquidity to the financial markets, as needed, until more normal market functioning is restored." In addition to this monetary stimulus, Congress had enacted a $40 billion emergency spending package to cover some of the 9/11-related costs, including the repair of the Pentagon and the cleanup of New York City.[19]

For those traveling to the Financial District, the commute remained disrupted. Bill Langan's usual Long Island Rail Road train halted just outside the Flatbush Avenue station in Brooklyn. After a half hour, the riders were told that the delay was due to police activity. "Upon hearing the announcement, the passenger seated in front of me began to shake uncontrollably," Langan recounted. "That continued until we were in the station." Many of those walking through lower Manhattan to their offices had their IDs checked by National Guard troops.

On his way to lower Manhattan, Dave Cosgrove, who had left his house in Westchester before 3 a.m., was stopped twice by police while driving down the Palisades Parkway. Cosgrove parked in Midtown and took the Lexington Avenue subway to the Bowling Green station, at the end of lower Manhattan. He would have exited one stop earlier, at the Wall Street station, but that stop was restricted to use by police and rescue workers. Emerging in the pre-dawn darkness, he encountered "smells that I associate with hunting. Huge lights and tents for National Guard troops, who were everywhere." Like all who would return to work in the Financial District, Cosgrove was disoriented by the void once filled by the Twin Towers.

Tom Costa took his customary ferry from Glen Cove to Pier 11, at the east end of Wall Street, to get to work: "When I got off, I always walked past the small fire house on Old Slip. The firemen were usually outside washing the trucks and stuff like that, and I'd say hi to them. This time, the firehouse was closed. I looked inside and it was empty. No trucks. And then it hit me that those guys were dead. I started crying."

Tom Wipf flew from London on Thursday night on a private jet with about a dozen Morgan Stanley colleagues. Landing in Toronto, they paid a van driver handsomely to take them to New York. "Took about ten hours, including some McDonald's stops, which was a foreign country for the investment bankers," Wipf recalled. "We had to make some interesting field decisions about how many bathroom stops to make." Arriving at Morgan Stanley's headquarters in Midtown, he noticed the makeshift memorial at the nearby fire house on 8th Avenue, and then "the reality really took hold." [20]

Reopening of the Stock Exchanges

A host of dignitaries, including Senators Clinton and Schumer, Governor Pataki, Mayor Giuliani, Treasury Secretary O'Neill, SEC Chairman Pitt, New York State Comptroller Carl McCall, and New York City Fire Commissioner Tom Von Essen, gathered on Monday at the New York Stock Exchange for the 9:30 a.m. opening ceremony. After observing two minutes of silence, a Marine officer sang "God Bless America," and members of the New York City Police and Fire Departments helped ring the opening bell.

The markets immediately plummeted. By the close of trading, the NASDAQ composite index had fallen 6.8 percent. The Dow Jones Industrial Average was down 684.81 points, more than seven percent, its largest one-day point decline ever which would not be exceeded until September 2008, soon after the

Lehman Brothers bankruptcy.[21] But the selling was orderly, and to the delight of operations and technology staff at the NYSE and NASDAQ, the operating systems worked, accommodating the highest volume of trading that had ever occurred in a single day: 4.5 billion shares for the two exchanges combined.[22] By the end of the week, the DJIA would be down 1,370 points, its largest one-week point drop, resulting in a loss in value for U.S. stocks of $1.2 trillion. However, the markets would regain all the ground lost within just a few weeks of trading.

The American Stock Exchange on 9/11 had been devastated. Left without a backup floor, Sal Sodano had initially thought there was no chance of it reopening by Monday. But it did. "It was miraculous," he emphasized years later. "To this day, I believe that God was standing right next to us." The NYSE, which ordinarily would have taken every opportunity to put the AMEX out of business (and which, in 2008, would acquire its rival exchange),[23] offered floor space for the AMEX's equities and exchange-traded funds (ETFs) activity. The AMEX had pioneered ETFs, which are packages of securities that trade like stocks, in the early 1990s; ETF activity was critical to that exchange.

Another rival, the Philadelphia Stock Exchange, gave the AMEX floor space for its options business. "It was really crowded on the Philly floor," remembered Sodano. "They were packed in like cattle."[24] And the SEC granted the AMEX emergency relief, permitting it to operate outside of its building, which was otherwise proscribed by regulation.

The AMEX had to shift connectivity to its computers over to the NYSE. That move was accomplished in a relatively short time because both exchanges used SIAC to manage their hardware and communication systems. Over the weekend, all of the AMEX's front-end terminals that hadn't been destroyed were moved to the NYSE and reconnected.[25]

Numerous AMEX staff had spent Sunday, September 16, on the floor of the NYSE rehearsing for the following day. "All our specialists and market makers were there," Sodano recounted. "There was a resourceful NYSE operations guy who, working with SIAC, helped us set up the telecommunications connections to the floor that we needed. We tested everything through the night on Sunday. And it all worked. We didn't miss a trade on Monday."

After the opening bell, Sodano stood in the AMEX area of the floor, reflecting on the events of the past week, including the deaths of ten AMEX traders who had been in the Trade Center, the crippling of his building, and the struggle to get back in business. He walked over to the NYSE side, where he was warmly greeted by the staff. When Sodano saw Bob Britz, an executive vice president (and soon-to-be president) of the NYSE, he thanked Britz and told him that the AMEX probably would be out of business if not for the NYSE's help. Britz shrugged and replied, "You would have done the same thing for us. It's the right thing to do."

Although the AMEX was small relative to the NYSE and NASDAQ, it provided much liquidity to the equity markets. If that liquidity had dried up, price discovery would have diminished, hindering the operation of the markets and potentially harming investors. Also, the exchange's market makers and specialists, who put up their own capital and had positions they may not have been able to unwind, could have been severely hurt or wiped out.

Sodano had pushed hard to resume trading that Monday: "If we hadn't opened up that Monday, we would have been out of business because all of those floor people wouldn't have sat by idly. They would have gone elsewhere to protect their franchise and capital. And who knows if they ever would have come back."

The New York Futures Exchanges Also Reopen

Both New York-based futures exchanges also reopened floor trading on Monday, with shortened hours. The facilities of the New York Board of Trade, which focused on traditional agricultural products, had been at Four World Trade Center and were completely destroyed. Fortunately, only limited trading, in cocoa and stock indexes, had been active when the attacks began. Recalled Pat Gambaro, NYBOT executive vice president of operations: "Because it was so early, we had only about 350 people on the floor. A half hour later, we would have had nearly 2,000 staff there, which would have made it likely that we would have lost some people in evacuating the building." On 9/11, twelve NYBOT employees had walked six miles, through midtown Manhattan and over the Queensboro Bridge, to their disaster recovery center in a turn-of-the century, three-floor warehouse in Long Island City, just on the other side of the East River.

NYBOT had been created in 1998 from the merger of the New York Cotton Exchange and the Coffee, Sugar, and Cocoa Exchange. The latter exchange had the foresight to have built the Queens backup after the 1993 Trade Center attack, when it came close to losing access to its trading floor for several weeks.[26] George Haase was President of the New York Clearing Corporation (NYCC), which cleared all of NYBOT's trades. "The bad news was that it was the only futures exchange that lost its entire floor," Haase said. "But the good news was that it was the only one with an operating backup floor."[27]

Through the prior weekend, NYBOT staff had worked to ensure that the Queens site would have sufficient connectivity to its member firms.[28] Gambaro, who had been instrumental in establishing the backup facility years earlier, led that effort. He was to have been in an 8:30 a.m. meeting on 9/11 at Cantor's offices to discuss the Cantor Exchange, an electronic exchange for the trading of U.S. Treasury futures that was a joint NYBOT-Cantor venture. His daughter had gone into labor the night before, causing him to reschedule the meeting, sparing his life.

On Saturday, September 15, Gambaro invited the entire NYBOT membership to the Long Island City facility. "We wanted them to see the new environment and mock trade," he explained. "If nothing else, it helped ensure that they knew where the place was." Members were given their booth assignments and phone numbers, together with a package of information containing directions on how to get to the site and nearby hotel and parking facilities.

NYBOT and NYCC management were concerned that members would start trading and then sustain losses due to lack of liquidity or connectivity. "To have a viable market, we needed a good majority of our members to trade through us," noted Haase. "A lot went into that, including having connections to phones on the floor." The inconvenient location of the Long Island City facility was mitigated by the NYBOT having implemented, just a few months earlier, a capability for its clearing members to download their key reports from the exchange rather than having to pick up paper.

The Queens site was operational on 9/11, but it had been designed as a temporary fix, not as a long-term home. No one had contemplated that NYBOT would have its main site destroyed.[29] The 3,000-square-foot backup trading area was one-quarter the size of NYBOT's original floor;[30] it had been set up in

1995 for a similarly-sized floor for the Coffee, Sugar, and Cocoa Exchange.

With only two pits – a larger one for futures trading and a smaller space for options on futures trading – NYBOT was forced to set up a staggered trading schedule.[31] Coffee, cocoa and sugar traded in the morning hours; cotton and juice trading followed in the afternoon. For products that generated lesser volume, such as currency contracts and the stock indexes of the New York Futures Exchange, a NYBOT division, trading was shifted to small corners of the building where phones were quickly installed.[32]

Within months, NYBOT had doubled its space, primarily by taking over the entire second floor of the building for use by staff and members. Realizing that the Queens contingency site, now its primary one, wasn't itself backed up, management established a new data center for that purpose at 39 Broadway. That location was chosen in part to demonstrate that returning to the Financial District was safe and viable.[33]

Having the Queens floor proved critical to NYBOT. In an environment in which available office space was at a premium, it would have taken at least a month to create a usable trading floor from scratch, a scenario that Haase reflected on years later. "What would have happened to our markets during that time? Coffee, sugar, and cocoa, for example, probably would have been taken by London [the London International Financial Futures Exchange, the largest futures exchange in Europe]. If those contracts had moved to London for any significant amount of time, it would have been hard to get them back. The backup site saved our ass."

The New York Mercantile Exchange, which until a couple of years before 9/11 had been in Four World Trade Center, also reopened that morning. It had been uncertain for most of the prior week whether NYMEX trading, still done largely by open outcry, could recommence by the following Monday and, if so, whether it would be in New York or Chicago. On 9/11, Vincent Viola, the NYMEX Chairman, called Pat Gambaro to ask if NYBOT could make time and space available to NYMEX should it be needed. But that wasn't feasible in the cramped Queens site.[34]

In Chicago, soon after the attacks began, Gill, the Chicago Merc's Clearing Division head, received a call from David Solomon, a consultant for the NYMEX responsible for strategy. Solomon told Gill that he was jumping in a car and driving to Chicago to arrange for the Merc to help NYMEX set up an alternate location.

The Chicago Merc shifted full bore into assisting its competitor exchange. "We had 70 people working here nonstop, living downtown, for the next five days to both set up an alternate trading floor for the NYMEX and to develop the contract specs and systems changes needed to list NYMEX products on our Globex electronic trading system," Gill remembered.

The Chicago Board of Trade, which was actively listing and promoting futures products that were in direct competition with the NYMEX's, also offered help. Bernie Dan of the CBOT told the NYMEX that his exchange could house them in Chicago: "We had our old, vacant floor at the Mid-American Commodity Exchange, still with power and quotes."

In the end, the NYMEX, working closely and at a furious pace with Verizon, other infrastructure providers, and New York City police and emergency staff, returned to its own floor in time. The lack of land access to the building, which was near Ground Zero on the water's edge, was overcome by the use of ferries.[35] NYMEX officials later expressed appreciation to the Chicago Merc and CBOT, although some NYMEX members had viewed the efforts of these exchanges with suspicion, worried that if trading in their products shifted to Chicago, they'd never get it back. [36] As one neutral industry veteran observed, "People don't realize how fragile a market is. When it's shut down, it's not a slam dunk that the market is going to come back up again. There's a critical mass of buyers and sellers that you might have lost."[37] (Ironically, in 2008, NYMEX would be acquired by the Chicago Merc.)

A Lack of Critical Settlement Information

Liquidity was strong and a more typical pricing mechanism had returned to the Govie market.[38] Having restored connectivity with BoNY,

GSCC used the weekend to fuel its own return to health. At the close of business on Friday, it had $404 billion in fails activity at BoNY; by Monday morning, this amount was down to $225 billion, in part due to pair-offs of settlement obligations.[39] All of downtown Manhattan east of Broadway was now accessible, and GSCC became host to several displaced members, including the brokers GFI, Maxcor, and Tradition, who began using its offices and terminals to process their activity.[40]

Not that all was well. At 11 a.m., GSCC issued an extraordinary notice for a clearing corporation whose role was to be the bedrock of the Govie market. It reported that it couldn't be certain whether the funds settlement requirements published in the daily reports "accurately reflect funds received from members since last Tuesday." As a result, the clearing corporation asked that netting members ignore the funds requirement statement issued to them on Friday.[41]

On the securities settlement side, the notice made clear that much remediation remained to be done. During all of Wednesday through Friday, when it was flying blind, GSCC had been forced to consider all securities positions as fails, generating new deliver instructions to participants that might have been unnecessary. The clearing corporation also acknowledged that the information received regarding the blind broker fails picked up on the evening of 9/11 might be inaccurate or incomplete. To help facilitate the settlement and reconciliation process, members were asked to give priority to GSCC's calls that tried to pair off clearance obligations.[42]

GSCC began a lengthy and massive reconstruction effort with the Street. Staff with Microsoft Excel® skills were in high demand. Jie Xie, of Sal Matera's technology group, built an extract of Garban's positions that was e-mailed to the broker on a daily basis. With only a small number of worn out staff, help was needed. Dave Buckmaster called an old friend, Bill Hughes, who for decades had run the back-office of Aubrey G. Lanston, a former primary dealer.[43] Hughes, retired for more than two years, understood how to read reports and manually balance positions, unlike many of those new to operations who knew only "what button to push." Hughes also had long-standing relationships with many key individuals in the operations areas of the dealer shops.

As Hughes would recount years later, "Dave asked me if I ever gave a thought to going back to work. And I said, 'No, never gave it a second thought. I'm enjoying myself.' Then he asked me if I could do him a favor and come in and help him with the reconciliation."

Hughes started on the following Monday: "I shifted from living in the Hamptons full time to staying in Brooklyn during the week." One day, weeks later, Buckmaster invited Hughes to dinner and asked him, "How much do you want to get paid?" Hughes responded, "What do you mean? I thought I was doing you a favor." They agreed on a market rate; Hughes ended up working at GSCC for nine months.[44]

While the back-end of the Govie market was only at the beginning of what would be a painful process of records restoration, the more visible trading side of the market had been substantially repaired. On Monday at 3 p.m., the BMA board, Calendar Committee, and Primary Dealers Committee held yet another joint conference call.[45] Although the backlog of reconciliations persisted, almost all the key players were now operating at full capacity and communicating with each other. Many on the call expressed their concern about the mental and emotional well-being of their exhausted staff members. Although early closes were recommended again for Tuesday and Wednesday, the group picked Thursday, September 20, as the day to resume usual trading hours. [46]

Monday night was the beginning of Rosh Hashanah, the Jewish New Year. Jews in the New York City area flocked to services in record numbers. One 45-year-old man walked up to the B'nai Jeshurun synagogue on the Upper West Side and said to an usher, "I don't have a ticket. I'm not a member of the synagogue. I just want to observe."[47]

A full week had gone by since 9/11. The U.S. financial industry had absorbed a savage body blow. The healing process would now begin in earnest.

CHAPTER 13

RECONCILIATION AND HEALING

"I did think at one point that the reconcilement would be impossible. As it turned out, we kind of ring-fenced where the problems going forward would be. It took two years, and we never proved to the penny, but we got down to a less than $100,000 gap. At that juncture, we realized there was no further point to it."

Al Clark, Senior Vice President, Chase Manhattan Bank[1]

Recurring fears that One Liberty Plaza would collapse led to frequent evacuations of nearby buildings during the week of September 17. One afternoon, a driver, upon hearing a rumor that the building was about to fall, jumped out of his large truck and ran, causing a frenzy in the nearby crowd.[2]

In the days immediately after 9/11, the Govie market had been a shell of itself. Market volume was significantly reduced and there was only minor inter-dealer broker activity. Securities lending was greatly curtailed. Price discovery was limited, with few market participants offering consistent financing capabilities, and term financing was nonexistent. Most dealers stayed in pure funding mode.[3]

Yet less than two weeks later, the market had fully revived on the trading side, spurred by the Fed's infusion of significant additional liquidity.[4] The restoration of most of the inter-dealer brokers also was critical. On Tuesday, September 18, Euro Brokers reopened with half of its surviving staff. By November, Euro Brokers had recaptured almost all of its pre-9/11 business.[5]

On the floor of the Chicago Board of Trade, along with the electronic displays listing the numerous price quotes for futures, there was a board devoted to cash bond quotes. That information was critical to the many CBOT members who engaged in "basis trading," which involved taking advantage of the spreads between cash and futures prices. After 9/11, that display was largely blank, containing only a few quotes from BrokerTec that had minimal market impact. Cantor's price quotes were key. And they weren't reaching the CBOT because that information stream had originated out of the Trade Center.

The CBOT worked to get connected to Cantor's London office. On Wednesday, September 19, Bernie Dan was on the floor: "All of a sudden, we started to see flickers of pricing from Cantor streaming onto the board. The entire floor stopped. Everyone began clapping and hollering, about 3,500 people, who truly were a bastion of competitors. In a show of admiration for Cantor's resiliency that I had never seen the likes of."

On Friday, September 21, the Open Markets area at the Federal Reserve Bank of New York reopened. Lori Santamorena of the Bureau of the Public Debt was there: "They had a beautiful little ceremony on the ninth floor, with a bagpipe player." In the days prior, the New York Fed had invited police, firefighters and emergency workers in the area to use its facilities, including its elegant dining room.[6] After the ceremony, Santamorena went into the ladies room, where a firefighter was scrubbing down.

On Monday, September 24, Tradeweb was back in operation. Lee Olesky was Tradeweb's Chairman at the time: "Thank God we had the London data center [opened earlier in the year], which contained a complete mirror of our technology in New York. If not for that, we might not have stayed in business. We were a small company, and everything in New York had been destroyed. If we had been snuffed out then as a business, you wouldn't have had this pretty significant company that we have today." (Nine years later, Tradeweb was a global company with 550 employees trading $300 billion a day in an array of products.)[7]

On Monday, October 1, the American Stock Exchange reopened trading in its building, in the middle of what continued to be a tightly restricted zone busy with emergency workers. Next to the front of the exchange was a makeshift morgue set up in a school building. Bodies were still being brought in. Rescue workers and their dogs took refuge in the back of the AMEX building, seeking sleep, food and coffee.

Sal Sodano had been on the phone virtually every day with Ivan Seidenberg, the CEO of Verizon. "They had an army of people in the exchange physically rewiring hundreds of individual telephone lines, without which we couldn't do business," Sodano recalled. "The city brought in water through a temporary pipe. Con Edison restored our steam power, which we needed to maintain the air conditioning. And we had generators brought in."

A makeshift tunnel had been built leading from Rector Street, where the subway stopped, to the AMEX's front door. "Everyone went through a checkpoint at Rector, to make sure that you belonged with the exchange," Sodano explained. "Then there were two more checkpoints before you could get into the building. If you didn't belong in the area, you would have had a rough time. They would have just carted you away." For weeks, the AMEX building was the only one in the area with employees working in it.

A New Matching System

At the same time, GSCC was completing its reconciliation. During the month after 9/11, it built a new matching system to finally and comprehensively compare the banks' physical transaction journals to GSCC's delivery obligations. Leading that project was Sal Matera: "By this time, transaction journals were flying in. We had to take what BoNY and Chase said we did and look at what our books and records said we did and match them up. Sometimes there was a round robin that led nowhere. Sometimes we cleared items for the wrong reasons. Sometimes we cancelled items and then reestablished them. It was difficult."[8]

To enable this, Matera and his team of data base administrators parsed information and created tables in Oracle®, which GSCC hadn't used before. Complicating matters was that Matera's wife had undergone surgery right after 9/11 and was recovering at the Hospital for Special Surgery on the Upper East Side. Matera, while working long hours downtown, took extended lunch breaks to visit her. "What amazed me was that New York City had a procedure in place to prepare hospitals for victims of emergencies like 9/11," he reflected. "All elective-surgery patients were asked to leave, to make room to care for those injured in the Trade Center attacks. But no survivors were ever treated at the hospital."

At first, Matera's team was overwhelmed. "We took all of the bank and GSCC data for the weeks after 9/11 and looked at it all as having been done in one virtual settlement day. That 'day' just increased every new real business day," he remembered. The group ended up processing about half a million transactions by the time it was finished in October.

Reconciling Funds

While the securities settlement process was being addressed, GSCC's focus during the week of September 17 and thereafter increasingly shifted to the funds settlement side. Because the clearing corporation had been flying blind without good records after 9/11, it had stopped paying out funds to members in a credit position. It was, on the other hand, still issuing daily funds settlement instructions to the Street, and some firms in a debit position were continuing to pay into GSCC.

A number of firms had made funds payments to BoNY that BoNY either had been unable to report to GSCC or didn't recognize. Other firms claimed they had given BoNY instructions to pay funds to participants, but those participants had never received them. Day by day, GSCC was sitting on more and more cash. By Friday, September 21, that cash balance was about $2 billion. Members were calling GSCC, demanding to be sent the payments owed them.

Because of his facility with Excel spreadsheets, not to mention his self-admitted anal retentiveness, Adrien Vanderlinden, the GSCC staffer who had just come from Brussels a few weeks before 9/11, had been assigned by Dave Buckmaster to work solely on funds reconcilement. Vanderlinden would devote much of his time to confirming whether BoNY had received certain funds payments or made others. Every piece of information was reflected in Vanderlinden's spreadsheets. "I had three different sets of records from BONY," he recalled. "I took the view that, if the member says that he paid, and if BoNY confirmed that it got the payment in two of its three records, I'd just assume that it got paid by the member. Same for outgoing payments by us."

Around 5 p.m. on Friday, September 21, as funds Fedwire's 6:30 p.m. closing approached, an anxious Tom Costa walked over to Vanderlinden's cubicle.

"Adrien, I need to pay out funds. How much do I have to pay out?"

"According to my calculations, 1.6 billion dollars."

"That's a lot of money! You want me to write a check for that big an amount? You sure about that?"

"Tom, there's a lot of uncertainty about the information that I got."

"That's not what I'm asking. Are your numbers correct?"

"Well, to the best of my knowledge. I've only been here a few months."

"Okay, here's what I'm gonna do. I'm gonna write a check for 1.6 billion dollars. But the first time I find out that there's an error in your numbers, I'm personally gonna put you on the first boat back to Belgium!"

And with that, Costa walked away. GSCC wired out the money minutes before the close of the Fedwire. Although Vanderlinden had his work continually reviewed by Buckmaster and others, he was dismayed: "I'm a peon who just arrived at the company, and based on a spreadsheet I put together, this guy just paid 1.6 billion dollars!"

The following morning, September 22, Vanderlinden was in a car headed to Maywood. The only way GSCC would truly reconcile its funds position was for him to go to the source – BoNY. Vanderlinden reviewed BoNY's funds records and TJs, and then started "ticking things off."

He ended up spending the weekend there. "Maywood was set up like a makeshift army base. There were rows and rows of staff, trying to reconcile hundreds of millions of dollars. Some women had their kids there also, who were running around and banging on keyboards. There were balloons and food all over the place," Vanderlinden described. Reviewing the TJs, he "freaked," as he could see that literally hundreds of millions of dollars had been wired out of GSCC's account that he was unaware of, throwing off his $1.6 billion assumption. "And I knew that I would have to go back to Tom and tell him that we needed to get back all that money."

As a result of Vanderlinden's work, GSCC reversed a number of payments the next Monday. It made other adjustments in the weeks that followed based on the ongoing review of TJs as well as records produced by participants or BoNY. The reconciliation of BoNY's internal funds records with GSCC's records would go on until November 30.

During that time, Vanderlinden was on numerous calls with various firms: "Very few people were in their normal offices. Often you'd talk to a guy for a few days and give him all the information and be working with him and then find out that he had been sent to another location." Some corrections were reversals of initial corrections. "There were some payments that had been executed properly, but since we hadn't gotten BoNY's confirmation that they had been paid through, we changed something that we shouldn't have. Most participants handled it in good spirit, even when I took them through a convoluted explanation. They understood the mess."

Bill Hughes was the final arbiter. Using TJs and records from Chase, as well as the Fed, Hughes spent months ensuring that every GSCC member was whole either money-wise or securities-wise. "If I thought that we owed a firm money, I wouldn't tell them the amount, because they would agree right away," he admitted. "I would give them the issues and tell them to look through their records to figure it out." One case involved a small company that appeared to be owed $1.3 million by GSCC. "When I went back to the original records," Hughes recalled, "I found a DK that meant that the firm in fact owed GSCC $2 million. When I told their guy about it, he said, 'I thought that you might find that.' He knew where the problem lay, but he wouldn't admit it."

Hughes sat in GSCC's small, cramped legal library with a hand-written list to which he continually added "open items" or crossed them off. "The firms didn't learn from '93," Hughes observed. "Some kept tapes in the basement of the World Trade Center, where there was a big vault, but didn't use them. I didn't understand the mindset. It's like having a checking account but never checking the bank's records against your own."

In October, GSCC retained PricewaterhouseCoopers (PwC) to review open settlement orders and bring closure to the reconcilement process.[9] PwC sent requests to 92 participants asking for verification of all outstanding positions. GSCC received 63 responses. The last position break reported to GSCC was settled by the following January.

GSCC's reconciliation effort formally ended in May 2002, when the results were wrapped up in a report to the board. On the securities side, the total dollar amount of positions reconciled exceeded $50 billion. Resolved on the funds side were more than 2,000 individual money differences involving 60 accounts totaling over $300 million. All but five members were able to balance their records with GSCC; those five were paid the amount that GSCC had calculated. GSCC was left with a total unresolved balance of less than $39,000.[10]

Through GSCC, the industry also mutualized and absorbed all the bank financing costs that the inter-dealer brokers had borne in the days following 9/11.[11] But GSCC itself entered into a dispute with BoNY over which company should bear the financing cost of the $31 billion in securities that had sat in GSCC's box at BoNY. In December, BoNY took $9 million from a GSCC account in settlement of interest owed. GSCC demanded its return, arguing that the expense was caused by BoNY's inability to maintain sufficient communications links and backup capability. BoNY countered that it had performed valuable services for GSCC, placing blame with the telecommunications companies and, ultimately, the terrorists. The following May, the matter was settled in mediation, with GSCC paying BoNY a total of $6 million in interest cost ($3 million less than BoNY claimed).[12]

Months of difficult reconcilement efforts, involving huge dollar amounts, would be the norm for major participants in the Govie industry. One day during the week of September 17, Una Neary, the New York Fed examiner on BoNY's premises, walked into Tom Perna's office and slammed the door. "Do you realize that you're out of proof $470 billion in your Fed account?!" Responded Perna, "Great! It was $495 billion yesterday." Perna later learned that Neary had called the heads of the New York Fed and BoNY to complain that he wasn't taking the reconcilement process seriously.[13]

Squaring the books was a particular problem for some brokers. As BrokerTec's Joe Grima, reflected: "We spent the next couple of weeks emphatically insisting to certain dealers that our records were good. A lot of back-office staff didn't realize that BrokerTec was an electronic platform. They just saw tickets; they didn't know where they came from or how they were generated." While trying to resolve its records differences, BrokerTec also hosted several dealer firms in Jersey City, letting them input data to BoNY and GSCC through BrokerTec terminals.[14]

Garban Reopens

Garban reopened for U.S. trading on September 24. HSBC provided offices for it in spare disaster recovery space it had in two buildings near the Newport-Pavonia PATH station in Jersey City. Garban eventually housed about 300 brokers in those facilities. Tom Kinnally was one. He had a view of the Trade Center site, from which smoke continued to billow.[15] "It was cramped," he recalled. "Everyone had a desk and their own phone number. It was like your phone at home, so if you were calling out and someone was trying to call you, they got a busy signal. Initially, some dealers traded with us purely as an accommodation, to help us pay the bills."

Soon after, Bloomberg LLC offered Garban an entire floor at 59th Street and Park Avenue, with Bloomberg terminals and PCs aplenty. Ron Purpora and the Garban management team placed another 125 brokers there. "They had a couple of dozen Bloomberg employees who acted as concierges for us," Purpora recalled. "They even bought us all breakfast and lunch for the first two weeks." Garban wouldn't see normal trading volumes until January.

Purpora oversaw the rehabilitation of Garban's operations: "We could have opened earlier, but we had the $1.5 billion outstanding, and our settlement processes were compromised. There were a lot of people afraid to write another ticket when we still had so much to resolve. Even opening up on the 24th created problems. If we had waited, we could have cleaned up the $1.5 billion earlier. But we would have lost traction."

Tony Scianna of SunGard participated in Garban's continual senior management meetings: "The fact of the matter was that right after 9/11 they had no system. No books or records. They had no way of knowing their positions or which trades were good or not or what had settled. They didn't know which repos were open versus closed." SunGard created a settlement system for Garban over the first weekend after 9/11, which was critical because Garban was still up and running in the U.K. and needed to book trades.

By the middle of the week of September 17, SunGard had obtained from GSCC a file of Garban's open repo positions. SunGard's John Schipano managed its deconstruction. "We received balance order information from GSCC, which only told us what amount of securities Garban owed or was owed, not the nature of the individual repos," Schipano explained. "We needed to know what repos still were open, so that we could maintain them, pair them off or otherwise close them out. So we went through weeks of research trying to recreate the actual trades." A grateful Purpora, on two occasions, walked into the consultants' room handing out hundred dollar bills to the SunGard staff.[16]

"What kept us in business was that everyone owned up to their trades," Purpora recounted.

"People who made large sales that were many millions of dollars under water owned up to them, when they easily could have tried to say that they bought instead of sold."[17] Recalled Schipano, "We saw that level of cooperation as well. We had people calling us to say that they owed us coupon interest when we had no way of knowing that ourselves." Garban ended up with not a single uncompared trade.

Weeks later, Garban, whose staff was spread out in various locations in Manhattan and New Jersey, was offered additional space by Bloomberg LLC in a warehouse on the corner of Houston and West streets in the West Village. Right after 9/11, that warehouse had been converted from a sales office into a rest station for emergency workers.[18] As Purpora later described:

> The space had high beams and pigtail lights. Dark, dank and dirty. But it was cavernous. You couldn't see the other side of the floor. The construction guy asked us if the space would be good for us. Now, space was at a premium in Manhattan, with downtown being compromised and Midtown taken up by the big guys. So we said that it's great space, but we can't wait the six to nine months to build it out. Putting in the trading floor, power, communications, bathrooms, etcetera would take time. The guy says, "Six weeks."

Bloomberg's construction crews quickly built a trading floor and other facilities for Garban. By early December, Garban had consolidated all of its non-operations staff in that single location.[19] Recalled Purpora, "It was tight, we were elbow to elbow, it was dark, and we had three or four executives in a closet with no windows, but we got in there within six weeks with direct lines to customers."

Record Level of Settlement Fails

Following 9/11, settlement fails in the Govie market, reflecting the selling side's inability or unwillingness to meet its obligation to deliver securities on the scheduled date, rose dramatically.[20] This threatened the market's healing process. Fails create risk; specifically, the potential for loss if one's counterparty to a trade goes bankrupt or becomes insolvent before making good on its settlement obligation, and the settlement isn't otherwise guaranteed. In turn, that risk began to limit secondary market trading.[21]

Initially, it was assumed that the fails rate had increased because of operational reasons, including the destruction of trade records and communication facilities. To help address this, the Fed loaned substantial amounts of needed securities to the Street. [22]

But the level of fails remained high, and the typical remedy – borrowing a security through a "special" repo – was ineffective because it became as costly as failing to deliver the security.[23] There was much speculation on the Street as to why the fails persisted. One theory was that there were several central banks that, given the uncertain environment, were holding a lot of the securities, refusing to lend them to the market.[24] Some just attributed it to the Street's ongoing reconcilement problems.

By early October, the availability of the "on-the-run" (or most current) 10-year Treasury note became severely restricted, making the functioning of the repo market progressively more difficult. In an attempt to alleviate the scarcity, the Fed raised its securities lending program limit, to no avail.

To break the fail cycle, on October 4, under Peter Fisher's direction, the Treasury Department held an unscheduled or "snap" auction on the 10-year note, selling $6 billion in those notes six weeks before the regular quarterly refunding. The sudden arrival of new supply sent the price of the 10-year note down sharply.[25] "That was a hard decision, and there were a lot of traders who were pissed off because we didn't announce this in advance, but it worked," noted Fisher. "It didn't add a risk premium to the Treasury market and it reduced the level of fails; plus we didn't have to reopen the five-year in order to reduce the fails in that note."[26]

In early October, the Treasury market became subject to a broad government inquiry into whether anyone with prior knowledge had profited from the attacks. Secret Service investigators contacted a number of bond traders regarding large purchases of five-year notes made prior to 9/11. As part of the probe, the SEC asked major firms to turn over customer accounts and stock trading records involving short-selling before that date.[27] The 9/11 Commission later concluded that there had been no insider trading.

New Crises

In the wake of 9/11, the number of jobs in New York City's securities industry fell dramatically. Some of the loss reflected a relocation of operations to nearby suburbs, mostly northern New Jersey.[28] And although the U.S. economy as a whole rebounded from contraction in the third quarter of 2001 to modest growth a quarter later,[29] not so in New York City. Within a half-year of 9/11, there were almost 135,000 fewer jobs in the city, with the area's unemployment level surging to nearly eight percent.[30]

However severe the harm to the financial markets caused by 9/11, it was a crisis hidden from most of the public, quickly fading from consciousness as disgrace emerged in corporate America. Just a month later, on October 16, Enron announced that significant revisions to its financial statements for the prior three years were necessary to correct accounting violations. By December 2, Enron had filed for bankruptcy, the largest one in American history at the time.

The wave of corporate implosions continued in 2002. Arthur Andersen, Enron's auditor and one of the five largest accounting firms in the world, admitted that it had destroyed documents related to the SEC's investigation of Enron. Arthur Anderson's conviction for obstruction of justice led to its demise. The deficiencies and doubts about the trustworthiness of corporate financial statements led fairly quickly to passage of the Sarbanes-Oxley Act on July 30, 2002, which changed the corporate governance landscape.

Less than ten days prior to the enactment of Sarbanes-Oxley, and also as a result of accounting misdeeds, WorldCom filed for Chapter 11 bankruptcy protection, overtaking Enron as the largest such filing in U.S. history (later surpassed by the collapses of Lehman Brothers and Washington Mutual in September 2008). Numerous other scandals rocked Wall Street in the years immediately after 9/11, including fraudulent analyst reports, IPO abuses, and mutual fund misdeeds involving late trading and market timing.

Personal Reassessments

The emotional scars brought about by 9/11 were laid bare in the weeks and months afterward, as the wrenching memorial services stretched on. For New Yorkers, the background music of their lives had changed forever. For those immersed in solving the operational mess, there was at least a sense of purpose that some described as overwhelming.

Many of those who worked in the Financial District reassessed their careers and lives. One Govie repo trader, who had escaped from the North Tower, for years afterwards battled depression and severe anxiety. He was later diagnosed as suffering from post-traumatic stress disorder.[31] This was not atypical.

Many Wall Streeters never returned to their jobs, while others were relocated. Thousands now had to report permanently to offices outside of lower Manhattan, turning Jersey City into even more of a financial hub. Those who returned to the World Trade Center area would need to adjust to the pervasive stink that emanated from Ground Zero, and to the disorientation created by the gap in the skyline. Many people avoided taking the subway. Some openly worried about contaminants still in the air.

Driving to work in Manhattan became more difficult, as many office building garages were either closed or restricted. The PATH train station at Exchange Place would be out of service for the next two years, so New Jersey residents who were used to taking the PATH one short stop to the Trade Center instead streamed out of the Grove Street station in Jersey City and walked to the ferry, flooding a normally empty area with people. One such commuter was Fran Glasser: "Each day I would just stare out the ferry window as we passed the Trade Center. The clearing of the debris seemed never ending. I would see the constant smoke, as if the fire was still there."

Larry Lemmon's son, who was 30, soon quit Merrill Lynch. "He took over a 50 percent pay cut to become a New York City fireman. We sat down and discussed it and he told me that it was something that he always wanted, and now he was determined to do it," Lemmon said. Rich Visco carried with him a photo of the Fire Department football team that he had coached, so many of its members now lost.

Steve Greenberg had dated a woman in the early 1990s with whom he hadn't spoken in years: "She was the love of my life, the proverbial one who got away. When she heard about the attacks, she kept going to the CNN and other websites every day to see if my name appeared." The two found each other by the end of September. "We rekindled our relationship, and got married a year later. Out of tremendous tragedy came the best thing in my life."

The financial industry mended its operational woes and moved on. But for any silver lining to be found, there would need to be a sufficient understanding of the lessons learned from 9/11. Some were obvious; others were more subtle. It would take years for them to be appropriately assessed and implemented.

CHAPTER 14

LESSONS LEARNED

"We were caught off guard as an industry. People talked a lot about the importance of having redundancy and geographic diversity, but it wasn't in place nearly to the degree it needed to be. And even more importantly, because it's more subtle, if you don't test it and keep it fresh and rehearse it, it's not worth the money you've invested in it. So 9/11 had a night-and-day impact on the whole continuity of business and disaster recovery industry."
Steve Randich, Chief Technology Officer, NASDAQ[1]

As the U.S. financial markets worked their way through the 9/11 crisis, they were fortunate in some important respects. The emergence of electronic communication and trading had made companies' physical location increasingly irrelevant, facilitating a gradual shift in the 1980s and 1990s to offices away from lower Manhattan. Firms in the Trade Center had incorporated lessons from the 1993 bombing. The Y2K preparations two years earlier had markedly improved the state of the industry's overall contingency planning.

Significantly, 9/11 did not raise questions about companies' creditworthiness. The financial institutions affected remained sound financially. This allowed for a level of trust essential for the Fed to lend funds to the Street and for firms to resume trading while they caught up on the settlement of money and securities they owed to each other.

A Revolution in Contingency Planning

9/11 changed the landscape for the management of operational risk, transforming it from an ad hoc, diffuse activity often split among various support areas to a valued, centralized discipline.[2] Regulators introduced a separate capital charge for banks to take into account operational risk, defined as "the risk of loss resulting from inadequate or failed internal processes, people and systems, or from external events."[3] Contingency planning went from being a technology management and back-office concern to a key responsibility for the CEO. Prior to 9/11, significant spending on disaster recovery was a tough sell at many firms; afterwards, it was difficult to justify *not* doing so.

The terrorist attacks raised issues that had never before been sufficiently considered, prompted by a redefinition of the concept of "disaster." After 9/11, everyone's imagination improved, revolutionizing contingency preparedness. When a massive power outage occurred in the Northeast during August 2003, financial firms reported little disruption to their operations, a result that many credited to post-9/11 enhancements.

This transformation in disaster planning was led by the various industry trade associations. In December 2001, the Securities Industry Association formed a Business Continuity Practices (BCP) Committee. This action essentially put an existing BCP industry-wide "management group" under the SIA umbrella, giving the committee far greater status and resources. Don Kittell chaired that committee: "All the firms had some degree of disaster recovery plans. But they were more data center and operationally focused. One of the things that 9/11 convinced everyone of was that the whole gamut of what a firm does, including trading desks and investment banking, has to be involved in contingency planning."

The BCP Committee created an industry disaster command center to link securities firms, exchanges, utilities, the New York City Office of Emergency Management, and federal and state regulatory agencies.[4] In addition, it brainstormed about potential calamities such as a poison gas attack or pandemic. Once the group scoped out the dimensions of a disaster, it then designed and tested a corresponding contingency plan. One participant likened the process to "war games."[5]

After months of imagining possible catastrophic scenarios and how to defend against them, the group realized that it was an endless task. Recalled Kittell, "We concluded that, rather than continue to do that, we would break out the elements that were functionally critical to a firm, and then make sure they were resilient and backed up. So whatever disaster you envisioned, the answer was sort of the same. What are the essential building blocks of your process, and how can they be made enduring no matter what happens?"

The other industry trade groups reacted in kind. The Bond Market Association established the Business Continuity Management Council to address business continuity issues specific to the fixed-income markets. In 2006, the BMA and SIA merged, facilitating coordination and communication between the fixed-income and securities industries.[6] By 2004, the Futures Industry Association had begun to orchestrate an annual disaster recovery test among all the major U.S. and international futures exchanges, clearinghouses, futures commission merchants, and clearing firms.

Prior to 9/11, market regulators had only a limited focus on operational issues, leaving contingency planning largely to individual financial institutions. In 2002, at the urging of the Treasury

Department, the Street formed the Financial Services Sector Coordinating Council to communicate between the private sector and federal regulators on business continuity issues. Over the next two years, the senior market regulators laid out, in a series of papers, their expectations for market participants' contingency plans. They insisted that those plans provide for a range of resiliency and protective measures, including multiple backup sites, long-term data storage, and communications testing.[7] For "core clearing and settlement organizations," it was generally agreed that the goal for recovery and timely resumption of critical operations after a disaster should be no more than two hours.

Post-9/11, many firms that had outsourced their disaster recovery capabilities had been faced with suppliers that could not simultaneously deliver to all their clients.[8] In response, the regulators pointed to the risks of entrusting business-critical functions to third-party vendors, and set standards and limitations regarding that.[9]

The SEC formed a new unit to deal with business continuity. By January 2002, the Street had been advised by a top Commission official that its inspectors would expect to see comprehensive contingency plans in place when they next examined firms.[10] In 2004, after much debate and fine-tuning, the SEC approved rule filings requiring every broker-dealer to establish and disclose a sufficient, written business continuity plan and to provide the regulators with emergency contact information.[11] By that year, the NASDAQ was offering disaster recovery tests for its entire customer base.[12] And in May 2004, many major Wall Street firms worked with federal and local law enforcement to simulate the handling of a bomb explosion in midtown Manhattan.[13]

Each of the exchanges raised the disaster planning bar. The AMEX built a backup trading floor. As AMEX's Sal Sodano recalled, before 9/11: "No one ever imagined the building would be physically devastated like it was. It was backed up from a technology perspective, but we had felt the building itself was just too big to be replicated." The NYSE also built a new contingency trading floor, as well as a remote network operations center. In all, the NYSE spent more than $100 million to bolster security and improve redundancy and business continuity.[14]

Ironically, while these plans were being implemented, physical backup for trading floors quickly became largely irrelevant. The level of activity taking place on them shrank significantly, and the concentration of trading in a few key exchanges evolved into a decentralized network of electronic trading platforms. In the United States, automated equity trading began to dominate order volume and eat away at the NYSE's preeminence. In response, the NYSE in 2007 introduced its "hybrid market," which affords immediate execution of stock brokers' orders in a fully automated manner as opposed to routing them to the trading floor for completion by live auction. A similar trend occurred in the futures world, as electronic trading volume quickly came to vastly overshadow pit activity.[15]

The increasing globalization of the markets rendered less threatening the prospect of an area's infrastructure being destroyed. In 2007, the NYSE merged with Euronext, a major European stock exchange, making it seamless for U.S. stock prices to be quoted abroad and further diminishing the risk of geographic concentration.

"Physical temples" would no longer be required. Never again would severe damage to floor space or buildings be a threat to the functioning of the equities or futures markets. Instead, cyber-terrorism would become the greater concern.[16]

Moving Out of the Financial District

The most visible impact of 9/11 was the acceleration of firms moving out of the Financial District to areas with different telecommunications and power infrastructures. Overall, of the 1,134 companies displaced by the Trade Center attacks, *only a little more than 25 percent* returned to lower Manhattan. Many of the firms that left permanently were in the financial sector.[17]

Even before 9/11, many companies had begun to move operations staff and processes out of Manhattan for economic reasons. The attacks hastened that, triggered by the stark reality that disaster planning must include the possible devastation of an entire geographic area. For the first time, many firms and industry utilities set up operating sites with separate staffs, applications, and hardware in locations hundreds or even thousands of miles from their headquarters. GSCC's parent company, the Depository Trust & Clearing Corporation, subsequently set up a large operations center in Florida, shifting a substantial number of staff there. BoNY eventually returned to all of its former sites in lower Manhattan, but not in the same numbers. It moved 1,400 employees to Brooklyn, 70 securities-processing and brokerage-clearing staff to Florida, and hundreds of administrative, clerical, managerial, and technical jobs to upstate New York.[18]

The events of 9/11 taught conflicting lessons. On the one hand, that greater distance was needed between primary and backup sites. But also that modes of transportation are at risk of severe disruption, with air travel particularly vulnerable. For firms that didn't have global locations with senior personnel on site, the focus shifted from relying on the ability to move *people* among sites to ensuring sound *telecommunications* links, including video conferencing.

Technological advancement did not diminish the desire of many firms to be near the New York City area's talent pool. Major Wall Street firms tended to shift their staff and facilities to locations relatively close by. One prominent example was Lehman Brothers. In the month after 9/11 it bought a Midtown tower being built by Morgan Stanley and eventually left lower Manhattan altogether. Morgan Stanley itself shifted about 1,500 staffers to Westchester after it bought the former Texaco headquarters in Harrison, New York. Merrill Lynch returned to Two World Financial Center, and Goldman Sachs completed its tower in Jersey City at the site of the former Colgate factory and in 2004 began construction on a global headquarters building catty corner from the Trade Center site. Cantor Fitzgerald took space in Midtown, while Garban ultimately relocated to Jersey City.[19] Tradeweb also relocated to Jersey City where it remained for nearly a decade before moving back to Manhattan in 2010. As Lee Olesky of Tradeweb explained, "Overlooking the Trade Center site still would have been emotionally difficult for many people, so we relocated in Midtown."

Aside from geographic dispersion, there would be a renewed focus on the adequacy of backup sites, particularly "dark" ones that are intended to be switched on only in an emergency. By their very nature, contingency sites tend to be less robust than primary locations. After 9/11, it was not uncommon for a firm to bring in folding tables and PCs by the dozens to its contingency site and set them up as "work space" for displaced staff. Companies often found that their backup facilities didn't have copies of their operating systems or of key application programs, were missing up-to-date hardware, or had systems not configured properly or tested sufficiently. Contingency planning would now need to provide details on how employees would travel to backup sites and how they would find adequate parking, work space, and food, perhaps for an extended time.

Some firms moved away from the notion of a primary location versus a backup facility, and towards a split-operations model in which two or more sites are equally active and provide backup for one another, including the ability to absorb the critical work of the other for a long period.[20] To make this model truly effective, those companies needed to make each site independently robust and conduct communications tests among all sites.

9/11 underscored the importance of local authorities providing access to *every* site a company has. In the days after 9/11, GSCC lost effectiveness as its staff had difficulty gaining entry to its Manhattan offices, in part because law enforcement authorities were unfamiliar with the company. Thereafter, New York City implemented an emergency system that facilitated access by key personnel to restricted areas.

Telecommunications is Key

The operational crisis created by 9/11 was, in many respects, based on lack of telecommunications capability and of redundancy. Most financial firms had a carefully constructed communications plan in place, including multiple connections to their banks and redundant lines and facilities. But those plans often were rendered useless.

Even the communication contingencies of firms that used entirely *different* phone companies for backup failed, as the phone companies shared facilities and all lines still may have been routed through a single point of failure. As the co-CEO of Verizon said three months later, "What 9/11 showed us is that true security lies in having a diversity of technologies that give customers redundant capabilities and provide alternative ways to communicate. You need to have more than just Verizon."[21] Paying heed to that admonition, within a year, SIAC developed for the Street a highly redundant communications access network, the Secure Financial Transaction Infrastructure (known as "Safety"), that replaced point-to-point circuitry with distributed pathways.[22]

Compounding the problem was the lack of an industry-wide plan for prioritizing reconnection of telecommunications services. Everyone on the Street was simultaneously vying for attention, and there were no clear procedures for determining which entities had the greater need. After 9/11, firms joined a federal program established for that purpose, designed to launch in the event of a wide-scale disruption.[23]

Protection of Data – and People

The financial markets never truly close; creation of trade and settlement data never stops. The 9/11 events caused a massive loss of data and attendant books and records. Firms came to understand that housing and protecting data is even more critical than maintaining functioning operational sites.

Post 9/11, restoring lost data was a slow process for many firms because they used "cold site" recovery. This required the transport of backup tapes to recovery sites, an inefficient method particularly in the days immediately following 9/11. Thereafter, as technology developed, companies began shipping records offsite more frequently and shifting to real-time communications (which GSCC later made a requirement for its netting members). Transactions and other vital data would be preserved on an up-to-the-minute basis at a remote "hot" backup site that was a mirror image of a company's main data center. All systems were configured to allow the backup site to be brought up to full production in a few hours.

The "human capital" plans of financial firms understandably failed on 9/11. Companies had difficulty reaching staff, relocating them to alternate sites, accommodating displaced employees, and putting them to work productively. Firms were unprepared to handle the large number of traumatized workers; Morgan Stanley alone hired more than 300 grief counselors to help distraught employees cope and to coach supervisors on how to deal with them.[24]

In the wake of 9/11, some lessons were manifest, such as instituting a procedure for maintaining and distributing contact lists. Others became more evident over time, including training staff in the basics of key operational processes. When the calculator doesn't work, can someone do the math on paper?

Firms had tended to focus their contingency planning on the preservation of computers and machinery, not people. But as Tom Wipf of Morgan Stanley observed, "We had a number of really bright senior guys in a room who made some remarkable decisions, on instinct, that were right and they convinced others of that. That was a lot more important than our contingency plan."

Companies recognized the need for better planning to ensure the protection of life. Businesses of any size no longer had all their staff members work in the same location, to minimize the chance of their entire workforces being decimated. Decentralization of a firm's "knowledge capital" became an industry norm. Companies enhanced their evacuation procedures and conducted more rigorously drills to that end.[25]

Market Dependencies

Global marketplaces have an interdependency that requires instant consultation in an emergency. In the days after 9/11, coordination among marketplaces was haphazard. For instance, the cash Govie market in New York had an insufficient, ad hoc process for communicating with the Chicago futures exchanges. As for the equities markets, traditionally, the NYSE and NASDAQ mimic each other on operating hours. If one market is down and the other trades, problems arise for investors; for example, with regard to composite products, such as stock indexes, which require market data from both systems. Because the 9/11 attacks occurred at a time close to when the two exchanges would make their decision to remain closed, certain electronic communication markets did open, trading briefly that morning.[26]

The Govie market had multiple regulators and an industry association whose recommendations were voluntary, leading to the suggestion that there should be a single entity with the power to make binding decisions about the market's closing and reopening. Soon after 9/11, the Bond Market

Association invited comment on whether it should seek authority to issue mandatory guidance in an emergency. No action ever came of that; the Street didn't want to give the Association that power. In any event, the 24/7 and remote nature of electronic trading erased the notion that the Govie market could ever really be closed.

Probably the most significant issue specific to the Govie industry was that of clearing-bank concentration. The vast majority of the securities settlements in the U.S. government market were conducted within two clearing banks: Chase and BoNY. Creating a fallback plan for continuing settlement in the absence of one seemed obvious.

In May 2002, the Fed and the SEC issued a white paper outlining issues raised by 9/11. In that document, they asked whether the clearing bank system might need to be restructured. [27] The BMA responded for the industry by arguing that wholesale changes weren't warranted, and indeed would carry their own risks.[28] Chase and BoNY filed similar comments, with Chase noting that direct access to the Fedwire is a form of backup if one of the banks were to be down.[29]

Given the critical importance of Govies, the Fed went further, setting up in November 2002 the Working Group on Government Securities Clearance and Settlement. Some of its recommendations, issued in a report released in December 2003, were fairly manifest, including the development of a "secure and resilient telecommunications structure" for the settlement of Govies. Others went beyond the lessons learned from 9/11, such as taking steps to reduce the threat posed by cyber-terrorism.

Under the leadership of Mike Urkowitz, who in the 1980s had been responsible for Chase's worldwide operations, data processing, and telecommunications, the Working Group developed the idea of establishing "NewBank," a dormant entity that would spring to life if needed should Chase or BoNY suddenly exit the clearing-bank arena. That idea eventually died, in part because of the large amount of capital it would have required and also because, as Urkowitz later noted, "other crises came along and took center stage."[30]

In the end, no basic change was made to the Govie settlement system other than a vast enhancement of its disaster recovery capability. As the Fed's Roger Ferguson would recount years later, "The government securities market resumed operating smoothly. We didn't need a wholesale restructuring, just more resilience in the system in the form of robust business continuity plans."

For regulators, policy makers, and the Street, 9/11 was a stark illustration of the essential lesson of the Paperwork Crisis that had crippled the equities markets over three decades earlier. Financial firms can trade all they want, night and day, with great sophistication, around the globe. And they can fine-tune all of the front-office, risk, legal, and regulatory considerations related to that trading. But none of that will matter if those transactions can't be adequately cleared and settled.

***

The Wall Street of the early morning of 9/11 is gone. The highly publicized scandals and financial calamities that ensued, the explosion of high-speed computerized trading away from the traditional exchanges, the dramatic business mergers and failures that occurred during the Great Recession, the impact of the Dodd-Frank legislation triggered by the financial crisis, and the unyielding passage of time have fundamentally remade the markets and far overshadowed the operational crisis of September 2001. In an ever more complex and interconnected environment, the Street now measures time from another September – the one in 2008, when Lehman Brothers failed and its contagion spread globally.

Yet the emotional wounds and indelible memories of 9/11 remain, and shape a greater wisdom that guides our lives. The ultimate lesson learned is timeless: that our strength, and our faith, come from a common sense of purpose. In an increasingly divisive world, when the next threat to our way of life comes, it will again be our collective spirit that must save us.

HOW IT AFFECTED US

My final question to most of those whom I interviewed was: "How did 9/11 affect you personally?" Here are some of the answers:

"It didn't change my lifestyle. Or my career. Or make me smell the roses more. It has made me see things more clearly. Too often people want to make things gray. But I'm sorry, there is black and white. There is good and evil. It's made me more emphatic about that...I also feel the need to prepare my wife and kids for the day when I might not come home."

"It gave me more empathy for what other people go through. In my case, it helped prepare me for all the other crazy things that were about to happen to me. That day, when I really thought I was going to die, I felt kind of calm about it, and I surprised myself by feeling calm instead of frightened. And I thought about that again when I got the cancer diagnosis. I think 9/11 honestly helped prepare me for dealing with other life-threatening things."

"There are numerous days that go by when I think that, but for the grace of God, I could have been in that building. Had a meeting with Cantor or Eurobrokers. Or been walking by. And I realize there are certain things in my life that may not be quite right that I want to change."

"It has impacted my politics. It's raised dramatically the level of importance to me of national security issues. Even to this day, regarding the balance between civil liberties and national security, I am much more conservative than I ever thought I would be. If they want to search bags at subway stations, go ahead. If they want to arrest someone and put him in Guantanamo without a warrant, go ahead. I see the world in black and white, because I realize that I could have been killed, that people targeted me for no good reason, that they hate me and would kill me and my family."

"It didn't make me want to leave the city or something like that. I knew this was my life and what I wanted to do with it. It did wake me up, being the sort of person that I am, who is a bit of a workaholic, that I need my kids and they need me. You realize the value of family a lot more. Shame it takes that to make you realize that."

"I remember that I wasn't able to talk to my family until late that afternoon. When I got home that night, my two daughters both begged me not to go back to work. My older daughter said to me, 'Those people are nothing to you. Don't go back there anymore. Why do you have to go back?' That really hit me."

"I felt an urgency to do everything I wanted to do right away. And I feel guilty that I'm alive when people with children died."

"I lost a lot of friends. After 9/11, I avoided going back to New York for three years. I couldn't bring myself to look at that hole."

"It didn't affect me as much initially as later. I was single at the time, with no kids. I was still going out three nights a week and having a good time. Now I'm married with kids. It hit me again, and more deeply, when I had my first child."

"I certainly have a greater sense that in a moment or two things can be so different. But you have to live your life."

"I was very angry at first. I smoked like a bandit, although I had quit before 9/11. I needed an outlet. Everyone wanted to get these people. If I was twenty years younger, I would have enlisted. You felt helpless."

"I went and cashed in all the rewards points I had. Any certificate I had I went and used. I carry more cash, in the event something happens. I started to live like I did in my early 20s. Someone asks me to go out, I go out. Someone asks me to take a trip, I'll take it now. I partied more for the next two years. Till I felt that things were looking better. That we weren't doomed."

"I enjoy life. But I've changed. I take more vacations with my family now. I want that more now.

I'm more aware of certain things. And I buy lottery tickets now. I win it, I'm gone."

"I changed jobs and left some money on the table in doing so. But being here, it's important to me that I like the people – they're smart and I'm growing more. And I never thought about stuff like that. It was all about dollars before."

"I still won't get on a crowded subway car, because I don't want to get stuck down there with the lights out. And I found that when I got on planes, if there was a delay or it was hot, I'd get claustrophobic. I never had that problem before."

"Having been away from home all week, it was pretty emotional when I finally got home. I never remember coming home and being as glad to see my kids as I was then. I think it had a big impact not just on the people who work in the financial industry but also on their children. You couldn't shield them from the events."

"I'm more cynical now. And I do get very angry when I see protests at the World Trade Center. Or people coming to New York for the first time and going to the Trade Center and pretending to know what happened that day. Or people selling cheap mementos. That angers me to no end. The commercialization of that. It wasn't a NASCAR race."

"I used to think of myself as a very open person. Now I'm very suspicious all the time. I walk around in a constant state of paranoia."

"I'm not afraid to come to the City, because I've taken the view that if I'm going to be in the wrong place at the wrong time, that's my fate. And I have to go on living. I've come to terms with that. But I was deeply upset. And if I hear the "Star Spangled Banner" or "America the Beautiful," I'm overwhelmed with emotion."

***

As for how 9/11 affected this author, I feel more vulnerable than I had before. And I see more clearly the immoral extremes, often clothed in righteousness, that taint this world. I had always been aware of the need to safeguard myself and my family. Now I understand that even more imperative is our mutual responsibility to protect our society and future generations from the evil on full display that day. Or what else matters?

This gut feeling only solidified over the years as I spent time researching on the Internet. So often I'd become sickened and disillusioned when coming across hateful nonsense written about 9/11, of which there is so much. I hope that, in some small way, this book helps to counter that.

ACKNOWLEDGEMENTS

My initial goal was limited: to interview my colleagues at GSCC and preserve their memories of the event. Gradually, I expanded my ambitions to writing an article, then a book, and then broadening the scope of the book to touch on all the major financial markets.

This book would not have been possible without the active assistance and interest of quite a number of people. Critical to writing the book were the more than 100 folks who took the time to speak with me and provide their reminiscences and insights. Many shared experiences that obviously were painful to revisit. For some, who had not allowed themselves to fully reflect back on that day, the emotions rushed back anew. I thank each one, and hope that I've done them justice.

Many interviewees already were friends or colleagues. Early on, Peter Fisher, whom I've known since the early 1980s when we both worked at the New York Fed, shared in an extremely thoughtful and frank manner his memories, and encouraged me to continue my effort. Later, other ex-senior government officials graciously agreed to speak with me, including Suzanne Cutler, Roger Ferguson, Jerry Hawke, Sara Kelsey, Paul Malvey, Jim Newsome, Brian Roseboro, and Jamie Stewart. Among the senior industry figures who were extremely supportive were

Jane Buyers, Dennis Dutterer, Ed Watts, and Tom Wipf.

My interview with Joe Blauvelt was invaluable, not just for his recollections and explanations regarding the trading side of the crisis, but also for the mound of contemporaneous e-mails and writings that he had kept.

I particularly want to thank those who were willing to meet and talk to a stranger. Sal Sodano, for example, welcomed me into his office, spoke to me at length about the amazing events that took place at the AMEX, and showed me dozens of remarkable photos he had taken.

Much of the value of the book stems from various interviewees' honesty about the difficulties encountered by their companies after 9/11. In this regard, I want to express special appreciation to Al Clark, Tom Costa, Tom Perna, and Ron Purpora.

Various industry trade association officials were important sources of information. I thank Will Acworth, John Damgard, Eric Foster, Micah Green, Don Kittell, Marc Lackritz, Brian Macwilliams, Omer Oztan, Andy Waskow and especially Paul Saltzman (who, among other things, wisely insisted on the keeping of minutes of the emergency meetings of the Bond Market Association that took place after 9/11) for their accounts and observations. Of great help in conveying to me the events that took place in the futures markets were Bernie Dan, Dennis Dutterer,

Pat Gambaro, P. Gill, George Haase, Tom Hammond, Dennis Murray, and Ira Polk. On the securities side, a vital source of information was the SEC Historical Society's website.

I truly enjoyed researching and writing the brief history of the Govie market. Many thanks to the "old-timers" who shared their reminiscences with me, including Al Clark, Griff Clarke, Chris Dark, Ben Fargione, Dave Gordon, Joe Malvasio, Chuck Moran, Ron Purpora, Tom Russo, Ed Watts, and especially my brother-in-law, Jerry Rubin, who has a deep understanding of the Govie market and a remarkable recollection of events that happened 30 or more years ago. I also want to thank Professor Dick Sylla of the Stern School of Business at New York University for taking the time to read the history chapters and for correcting errors that I had made in writing about the early history of the market.

I learned quickly that writers need readers. Griff Clarke, Suzanne Cutler, Jon Flaute, Marisa Lago, Gary Lewitzky, Sal Matera, Omer Oztan, Richie Shadick, Inge Shumer, Jamie Stewart and many others read one or more drafts and provided valuable edits and corrections. Early on, Denise Raymond offered thoughtful ideas including a suggestion to add a chronology and diagrams. Kate Connelly gave me constructive tips on how to write in a more interesting, readable style. Larry Bergmann assisted with conveying the aspects of regulatory relief granted to the industry. Sal Matera helped me to better understand and more accurately portray various technical issues. Ken Garbade, who is as knowledgeable about the Govie market and its history as anyone, graciously took the time to give me voluminous comments. Mike Urkowitz led me to more fully appreciate the true lessons learned from 9/11.

The heart of the book is the GSCC story, and I thank the more than 20 GSCC friends and colleagues who shared their remembrances with me. I'm especially grateful to Dave Buckmaster. Over the years, whenever I would see Dave, he would ask me how the book was coming along, which would prompt me to get back to writing it. Dave also patiently read and reread many versions of the book, always supplying blunt but welcome criticism as well as important corrections and facts. Much appreciation also to Marc Golin for his meticulous reading of several drafts, and to Adrien Vanderlinden for his detailed and candid recollections and for the stack of documents that he had kept.

Many thanks to my editors, Ruth Mills and Pat Egner, who aside from excellent editing provided me with much wise counsel, including how to best organize the book in a logical fashion and to tell the story in a more coherent and compelling manner.

Many people have asked why I'm not in the book. I certainly was in the midst of the handling of the crisis in the Govie market and a firsthand witness to much that occurred. But it's not false modesty to say that I wasn't a major player.

My role was destined to be a chronicler of those extraordinary events. But only some of them. To learn more about the vast story of the regeneration of the markets, one must read other sources, including Tom Barbash's book *On Top of the World: Cantor Fitzgerald, Howard Lutnick and 9/11: A Story of Loss and Renewal* (HarperCollins, 2003); Charles Gasparino's book *King of the Club: Richard Grasso and the Survival of the New York Stock Exchange* (HarperCollins, 2007); Jeffrey Lacker's article "Payment System Disruptions and the Federal Reserve Following September 11, 2001," Federal Reserve Bank of Richmond Working Paper Series (WP 03-16, December 2003); and the record of the 2005 Annual Meeting of the SEC Historical Society, "Crisis and Resolve: The SEC and the Securities Industry Remember September 11, 2001." Hopefully, other accounts will be written in the future.

As always, my family was there for me. Much love and appreciation to my talented daughter, Arielle, for creating the cover and various graphs, to my son Craig for his great encouragement and enthusiasm for the book, and to my son-in-law Adam for his scrupulous readings, support, and suggestions. And to all three, thanks also for all of the brainstorming sessions and for enduring my constant chatter about the book.

My final and most important thanks go to my wife, Linda, who was an unfailing source of support over the many years of this effort. Linda read every interview and draft of the book, supplying a layperson's perspective that was much needed. She encouraged me to get out of my detached, lawyerly head and draw out the human aspects of the financial drama. Her love, wisdom, and beauty give me faith that this world can find the right path.

January 2011

Selective Timeline of Events on September 11, 2001

(Times are Eastern Standard/New York City; some are approximate)

7:00 a.m.: The Govie repo market begins active trading.

8:46 a.m.: American Airlines Flight 11 flies into floors 93 through 99 of One World Trade Center, known as the "North Tower."

9:03 a.m.: United Airlines Flight 175 flies into floors 77 through 85 of Two World Trade Center, known as the "South Tower."

9:15 a.m.: The Port Authority of New York and New Jersey begins closing New York City bridges and tunnels (including all five that cross into lower Manhattan) to all but emergency vehicles and to pedestrians leaving Manhattan

9:25 a.m.: The Federal Aviation Administration orders the first-ever nationwide ground stop, prohibiting the take-off of flights.

9:30 a.m.: Opening time for the U.S. stock exchanges, but they remain closed; the SEC issues a supportive press release.

The Empire State Building is shut down.

9:37 a.m.: American Airlines Flight 77 flies into the west wall of the Pentagon.

9:44 a.m.: A message is sent to banks over the Fedwire system stating that the system "is fully operational at this time and will remain open until an orderly closing can be achieved."

9:50 a.m.: The FAA orders all U.S. airports closed and all non-departed flights cancelled.

9:59 a.m.: The South Tower falls.

10:03 a.m.: United Airlines Flight 93 crashes near Shanksville, Pennsylvania.

10:15 a.m.: The Chicago Board of Trade suspends all trading.

10:20 a.m.: The New York City Transit Authority halts all subway service.

10:28 a.m.: The North Tower falls.

10:30 a.m.: New Jersey Transit stops all rail service into Manhattan's Penn Station.

10:41 a.m.: All federal office buildings in Washington D.C. ordered to evacuate.

10:45 a.m.: PATH service between New Jersey and Manhattan is suspended.

10:57 a.m.: New York Governor George Pataki orders all New York government offices closed.

11:02 a.m.: New York City Mayor Rudolph Giuliani urges New Yorkers to remain calm and to do what they can to evacuate lower Manhattan below Canal Street.

Noon: The Board of Governors of the Federal Reserve System issues a press release stating, "The Federal

Reserve System is open and operating. The discount window is available to meet liquidity needs."

2:49 p.m.: Mayor Giuliani announces at a news conference that subway and bus services are partially restored in New York City.

3:50 p.m.: The White House reports that, while some federal buildings had been closed, the government remains in full operation.

4 p.m.: Governor Pataki issues a proclamation allowing banks to close at their discretion.

4:25 p.m.: The American Stock Exchange, the New York Stock Exchange, and the NASDAQ jointly announce that they will remain closed on September 12.

5 p.m.: An official announcement of the close of the Govie market is made by the Bond Market Association via CNN.

5:20 p.m.: Seven World Trade Center collapses.

6:00 p.m.: Amtrak resumes rail service. Fixed-income trading opens in Tokyo.

6:10 p.m.: Mayor Giuliani urges New Yorkers to stay home on Wednesday.

7:15 p.m.: The securities portion of Fedwire closes, four hours later than normal.

8:15 p.m.: The Office of Personnel Management announces that all federal agencies at all locations will be open on Wednesday.

8:30 p.m.: President George W. Bush addresses the nation, stating, "Our financial institutions remain strong, and the American economy will be open for business as well."

<u>9:00 p.m.</u>: The funds portion of Fedwire closes, two and a half hours later than normal.

NOTES

Preface

[1] Personal interview, Ron Purpora, August 13, 2009.

[2] Personal interview, Tom Wipf (head of the Finance Desk at Morgan Stanley), April 12, 2004.

[3] "The fiercest of competitors cooperated like the closest of friends. This happened on everything from sharing trading floors to sharing strategies on trading halts to coordinating on the united reopening of the markets." (remarks by Mary Schapiro, President, NASD Regulation Inc., at the A. A. Sommer Lecture, Fordham Law School, November 13, 2001).

Chapter 1

[1] Personal interview, Brian Roseboro, September 15, 2006.

[2] Gordon R. England (first Deputy Secretary for Homeland Security), "Remarks to the Bond Market Association" New York City, April 11, 2003.

[3] "Of the 1,134 firms located in the affected buildings, 28 percent were engaged in the financial services industry." (New York Metropolitan Transportation Council, "Demographic and Socioeconomic Forecasting Post September 11th Impacts" 3.1-3, 2002).

[4] Government Accounting Office, "Potential Terrorist Attacks: More Actions Needed to Better Prepare Critical Financial Markets", GAO-03-468T, February 12, 2003. At the end of 2000, over 200,000 persons were estimated to have been working in New York City's securities and commodities industries. See http://www.nycp.org.

[5] Eric P. Nash, *Manhattan Skyscrapers* (Princeton Architectural Press, 1999), 133.

[6] On Sunday, September 23, the Rev. Dr. Daniel Paul Matthews, Rector of Trinity Church, spoke at what was known as "Trinity South" – the Shrine of St. Elizabeth Ann Seton, on State Street. He began his sermon with one word: "Dust."

> We couldn't imagine how the whole of south Manhattan island could be covered with dust. It wasn't long before we began saying, what should we dust off first? What should be the priority in getting rid of some of the dust?

http://www.trinitywallstreet.org.

[7] The attack on the World Trade Center destroyed 13.4 million square feet of office space and damaged an additional 21 million square feet. See http://www.fdic.gov/bank/analytical/bank/bt0204.html.

[8] Federal Reserve Bank of New York, 2001 Annual Report.

[9] Terry Pristin, "After the Attacks: Utilities; Phone Service Improving, But Many Still Lack Power," *New York Times,* September 14, 2001. Con Edison, the local power provider to lower Manhattan, lost three power substations and more than 33 miles of cabling. As a result, more than 13,000 business customers lost power. See Suburban Emergency Management Project, "Has U.S. Financial Infrastructure Protection Improved Since 9/11?" October 28, 2004. Available at http://www.semp.us/publications.

[10] Approximately 8,000 Intel servers and 5,000 UNIX servers were lost. See Dave Shore, "September 11 Teaches Real Lessons in Disaster Recovery and Business Continuity Planning," *Technology Republic,* May 17, 2002. Salomon Smith Barney alone lost about 400 servers when Seven World Trade Center collapsed. (personal interview, Luis Guerriero, senior vice president, Salomon Smith Barney, October 30, 2007).

[11] Seven World Trade Center fell at 5:20 p.m. on 9/11. Because of a number of reasons – it was not struck by a plane, it fell straight down instead of tumbling over, the commonly available views of the exterior didn't show significant damage, and no skyscraper previously had fallen solely because of fire – the collapse of Seven World Trade

Center is cited in hundreds of websites and books as compelling evidence that each of the towers was destroyed by secretly planted explosives. See Eric Lipton, "Fire, Not Explosives, Felled 3rd Tower on 9/11, Report Says," *New York Times*, August 22, 2008. Conspiracy theorists point to the collapse of Seven World Trade Center as evidence that the U.S. government orchestrated the 9/11 attacks. Since Seven World Trade Center housed Secret Service and CIA offices, some claim that the building was destroyed in a controlled demolition in order to eliminate evidence of the government's complicity in the terrorist attacks.

In August 2008, the National Institute of Standards and Technology released its long-awaited report on the collapse of Seven World Trade Center. After a three-year investigation involving more than 50 federal investigators and the use of elaborate computer models, the 915-page report confirmed that the collapse was caused primarily by the heat from uncontrolled building fires, which caused girders to expand and weakened structural elements. There were other factors as well, including that the water supply for the sprinkler system had been cut off and that debris from the falling towers damaged structural columns. See http://wtc.nist.gov.

[12] Damage to the facility was compounded when water from broken mains and fire hoses flooded cable vaults located in the basement of the building and shorted out remaining cables that hadn't been directly cut by debris. Water being used by firefighters got into the lower floors of the communications center at the West Street building. It went up the cabinet rungs, ruining the communications gear. See Government Accounting Office, "Potential Terrorist Attacks."

[13] Ivan Seidenberg, Co-CEO of Verizon Communications, remarks before the National Press Club, December 3, 2001.

[14] See Government Accounting Office, "Potential Terrorist Attacks" and Jeffrey M. Lacker, "Payment System Disruptions and the Federal Reserve Following September 11, 2001," The Federal Reserve Bank of Richmond *Working Paper Series* (WP 03-16, December 2003).

[15] Jamie B. Stewart, first vice president and Chief Operating Officer of the Federal Reserve Bank of New York, "Challenges to the Payments

System Following September 11: Remarks Before the Bankers Association for Finance and Trade," April 25, 2002.

[16] The GAO reviewed 15 organizations, including exchanges, clearing organizations, electronic communication networks, and payment system processors, that perform trading or clearing and found that four had no backup facilities and six had facilities located between two and ten miles from their primary sites. See Government Accounting Office, "Potential Terrorist Attacks."

[17] Six days after 9/11, John Mack, Chief Executive Officer of Credit Suisse First Boston, disclosed in a PBS interview with Charlie Rose that his firm, which had 842 employees in Five World Trade Center, was still trying to determine for certain whether one particular staff member had perished.

[18] Shore, "September 11 Teaches Real Lessons in Disaster Recovery and Business Continuity Planning."

[19] Barnaby J. Feder, "After the Attacks: The Recovery Experts; Trying to Plan for the Unthinkable Disaster," *New York Times*, September 17, 2001.

[20] Recollection of Ed Kwalwasser, head of New York Stock Exchange regulation, 2005 Annual Meeting of the SEC Historical Society, "Crisis and Resolve: The SEC and the Securities Industry Remember September 11, 2001." Available at http://c0403731.cdn.cloudfiles.rackspacecloud.com/collection/programs/Transcript_2005_0609.pdf.

[21] Susanne Craig, "Morgan Stanley Faces Questions on Lost Records Its Clients Need," *Wall Street Journal*, November 29, 2002.

[22] Ultimately, the office was able to reconstruct all key records. Recollection of Wayne Carlin, SEC Northeast Regional Administrator, 2005 Annual Meeting of the SEC Historical Society, "Crisis and Resolve." Available at http://c0403731.cdn.cloudfiles.rackspacecloud.com/collection/programs/Transcript_2005_0609.pdf.

[23] European markets remained officially open, but "most traders found it difficult to do much business." (Michael Schroeder, Kate Kelly and Antonio Regalado, "Attack Shuts Down U.S. Markets and Causes Global Declines," *Wall Street Journal*, September 12, 2001 B1).

[24] See http://isu.indstate.edu/guell/ecn100/Sept11th.PDF
Open outcry trading of Treasury futures on the Chicago Board of Trade began at 8:20 a.m. New York time and continued for less than an hour. The CBOT and Chicago Mercantile Exchange were evacuated soon after the second plane hit, and each didn't reopen until Thursday, September 13. See Government Accounting Office, "Potential Terrorist Attacks." At the New York Board of Trade, located in Four World Trade Center, trading in cocoa and stock indexes had started at 8 a.m. (telephone interview, Pat Gambaro, May 13, 2010).
The NASDAQ Stock Market, whose primary and backup technology centers were outside Manhattan, was not affected, and could have been open on 9/11. NASDAQ, however, made the determination to open only when major market participants were fully prepared and simultaneously with other markets. See Steven J. Randich, "Electronic Communications Networks in the Wake of September 11th," testimony before the Subcommittee on Commerce, Trade and Consumer Protection, Committee on Energy and Commerce, U.S. House of Representatives, December 19, 2001.

[25] The NYSE depended on a Verizon switching center on Broad Street that handled about 80 percent of its data lines; that center lost its power after the attacks. See Pristin, "After the Attacks: Utilities; Phone Service Improving, But Many Still Lack Power."

[26] See http://www.nyse.com/pdfs/closings.pdf. Government Accounting Office, "Potential Terrorist Attacks."

[27] Letter from Michael Oxley, Chairman of the House Committee on Financial Services, and John J. LaFalce, Ranking Member of the Committee on Financial Services, to David M. Walker, Comptroller General, October 11, 2001 (calling on the Government Accounting Office to examine the effects of the recent terrorist attacks on the nation's financial institutions and markets).

[28] NYBOT traced its roots back to 1870, when the New York Cotton Exchange was formed. Its trading floor was the setting for a scene near the end of the 1983 movie *Trading Places*.

[29] Federal Reserve Bank of New York, 2001 Annual Report.

[30] James J. McAndrews and Simon M. Potter, "Liquidity Effects of the Events of September 11, 2001," *FRBNY Economic Policy Review* (November 2002).

[31] Gail Makinen, "The Economic Effects of 9/11: A Retrospective Assessment," Congressional Research Services, Report for Congress, Coordinator Specialist in Economic Policy Government and Finance Division, September 27, 2002, CRS-4. On Thursday, September 13, the Federal Aviation Administration gave check couriers approval to resume their chartered flights. See Lacker, "Payment System Disruptions," 7.

[32] "The flames raged from sixteen to twenty-four hours, swept away six hundred and seventy-four buildings, covering seventeen blocks, and fifty acres of ground....It destroyed the section which contained the banks, the Stock Exchange, the Post Office, two churches, the dry goods warehouses, and some of the finest buildings in the city." (History of the Fire Department of the City of New York, Chapter 18, Part I).

[33] "The 1967-68 boom in business, coupled with the 1969-70 bust would have created trouble in the best of circumstances. The back-office problems turned the situation into a disaster, however, by depriving many firms of control over their records and costs. Almost every firm that went under suffered greatly from confusion in its back-office....record-keeping problems accounted for 90 percent of the money spent by the NYSE to liquidate the ten firms that had failed by mid-1970, and chaos in their back-offices precipitated the collapse of Hayden, Stone, Goodbody, and Dupont." Wyatt Wells, "The Remaking of Wall Street, 1967 to 1971" (Harvard Business School's Business History Review, October 2000).

[34] Stephen J. Nelson, "Crisis In and Out of the Financial Markets," *Traders Magazine,* April 17, 2008.

[35] SEC Historical Society, "Keeping the Markets Open: Lessons Learned from the 1987 Market Break," November 1, 2007. Available at http://c0403731.cdn.cloudfiles.rackspacecloud.com/collection/programs/Transcript_2007_1101_MarketsOpen.pdf.

[36] Stuart Johnson, "The Impact of Recent Disasters," *Disaster Recovery Journal* (1999). The Great Chicago Flood forced the Chicago Mercantile Exchange to halt trading and close. See Patrick T. Reardon, "The Loop's Great Chicago Flood" *Chicago Tribune,* April 13, 1992.

Chapter 2

[1] Personal interview, Tom Kinnally, May 10, 2004. Kinnally had dropped out of college and started on Wall Street at A. G. Becker & Co., an investment bank based in Chicago. He then went to Euro Brokers, an inter-dealer broker located in the World Trade Center, where he spent 15 years, eventually ending up as head of the repo desk. Thereafter, Kinnally worked at Garban and Cantor Fitzgerald, two other inter-dealer brokers.

[2] Those commuting to work read about the assassination over the weekend of Ahmad Shah Massoud, the military leader of the anti-Taliban Northern Alliance forces in Afghanistan, by suspected al-Qaeda agents posing as journalists. For those listening to the radio that morning, there was breaking news that Michael Jordan would be coming out of retirement to return to play in the NBA. See Sarah Boxer, "Eyewitnesses; One Camera, Then Thousands, Indelibly Etching a Day of Loss," *New York Times,* September 11, 2002.

[3] By the time that trading stopped that morning, 7,062 buy-sell transactions, valued at $81.1 billion, and 9482 repo transactions, valued at $434.7 billion, had been executed. Of note is that this amount only reflects trading among GSCC members; the amount of Govie trading that had been done that morning by or with non-members is unknown.

[4] There are a number of reasons for this. Firms that have bought securities and are borrowing money through repos to finance those securities positions want to do so early, because that's when the greatest supply of money is available. Conversely, firms lending money through repos want to enter the market when the demand for funds is strong and before the supply of securities available for collateral is exhausted. As repos normally begin on the day that they're entered into, market participants also need time to make the movements of securities and cash necessary to start those transactions.

Yet another strong incentive for firms to trade repos early was created in April 1994 when the Federal Reserve began to charge a fee on the intraday credit that it provided to market participants, also known as *daylight overdraft*s. Government securities dealers began to arrange repo transactions earlier in the day and to deliver securities used as collateral more quickly to cover overdrafts generated by the repayment of maturing repos and receipt of securities purchased.

[5] *The 9/11 Commission Report: Final Report of the National Commission on Terrorist Attacks Upon the United States* (W.W. Norton & Company 2004) 285; Jim Dwyer and Kevin Flynn, *102 Minutes: The Untold Story of the Fight to Survive Inside the Twin Towers* (Times Books, 2005), 20.

[6] Personal interview, John Salemmo, March 7, 2008.

[7] Salemmo interview.

[8] The Marriott World Trade Center Hotel, located at Three World Trade Center, was a 22-story steel-framed building with 825 rooms. When it opened in 1981 as the Vista Hotel, it was the first hotel to open in lower Manhattan since 1836. Originally owned by the Port Authority of New York and New Jersey, it was sold in 1995 to Host Marriott Corporation. Many commuters walked through the hotel to get to the towers.
Firefighters used the hotel lobby as the staging area, and had reported bodies on the roof (the people who had jumped or fallen from the burning towers). The collapse of the South Tower split the hotel in half, and the collapse of the North Tower destroyed most of the rest of

the hotel. Part of the lobby turned out to be a safe zone, shielded by reinforced beams that had been installed after the 1993 bombing. Two hotel employees were killed and 11 of the 940 registered hotel guests were unaccounted for. At least 41 firefighters helping to evacuate hotel guests also died in the hotel. See Jim Dwyer and Ford Fessenden, "One Hotel's Fight to the Finish; At the Marriott, a Portal to Safety as the Towers Fell," *New York Times,* September 11, 2002. Marriott International ultimately received $36.25 million from the property insurer for the loss of the World Trade Center hotel.

[9] Personal interview, Barbara Blumberg, May 6, 2009. Dozens of stories from the 9/11 survivors of the Marriott World Trade Center Hotel can be found at http://www.sept11marriottsurvivors.org/survivors_stories.php.

[10] Ultimately, five Islamic fundamentalists, led by Ramzi Yousef, were convicted of committing the bombing.

[11] USA TODAY interviewed a number of survivors of the South Tower attack. The newspaper determined that there were four significant factors at work, often in combination, in determining who on the 78th floor and above of the South Tower got out in the 16 minute window that they had between the times that the two planes hit:

1) The sight of people jumping to escape smoke and fire spurred evacuation.
2) People lived and died in groups, influenced to stay or go by those around them.
3) Announcements that the building was "secure."
4) People who had experienced the 1993 terrorist bombing of the World Trade Center reacted in two different ways. Many ran to evacuate because they remembered how long it had taken to get out in 1993. Having been down the stairwells before, they knew how to get out in a hurry. But others delayed, confident that everyone would be helped by firefighters and that the buildings would survive, as they had before.

Martha T. Moore & Dennis Cauchon, "Delay meant death on 9/11," *USA TODAY,* http://www.usatoday.com.

[12] Telephone interview, Joe Malvasio, August 24, 2010.

[13] In 1993, Carroll McEntee, which later became HSBC Securities (USA) Inc., provided its backup facilities to Yamaichi Securities, one of the displaced firms.

[14] Personal interview, Dave Buckmaster, October 6, 2003.

[15] Refco was founded in 1969 as Ray E. Friedman and Co. In August 2005, Refco conducted a successful initial public offering of common stock. However, two months later, it was revealed that the firm had for years secreted hundreds of millions of dollars of uncollectible receivables with a related entity controlled by Phillip Bennett, the company's Chairman and Chief Executive Officer. This caused Refco to collapse; its bankruptcy at the time was the fourth largest in U.S. history.

[16] Personal interview, Nick Gialanella, June 20, 2004.

[17] Personal interview, Murray Pozmanter, March 29, 2007.

[18] Although Treasury securities are officially registered at the NYSE, for decades only an insignificant amount of Treasury trading has been done there.

[19] "As recently as the 1960s, Manhattan witnessed a daily Dickensian spectacle of messengers scurrying through the Financial District with pouches of stock certificates and checks. Only when mountains of paperwork were processed could each day's books close." Jonathan Rauch, "Post-9/11, Financial Security Has a Whole New Meaning," *Reason Magazine*, August 4, 2004.

[20] The origins of the BMA went back to 1912, with the founding of the Investment Bankers Association of America. The BMA had previously been known as the Public Securities Association; it changed its name to The Bond Market Association in 1997 to more accurately reflect its broad membership. In November 2006, the BMA merged with the Securities Industry Association to form the Security Industry and Financial Markets Association (SIFMA). www.sifma.net.

[21] Tom Barbash, *On Top of the World: Cantor Fitzgerald, Howard Lutnick and 9/11: A Story of Loss and Renewal* (HarperCollins, 2003), 7.

[22] Windows on the World was on the 107th floor of the North Tower. It boasted a popular "New American" style menu and a first-class wine list. See Janice Stern, "Windows on the World – The Unwritten Story," available at http://www.unpublishedarticles.com/stories/windowsontheworld.html (June 14, 2003).

One of the many memorable experiences of visiting Cantor's executive offices involved simply going to the bathroom there. "Floor-to-ceiling windows. The toilet faced out the window. No window treatments. You could see the curvature of the earth. The only one looking in the window was Lady Liberty. The view was spectacular. A view of the world." (personal interview, Rob Palatnick, managing director and Chief Technology Officer of GSCC, January 18, 2005).

[23] Lori Santamorena, long-time Executive Director of Government Securities Regulation Staff at the Treasury Department, remembered seeing the initial TV coverage and immediately thinking of Cantor Fitzgerald: "I knew right away that there was going to be a problem for the market." (personal interview, Lori Santamorena, December 28, 2006).

[24] In the North Tower, everyone on the 92nd floor and above died. See "Inside the World Trade Center, 9/11/2001: Dennis Cauchon," *USA Today*, September 6, 2002.

[25] Maureen Fan, "Victimized Company Tries to Get On with Business," *Knight Ridder Tribune,* September 30, 2001.

[26] ICAP had been formed two years earlier by the merger of Garban Plc and Intercapital Plc.

[27] The ICAP board room was subsequently named in honor of Seymour-Dietrich. In a sad coincidence, her nephew, Mel Seymour, was born on 9/11. http://www.legacy.com.

[28] Stern, "Windows on the World – The Unwritten Story."

[29] Euro Brokers Inc. started in 1970, and was acquired by the Maxcor Financial Group in 1996. After the 1993 Trade Center bombing, Euro Brokers moved up the tower from the 32nd floor. In May 2005, BGC Partners, LP, an inter-dealer broker that had spun off from Cantor Fitzgerald, acquired Euro Brokers as part of the acquisition of Euro Brokers' parent, Maxcor Financial Group Inc.

[30] *The 9/11 Commission Report*, 285.

[31] "Inside the World Trade Center, 9/11/2001: Dennis Cauchon."

[32] Dwyer and Flynn, *102 Minutes*. This book includes a firsthand account by some of the Euro Brokers survivors.

[33] Personal interview, Joe Grima, managing director in charge of Operations and Risk at BrokerTec, June 16, 2009.

[34] Ivy Schmerken, "E-Bond-Trading Systems Consolidate, Two Heavyweights Emerge," *FinanceTech,* February 5, 2002.

[35] Gregory Ferris, "Response and Recovery at Morgan Stanley," *Risk Management Magazine*, New York, December 2002.

[36] Other dealers with offices in the World Trade Center included Bank of America, Citigroup, Credit Suisse, Deutsche Bank, Fuji Bank, Nikko Securities, and Sumitomo Mitsui. Merrill's headquarters sustained some damage, including broken windows and fallen debris, but the main difficulty for the company became access to the building. Merrill also used several other office buildings in the area that were affected. In all, almost 9,000 employees were displaced. Janette Ballman, "Merrill Lynch Resumes Critical Business Functions Within Minutes of Attack," *Disaster Recovery Journal,* Summer 2001.

[37] Paul Blustein and Kathleen Day, "Industrialized Nations Act to Reassure World," *Washington Post,* September 13, 2001. There were 25 primary dealers on 9/11.

[38] In the early 1980s, there were five clearing banks but, primarily because of mergers, by the early 1990s, only two remained. See Working Group on Government Securities Clearance and Settlement, "Report to the Federal Reserve Board" (December 2003).

[39] The Bank of New York can trace its history back to 1784. Alexander Hamilton wrote the bank's constitution and, during the early years, remained the individual most actively involved in the organization. In 1789, the bank, together with the Bank of North America, extended $170,000 to cover the first installments on the salaries of the President, Vice President, and the members of Congress, and for certain other vital expenses. See William J. Schultz and M.R. Caine, *Financial Development of the United States*, (Prentice-Hall, 1937), 92-116. In 2007, BoNY merged with Mellon Financial Corporation to become The Bank of New York Mellon.

[40] Chase traces its history back to the Bank of the Manhattan Company, established in 1799, which was created by Aaron Burr. Chase had been acquired by Chemical Bank in 1996, but the Chase name was kept. Two months after 9/11, Chase merged with Morgan Guaranty Trust Company of New York to become J.P. Morgan Chase Bank.

[41] At the time of 9/11, BoNY transferred about $900 billion a day in funds (12 percent of overall U.S. funds transfers) and cleared another $1 trillion a day in Govies. See "Bank of New York Overdue on $100 Billion Owed Last Week," *Wall Street Journal*, September 21, 2001. Chase processed an average of 87,000 securities transactions per day, reflecting general ledger activity of about $1.75 trillion. That included tri-party repo activity of about $450 billion daily. See Letter by JP Morgan Chase Bank to the Board of Governors and SEC regarding Interagency White Paper on Structural Change in the Settlement of Government Securities (August 12, 2002).

[42] The banks provided significant intraday liquidity to the Govie market through the extension of secured credit to cover daylight overdrafts generated by Fedwire securities clearance transactions. They also selectively provided unsecured intraday credit and overnight financing to broker-dealers via reverse repos and secured loans.

[43] Institutional investors relied on those two banks to place large volumes of funds in the tri-party repo market. BoNY and Chase each also was a significant tri-party custodian for other markets such as corporates and munis. Even the New York Fed maintained custody accounts with each bank for its domestic open market operations. The Fed also was dependent on the two banks' records, and the U.S. Treasury relied on the two banks for the settlement of auction issuances.

[44] Personal interview, Al Clark (senior vice president, JP Morgan Chase Bank), August 15, 2005.

[45] Saul Hansell and Rita Atlas, "Wall St. Lifeline Shakes Off Dust, and Critics; Disruptions Put The Bank of New York to the Test," *New York Times,* October 6, 2001.

[46] New York Metropolitan Transportation Council, "Demographic and Socioeconomic Forecasting Post September 11th Impacts" (2002). BoNY also had offices at 100 Church Street, a few yards from the Barclay Street site, and its treasury and trading operations were housed at 32 Old Slip, just three blocks from its headquarters. See "Emerging Stronger from 9/11/01: An Interview with Todd Gibbons," *RMA Journal* (December 2001).

[47] The building, completed in 1924, was modeled after the Strozzi Palace in Florence, which was built in 1489 for the banker Filippo Strozzi as a sign of supremacy over his rivals. The structure, with a stone base banded by barred windows within pointed Florentine arches, is designed to project strength and security. Over the years, the building had acquired a black crust, and a year-long façade cleaning had just been completed before 9/11. See Christopher Gray, *New York Streetscapes: Tales of Manhattan's Significant Buildings and Landmarks* (Abrams, 2003), 23-24.

[48] Fedwire provides only basic settlement services. It doesn't provide certain services that are essential to active dealers, such as automated position management, collateral management, and support for overnight and term financing of positions, thus the need for the two

clearing banks. See Working Group, *Report to the Federal Reserve Board*, 10.

[49] Personal interview, Jamie Stewart (first vice president, Federal Reserve Bank of New York), July 7, 2009.

[50] "We thought that someone might try to fly into our building as well, even though that would have been an incredible feat of aeronautics skill." (Stewart interview).

[51] Federal Reserve Bank of New York, 2001 Annual Report.

[52] Lacker, "Payment Systems Disruptions," 10.

[53] On 9/11, GSCC had 122 members, which themselves had over 450 correspondent institutions that used GSCC for comparing trades. On a daily basis, about 60,000 transactions, totaling approximately $1.3 trillion, were netted by GSCC into roughly 12,000 settlement obligations totaling around $400 billion.

[54] The 55 Water Street building, near the tip of Manhattan, was finished in 1972. With 278,800 square meters of rentable office space, it took over the Pan Am Building's title of world's largest commercial office building. Critical to its ability to remain open on 9/11 was its emergency power plant, which had 31 megawatt output. See http://www.skyscrapercity.com/showthread.php?t=49751

[55] Personal interview, Rich Visco, February 2, 2006. For the story of the falcons at 55 Water Street, see http://falcons.55water.com/

[56] Personal interview, Bob Trapani, March 6, 2003.

[57] Peter Field, "Remembering 9/11: The Day I'll Never Forget," available at http://db.riskwaters.com.

[58] Personal interview, Kate Connelly (GSCC vice president), October 15, 2003.

[59] In the time between the attacks by the two planes, most Morgan Stanley staff on the high floors in the South Tower had evacuated. See

Catherine Walsh, "Leadership on 9/11: Morgan Stanley's Challenge," *Harvard Business School: Working Knowledge for Business Leaders,* December 17, 2001. As one expert has noted, most companies in the World Trade Center did not take evacuation drills seriously enough and had an inadequate evacuation plan; Morgan Stanley was a clear exception. See Walker, "What Has the Private Sector Learned from 9/11?."

Rescorla died on 9/11 while searching for employees still in the building. James B. Stewart wrote a biography of Rescorla, *Heart of a Soldier*, which was published in 2002. Rescorla also was the subject of a 2005 documentary "The Man Who Predicted 9/11."

[60] Personal interview, Jane Buyers, April 27, 2004.

[61] Personal interview, Joe Blauvelt, March 22, 2006.

[62] Personal interview, Bob Sbarra (HSBC Bank), July 29, 2009.

[63] David E. Sanger, "Where they were: Frozen in Memory, the First Moments of a Transformed World – Condoleezza Rice; National Security Adviser," *New York Times,* September 11, 2002, and Rudolph W. Giuliani, *Leadership* (Miramax Books, 2002), 5.

[64] When Joe Grima of BrokerTec, in a meeting across the Hudson River in Jersey City, was told about the first plane crash, he recalled, "The first thing that crossed my mind was the plane that I had heard back in grammar school had hit the Empire State Building. So I thought it was no big deal, just one of these little planes that got too close. And we resumed the meeting" (Grima interview).

Some conspiracy theorists point to the 1945 event as proof that commercial planes could not have brought down the Towers. But there were many critical differences between the 1945 and 2001 incidents: 1) the Empire State Building has a "massively over-built" concrete-clad steel frame and masonry exterior; 2) the bomber was going only 200 miles per hour, less than half the speed of the planes that hit the North and South Towers; 3) the bomber was less than one-tenth the weight of the 767s that hit the towers and carried only one-tenth as much fuel; 4) the bomber's wings were flat instead of banked and therefore hit just the 79th floor rather than multiple floors; and 5) the bomber's fuselage hit just to the right of a major column instead of shearing multiple load-bearing columns. See David Dunbar and Brad Reagan (editors), *"Debunking 9/11 Myths: Why Conspiracy Theories Can't Stand Up to the Facts,"* (Hearst Books, 2006), 32.

Chapter 3

[1] Personal interview, Ann Marie Hanley, October 28, 2009.

[2] Personal interview, Dave Cosgrove, June 9, 2003.

[3] See http://hoosierarmymom.wordpress.com/2009/02/20/911-victim-adam-arias-remembered-by-his-sister.

> "According to the New York City coroner's office, my brother's remains were the eighth set of remains found on 9-11, outside of Tower 2." (e-mail of May 3, 2010 to the author from Don Arias, Lt Col, USAF, retired).

[4] National Transportation Safety Board, "Path Study – United Airlines Flight 175" (2002-02-19). Available at http://www.ntsb.gov/info/Flight_%20Path%20_Study_UA175.pdf.

[5] Palatnick interview.

[6] Telephone interview, Marc Lackritz, February 17, 2010.

[7] Personal interview, Sal Sodano, January 22, 2010.

[8] Blauvelt interview.

[9] Personal interview, Ron Purpora, August 13, 2009.

[10] Personal interview, Tom Costa, October 12, 2006.

Under federal regulations, in urban areas, airplanes must fly at least 1,000 feet above obstructions such as buildings and bridges. See A. G.

Sulzberger and Matthew L. Wald, "U.S. Jet Frightens New York in Photo-Op Gone Wrong," *New York Times,* April 28, 2009, A18.

[11] Personal interview, Bill Peterson, August 20, 2009.

[12] At 8:52 a.m., the PATH service operator instructed Manhattan trains to begin evacuation of the PATH World Trade Center station. By 9:10 a.m., three trains were able to carry everyone from the World Trade Center station to New Jersey. See U.S. Department of Transportation, "Effects of Catastrophic Events on Transportation System Management and Operations, New York City – September 11" (April 2002).

[13] "Unfortunately, there were too many volunteers and too few victims to treat." (Matthew Klam, "Bodies; Waiting," *New York Times*, September 23, 2001).

[14] Personal interview, Raj Manian, August 3, 2007.

[15] Personal interview, Sara Kelsey, January 4, 2010.

[16] A year after 9/11, because of structural damage, George's Restaurant had to be demolished. But it was soon rebuilt. http://www.georges-ny.com.

[17] For weeks afterward, Peterson's five-year-old daughter, asked him incessant questions: Why are there evil people in the world? Who is this Osama, and why don't they get him? She drew pictures of her father running away from the Trade Center and planes hitting the buildings. (Peterson interview).

[18] Personal interview, Tom Perna, October 1, 2009.

[19] Federal Reserve Bank of New York, videotape "Attack on the World Trade Center: September 11, 2001" (compiled largely from FRBNY security camera footage)

[20] Federal Reserve Bank of New York, 2001 Annual Report.

[21] Bill McDonough, attending a bankers conference in Basel, Switzerland, told Reuters on 9/11 that the Fed is "coping" with the

situation. See "Fed Stresses It's Open; Banks Report No Big Woes,"
Baltimore Sun, September 12, 2001.

[22] Federal Reserve Bank of New York videotape "Attack on the World
Trade Center: September 11, 2001."

[23] Personal interview, James McLaughlin, June 25, 2009; Stewart
interview.

[24] Personal interview, Dave Gordon, January 28, 2010.

[25] Personal interview, Barry Mandel, January 30, 2009.

[26] Personal interview, Omer Oztan, August 16, 2005.

[27] Barton Gellman, "I Saw Bodies Falling Out – Oh, God, Jumping,
Falling," *Washington Post*, September 12, 2001.

[28] Personal interview, Jean Donnelly, March 7, 2006.

[29] Personal interview, Allison Mansfield, May 7, 2003.

[30] Metro Tech Center, which was formed in 1992, lies between
Flatbush Avenue and Jay Street in Brooklyn, north of the Fulton Street
Mall and south of Tillary Street, close to Brooklyn's Civic Center and
Brooklyn Heights.

[31] SIAC was formed in 1972 as a subsidiary of the New York and
American Stock Exchanges. Over the years, it developed and
implemented automated information handling and communication
systems to support order processing, trading, market data reporting,
clearance and settlement. In November 2006, SIAC became wholly
owned by the NYSE Group, and it's now known as NYSE
Technologies.

[32] Palatnick interview.

[33] Personal interview, June Carey, October 6, 2008.

[34] Somini Sengupta, "A Day of Terror: The Rivers; A Battered Retreat on Bridges to the East," *New York Times*, September 12, 2001.

[35] Sengupta, "A Day of Terror: The Rivers ."

[36] Personal interview, Bart Schiavo, March 25, 2003.

[37] Personal interview, Fran Glasser, October 12, 2006.

[38] By striking coincidence, the cornerstone for the building had been laid almost exactly 100 years earlier, on September 9, 1901. See http://NYSE.com/about/history.

[39] Charles Gasparino, *King of the Club: Richard Grasso and the Survival of the New York Stock Exchange* (HarperCollins, 2007), 11-12.

[40] Personal digital assistants (PDAs) worked well because their wireless network had more capacity than the wireless voice channel. See Walker, "What Has the Private Sector Learned from 9/11?"

[41] The New York Stock Exchange was the largest stock exchange in the world. Its trading floor was located at 11 Wall Street, while its main building was at 18 Broad Street, between the corners of Wall Street and Exchange Place.

[42] Personal interview, Marc Golin, February 19, 2003.

[43] Other subway lines had halted service earlier. At 8:47 a.m., an R train operator felt the impact of the plane crash while in the Cortlandt Street subway station, which is located under Church Street, between Fulton and Cortlandt streets. He radioed the Subway Operations Control Center, which sent the train to City Hall station. This was the last to enter or leave the Cortlandt Street station before it was essentially destroyed when the towers collapsed. See U.S. Department of Transportation, "Effects of Catastrophic Events."

[44] Personal interview, Paul Saltzman, January 26, 2006.

[45] The original Trinity Church, built in 1698, was burned down in 1776 during the British Army's occupation of Manhattan. At the time, it was

the tallest structure in New York City. One historian, Mark Caldwell, has described its burning as "an eerie pre-echo of 9/11." See John Strausbaugh, "Home on the Corner of Boom and Bust," *New York Times*, January 2, 2009, C31. A second Trinity Church was completed in 1790 with a 200-foot steeple and large Gothic windows. It was later deemed structurally unsound and replaced with a house of worship designed by Richard Upjohn in the Gothic Revival style. When this building, the current Trinity Church, was completed in 1846, the church again was the tallest structure in the city. See Robert Gambee, *Wall Street: Financial Capital,* (W.W. Norton & Company, 1999), 94. The church was not damaged by the falling towers; however, its historic pipe organ was harmed by dust and had to be replaced. See http://www.sacred-destination.com/use/new-york-city-trinity-church.

[46] On 9/11, GSCC and MBSCC were separate companies, but they were well into the process of functionally integrating. As a part of that integration, the first joint GSCC-MBSCC board meeting had been held in May 2001. Much of 2001 was spent consolidating and combining staff, operations, technology, and expertise. In January 2002, MBSCC and GSCC became operating subsidiaries of the Depository Trust & Clearing Corporation. See Jeffrey F. Ingber, "From Birth to Central Counterparty Status: The 25-Year History of MBS Clearing," *Journal of Securities Operations* (Spring 2004).

[47] Personal interview, Tony Scianna, July 12, 2010.

[48] U.S. Department of Transportation, "Effects of Catastrophic Events."

[49] Richard Pyle, Detroit Free Press/AP, "Museum Tells Story of 9/11 Evacuation," July 5, 2006.

[50] The story of the mass evacuation of Manhattan by water was told in a 2006 exhibit "All Available Boats," at the Seaman's Church Institute at 241 Water Street, near the South Street Seaport. See "Seafarers International Union Exhibit Recalls 9/11 Evacuation" (July 2006), available at http://www.seafarers.org/HeardAtHQ/2006/Q3/aab.xml.

The evacuation of lower Manhattan by boats and ferries also was the subject of a study by Tricia Wachtendorf, Assistant Professor of sociology and criminal justice and a faculty member of the University of Delaware Disaster Research Center, and James Kendra, Coordinator of the Emergency Administration and Planning Program at the University of North Texas. See University of Delaware Archive, "Study Focuses on 9/11 Evacuation of Manhattan by Water," September 8, 2006, available at http://www.udel.edu/PR/UDaily/2007/sep/evacuation090806.html.

[51] U.S. Department of Transportation, *Effects of Catastrophic Events on Transportation System Management and Operations: New York City - September 11*, April 2002.

[52] Gellman, "I Saw Bodies Falling Out."

[53] U.S. Department of Transportation, "Effects of Catastrophic Events."

[54] Giuliani, *Leadership,* 16; U.S. Department of Transportation, *Effects of Catastrophic Events.*

[55] U.S. Department of Transportation, *Effects of Catastrophic Events.*

[56] USA Today, "Desperation Forced a Horrific Decision," September 2, 2002.

[57] Suhr had continued to serve as an assistant coach at South Shore High School in Brooklyn (http://www.footballfoundation.com/news). He also played on the FDNY football team. Pudgie Walsh, the coach of the Brooklyn Mariners, also was coach of the FDNY football team. For one of many tributes to Danny Suhr, including memories of him by Walsh and Visco, see Jerry Izenberg, "It's a Loss No Coach Can Ever Overcome," *Star Ledger,* September 9, 2005.

[58] Visco interview.

[59] Over 50 Hoboken residents died on 9/11, the most of any city in New Jersey. All but three of these victims were under the age of 40. Hoboken's emergency response teams triaged more than 10,000 survivors at the Hoboken train station. As news of the event's

magnitude spread, 3,000 community members reported to St. Mary's Hospital in Hoboken to volunteer. See http://www.hoboken911.com.

[60] Many of New York City's significant buildings were shut down on 9/11, including the Chrysler Building, Rockefeller Center, Lincoln Center, the Metropolitan Museum of Art, and the United Nations. See Randall C. Archibold, "A Day of Terror: Security; Fear's Ripple: Closing Down, Tightening Up," *New York Times,* September 12, 2001.

[61] Personal interview, Larry Lemmon, May 18, 2006.

[62] C. J. Chivers, "A Nation Challenged: The National Guard; After a War Starts at Home, the Guard Prepares to Take It Abroad," *New York Times,* September 18, 2001.

[63] Personal interview, Bill Langan, April 1, 2003.

[64] Personal interview, Steve Greenberg, October 22, 2003.

[65] Personal interview, Nikki Poulos, May 7, 2003.

[66] Federal Reserve Bank of New York videotape "Attack on the World Trade Center: September 11, 2001."

[67] Cutler interview.

Chapter 4

[1] Personal interview, Eric Foster, September 16, 2009.

[2] Micah S. Green, President, The Bond Market Association, testimony before the Subcommittee on Capital Markets, Insurance, and Government-Sponsored Enterprises, Committee on Financial Services, U.S. House of Representatives, February 12, 2003.

[3] "There is no fixed-income market that is more crucial to the global economy, nor more liquid, than today's primary and secondary market for U.S. government securities." (Bond Market Association letter of August 19, 2002 to the Board of Governors and SEC regarding Docket

No. R-1122, Interagency White Paper on Structural Change in the
Settlement of Government Securities: Issues and Options).

[4] The liquidity of the Government securities market allows dealers to
sell Government securities without necessarily owning such securities
(known as going "short"), because of the ready ability to cover such a
position later on, through the cash, repo or securities lending markets.
BMA letter of August 19, 2002 to the Board of Governors and SEC.

[5] Treasuries include bills (which are sold at a discount and mature in
one year or less); notes (which pay semi-annual coupons and have a
maturity of up to and including ten years); bonds (which are similar to
notes, but have a maturity of more than ten years and up to 30 years);
Treasury Inflation-Protection Securities or TIPS (which were first
issued in 1997; their payoff is linked to changes in the Consumer Price
Index); and non-marketable savings bonds for retail investors.

There's also a market for zero-coupon bonds (also known as Separate
Trading of Registered Interest and Principal of Securities or STRIPS)
that are created by the Treasury through an accounting system that
separates coupon interest payments and principal. The Treasury does
not directly issue STRIPS and they can't be bought through
TreasuryDirect, the web-based, book-entry system run by the Treasury
Department that allows individuals to purchase Treasuries directly from
the government at original issue and hold them to maturity. Rather,
STRIPs are formed by investment banks or brokerage firms and then
the Treasury registers them in its book-entry system. See Bruce
Mizrach and Christopher J. Neely, "The Microstructure of the U.S.
Treasury Market," Federal Reserve Bank of St. Louis Research
Division Working Paper Series (December 2007).

[6] Robert P. O'Quinn, "Economic Benefits from U.S. Treasury
Securities," Report of the Joint Economic Committee, U.S. Congress,
107th Congress, Second Session, February. 2002.

[7] The Bond Market Association, "An Investor's Guide to U.S. Treasury
Securities" (2001).

[8] Department of the Treasury, Securities and Exchange Commission, and Board of Governors of the Federal Reserve System, "Joint Study of the Regulatory System for Government Securities" (March 1998). The Federal Open Market Committee, which oversees the implementation of monetary policy, meets approximately every six weeks to review economic conditions and determine a target for the federal funds rate, the rate at which U.S. banks borrow and lend reserve balances among themselves. The manager of the Open Market Desk at the Federal Reserve Bank of New York is responsible for ensuring that the average federal funds transaction is close to that target rate by buying and selling Treasuries. In practice, the Treasury accomplishes this in large part by engaging in repo transactions. See Mizrach and Neely, "The Microstructure of the U.S. Treasury Market."

[9] "U.S. government securities" can best be defined as all securities that are issued, maintained, and transferred through the Federal Reserve's Fedwire Securities Service. See Mizrach and Neely, "The Microstructure of the U.S. Treasury Market."

[10] In general, government sponsored enterprises are required to obtain the approval of the Treasury Department on the timing, maturity, and pricing of their debt offerings. Issuances of agency securities, except for Farmer Mac, historically have been exempt from registration under the Federal securities laws. Joint Report on the Government Securities Market (1992).

[11] Some entities, like Freddie Mac, Fannie Mae and Sallie Mae, are privately owned and, thus, issue securities that are not backed by the full faith and credit of the U.S. government. Others, such as Ginnie Mae, are arms of the U.S. government and their securities have a "full faith and credit" backing.

[12] The government securities market has two basic phases. One is the initial (or primary) market. Treasuries are introduced to the market through auctions. Treasury bills were first auctioned when they were introduced in 1929; Treasury coupon-bearing securities began being auctioned in 1970. The best-known feature of a Treasury auction – the single price format – was introduced in 1992. In a single-price auction, a participant can bid its actual reservation yield for a new security; that is, the minimum yield at which it's willing to buy the security. If the

auction stops as a higher yield, it will get the full benefit of buying at that higher yield. In contrast, the multiple-price format encourages a participant to bid higher than its reservation yield in hopes of getting the security on more favorable terms. See Kenneth D. Garbade and Jeffrey F. Ingber, "The Treasury Auction Process: Objectives, Structure, and Recent Adaptations," Federal Reserve Bank New York Current Issues in Economics and Finance (February 2005). In contrast to Treasuries, most agency securities are distributed through selling groups composed of large dealers and banks. See "Joint Report on the Government Securities Market" (1992).

The second phase is the secondary market, where trading occurs. For Treasuries, secondary-market trading exists for "when-issued" securities (those that are about to be issued; the when-issued market allows dealers to pre-sell to customers ahead of the auction date and then cover the sale in the auction), "on-the-run" securities (those most recently issued), and "off-the-run" securities (those less recently issued). A common way for traders to profit is to sell the securities before the auction. If the auction draws a yield higher than in the "when-issued" market, traders can buy the new debt at a lower price, pocketing the difference as profit. Bond prices move inversely to yields.

When-issued trading is important because it serves as a price-discovery mechanism, thus reducing uncertainties surrounding Treasury auctions. In determining how to bid at an auction bidders look to when-issued trading levels as a gauge of market demand. See "Joint Report on the Government Securities Market" (1992). Interestingly, the Treasury twice restricted pre-auction when-issued trading – in 1970 and again in 1977 (after lifting the restriction in 1975) – but ultimately eliminated the restriction in 1981. See Garbade and Ingber, "The Treasury Auction Process."

[13] Treasury futures trading began in January 1976, when the International Monetary Market, which had been created by the Chicago Mercantile Exchange, began to offer a Treasury bill contract. The following year, the Chicago Board of Trade launched the U.S. Treasury bond futures contract, which became the most actively traded futures

contract in the world. In July 2007, the CBOT was acquired by the CME, its long-time rival.

There's also an OTC market in options on Treasuries and options on Treasury contracts.

[14] Although any type of security can be used for repo transaction purposes, underlying securities used most frequently are Treasury and Agency securities, because they are highly liquid and generally regarded as carrying no risk of default.

[15] Letter from Sarah A. Miller, General Counsel, ABA Securities Association, to Florence E. Harmon, Acting Secretary, SEC, and Jennifer J. Johnson, Secretary, Board of Governors, September 8, 2008 (regarding the status of bank repurchase and reverse repurchase agreement activities involving non-exempt securities under the Securities Exchange Act of 1934).

[16] Federal Reserve Banks used repos to extend credit to member banks as early as 1917. See Kenneth D. Garbade, "The Evolution of Repo Contracting Conventions in the 1980s," *Federal Reserve Bank of New York Economic Policy Review* (May 2006).

[17] Repos are used extensively for investment purposes. "Reversing in" securities offers institutions a safe means of investing cash on a day-to-day or flexible-term basis at favorable rates. The adjustability of the term of a repo makes it a useful financial management tool for institutions investing temporary cash balances.
Reverse repos also serve as a low-cost and flexible means of borrowing specific securities on a temporary basis. This typically occurs when a dealer needs to cover a short position. In effect, the availability of repos makes short selling more viable. The major suppliers of specific securities to dealers are banks (especially via their trust or custody departments).

Many large dealers engage in "matched book" trading in repos, simultaneously entering into repo and reverse repo positions as a form of arbitrage on rates. The dealer attempts to borrow funds at one rate and re-lend them at a higher rate to earn a spread. If a dealer repos out securities for the same maturity period that it reverses them in, it's running a "true" matched book. This is a relatively riskless form of matched book trading, with no interest rate risk. The dealer is profiting simply through the spread in interest rates between the two contracts. Dealers also mismatch asset and liability maturities in their books, as a play on the direction of interest rates.

The safety, flexibility and low-cost of repos also are why the repo portion of the Government securities market is where virtually all of the Fed's monetary policy operations are conducted. See Peter R. Fisher (Manager of the System Open Market Account managed by the New York Fed), "Views on the Repo Market," remarks before the PSA Annual Repo and Securities Lending Conference, January 16, 1997. The New York Fed uses repos domestically as the primary tool to implement the interest rate targets of the Federal Open Market Committee. These domestic repos are not yield transactions, and any returns are incidental to monetary policy goals. In contrast, the New York Fed's international repo operations are designed to increase yield and generally are not used as a tool of policy implementation. See Thomas C. Baxter and Robert B. Toomey, "Agreements Used by the Federal Reserve Bank of New York in Reserve Asset Investment and Monetary Policy Implementation," available at http://www.cemla.org/pdf/legales/leg-06-Baxter.pdf.

[18] Working Group, "Report to the Federal Reserve Board" (December 2003).

[19] Michael J. Fleming, "The Benchmark U.S. Treasury Market: Recent Performance and Possible Alternatives," *Federal Reserve Bank of New York Economic Policy Review* (April 2000) and BMA letter of August 19, 2002 to the Board of Governors and SEC regarding Docket No. R-1122, Interagency White Paper on Structural Change in the Settlement of Government securities: Issues and Options.

[20] The next day, the Reserve Primary Fund, the country's oldest money-market mutual fund, which held $785 million in Lehman debt securities, "broke the buck"; the first time that such a fund open to the general public had fallen below a $1 net asset value. That triggered a run on money market funds, which in turn paralyzed the commercial paper market, as money market funds are the major buyers of such

paper. To resolve those problems, Treasury Secretary Henry Paulson issued a federal guarantee for all deposits in money-market-funds. See James B. Stewart, "A Year Later, How Safe is Safe?" *Wall Street Journal*, September 16, 2009, D2.

The shock after the failure of Lehman Brothers in 2008 has been described "to be worse and more complicated than the one that caused the Great Depression." Confidence in the creditworthiness of businesses around the world was shattered, and banks became reluctant to lend to each other. See David Wessel, "Government's Trial and Error Helped Stem Financial Panic," *Wall Street Journal*, September 14, 2009, A1. World stock markets lost more than six percent of their value in three days, and more than a quarter of their value within a month, while Treasuries rose in price and their rates plummeted (Treasury bills carried a rate of near zero) as investors sought "full faith and credit" protection. See Bob Ivry, Christine Harper and Mark Pittman, "Missing Lehman Lesson of Shakeout Means Too Big Banks May Fail," Bloomberg.com, September 14, 2009.

Within ten days of the Lehman bankruptcy filing, the financial system experienced both the bailout of the largest U.S.-based insurance company (American International Group) and the largest bank failure in U.S. history (Washington Mutual). Massive government intervention was needed to ensure that the largest and more important financial institutions would not also fail, and the severity of the financial difficulties of that time rose to an even higher level. See Sam Jones, "Why Letting Lehman Go Did Crush the Financial Markets," *Financial Times,* March 12, 2009.

[21] Rafael A. Bayley, "The National Loans of the United States of America from July 4, 1776 to June 30, 1880 as Prepared for the Tenth Census of the United States" (Washington D.C.: U.S. Government Printing Office, 1883). In 1776, the Continental Congress authorized the country's first interest-bearing loan - $5 million of 4 percent securities payable in three years. See Richard H. Hoenig, "Selling Uncle Sam," Financial History (first quarter, 1992).

[22] Early on, Congress delegated this authority to the President, who gave it to the Secretary of the Treasury. See Hoenig, "Selling Uncle Sam."

[23] William J. Schultz and M.R. Caine, *Financial Development of the United States*, (Prentice-Hall, 1937), 92-116.

[24] Robert E. Wright, *One Nation Under Debt: Hamilton, Jefferson, and the History of What We Owe* (McGraw Hill, 2008), 282.

[25] William J. Schultz and M.R. Caine, *Financial Development of the United States*.

[26] *Hamilton and the National Debt,* 42.

[27] Jerry W. Markham, *A Financial History of the United States* (M.E. Sharpe, 2002).

[28] See http://www.nyse.com

[29] Joint Report on the Government Securities Market (1992). "The New York Stock Exchange, in fact, originated in 1792 as a bond exchange." (remarks by SEC Chairman Arthur Levitt in a speech "The Importance of Transparency in America's Debt Market," at the Media Studies Center, New York, September 9, 1998.)

[30] Email to the author from Professor Richard Sylla, Henry Kaufman Professor of the History of Financial Institutions and Markets and Professor of Economics, Stern School of Business, New York University, April 1, 2010.

[31] Levitt speech, "The Importance of Transparency in America's Debt Market."

[32] Ultimately, the bubble in debt-burdened railroad investments burst, contributing to the Financial Panic of 1873. See Catherine Rampell, "Same Old Hope: This Bubble is Different," *New York Times*, September 14, 2009, B1.

[33] Treasury and Federal Reserve Study of the Government Securities Market (1959) and Dominique Dupont and Brian Sack, "The Treasury Securities Market: Overview and Recent Developments," *Federal Reserve Bulletin* (December 1999).

[34] Steve Fraser, *Every Man a Speculator: A History of Wall Street in American Life* (Harper Perennial, 2005) 36.

[35] See http://www.ustreas.gov/education/history/events.shtml.

[36] See http://www.publicdebt.treas.gov/history/1800.htm.

[37] Greenbacks were the first non-interest bearing notes created by the government. See http://www.treasury.gov/education/history/events/1800-1899.shtml#7.

[38] See http://www.tax.org/Museum/1861-1865.

[39] Starting in August 1861, all incomes over $800 were taxed three percent until the year 1872, when the tax was repealed. See http://www.treasury.gov/education/history/events/1800-1899.shtml#7

[40] See http://www.tax.org/Museum/1861-1865. Congress also passed the National Banking Act, allowing for the chartering for the first time of national banks to create a uniform national currency and help fund the Civil War. See http://www.treasury.gov/education/history/events/1800-1899.shtml#7. National banks, by virtue of their higher level of financial credibility, had easier access to capital markets. See Rose Razaghian, "The Financing of the Civil War: Confederate and Union Efforts," paper presented at the annual meeting of the Midwest Political Science Association, Palmer House Hilton, Chicago, Illinois, Apr 15, 2004. Available at http://www.allacademic.com/meta/p83336_index.html

Selling those bonds proved difficult, so Treasury Secretary Salmon Chase enlisted the help of Jay Cooke and Company, a Philadelphia private bank. See Fraser, *Every Man a Speculator*, 90. Cooke also coordinated sales by telegraph, resulting in the "first wire house." See Charles R. Geisst, *Wall Street: A History from its Beginnings to the Fall of Enron* (Oxford University Press 1997), 54.

[41] Comments of Ken Garbade, January 2010.

[42] C.F. Childs and Company, "Golden Anniversary 1961."

[43] "A Study of the Dealer Market for Federal Government Securities," prepared for the Joint Economic Committee of Congress, 1960.

[44] Ira O. Scott, Jr., *Government Securities Market*, (McGraw Hill, 1965), 2.

[45] In mid-1914, there was only $968 million of interest-bearing Treasury debt outstanding. By mid-1919, the debt had grown to $25.2 billion. See Kenneth D. Garbade, "Why the U.S. Treasury Began Auctioning Treasury Bills in 1929," *FRBNY Economic Policy Review* (July 2008).

[46] Geisst, *Wall Street: A History,* 157.

[47] In the initial years of the Federal Reserve, the Fed's assets consisted primarily of short-term privately issued paper such as bankers' acceptances, trade acceptances and bills of exchange. But the war was funded largely by government debt, and the Fed's open market purchases of Treasury securities increased dramatically. See David Marshall, "Origins of the Use of Treasury Debt in Open Market Operations: Lessons for the Present," *Federal Reserve Bank of Chicago Economic Perspectives* (2002).

[48] Rudolf Smutny, "Government Securities and the Money Market" (remarks at the Life Officers Investment Seminar, June 1955). After the Civil War, the greater part of trading in government issues shifted to the auction market on the New York Stock Exchange. In the decades that followed, the level of public debt would fluctuate and there would be trading of government securities both on the NYSE and the over-the-counter markets.

[49] Also, in the 1920s, the Treasury Department relied on certificates of indebtedness and notes, which were never listed on the NYSE. (comments from Ken Garbade, January 2010).

[50] As a result, the Federal Reserve Bank of New York in 1925 shifted its operations for the Treasury account to the OTC market. In December 1929, the Treasury bill was introduced, which provided the Fed with an alternative to bankers' acceptances as a short-term instrument for open market operations. See Marshall, "Origins of the Use of Treasury Debt." The Treasury introduced this new financial instrument to mitigate several flaws in the structure of Treasury financing operations, such as new debt offerings being chronically oversubscribed. See Garbade, "Auctioning Treasury Bills," 31. The Treasury bill was not even listed on the NYSE; rather the Treasury began to sell bills at competitive auctions as soon as they were introduced. Exchange-listed Treasuries became traded mostly by foreign mutual funds required to trade through exchanges. See 1992 Joint Report.

[51] In 1935, Congress determined that the Federal Open Market Committee should include the seven-member Board of Governors as well as the 12 Reserve Bank Presidents. Congress also decided that only five of the 12 Reserve Bank Presidents would vote at any one time along with the seven members of the Board of Governors. The President of the Federal Reserve Bank of New York serves continuously, while the Presidents of the other Reserve Banks rotate in their service of one-year terms. The FOMC, which oversees the implementation of monetary policy, meets approximately every six weeks to review economic conditions and determine a target for the Federal funds rate, the rate at which U.S. banks borrow and lend reserve balances among themselves. The manager of the Open Market Desk at the Federal Reserve Bank of New York is responsible for ensuring that the average Federal funds transaction is close to that target rate by buying and selling Treasuries. In practice, the Treasury accomplishes this in large part by engaging in repo transactions. Mizrach and Neely, *The Microstructure of the U.S. Treasury Market*.

[52] Gordon interview.

[53] Allen H. Meltzer, *A History of the Federal Reserve, 1913-1951* (University of Chicago Press, 2003).

[54] *FRBNY Fedpoint 2: Primary Dealers.* All 18 have since either been acquired by other companies or gone out of business.

[55] Robert E. Kelly, *The National Debt From FDR to Clinton,* (McFarland & Company, Inc., 2000), 16.

[56] See http://www.treasurydirect.gov/govt/reports/pd/histdebt/histdebt_histo3.htm.

[57] Robert L. Heilbroner and Peter L. Bernstein, *A Primer on Government Spending*, (Vintage Books 1963), 94-95.

[58] During World War II, the Fed pledged to keep the interest rate on Treasury bills fixed at 0.375 percent. It continued to support low cost government borrowing after the war ended, even though the Consumer Price Index rose 14 percent in 1947 and 8 percent in 1948, and the economy was in recession. In 1948, President Harry Truman replaced Fed Chairman Marriner Eccles, who had opposed this policy, with Thomas B. McCabe, although Eccles's term on the board would continue for three more years. The reluctance of the Fed to continue monetizing the deficit became so great that, in 1951, Truman invited the entire Federal Open Market Committee to the White House to resolve their differences. William McChesney Martin, then Assistant Secretary of the Treasury, was the principal mediator. Three weeks later, he was named Fed Chairman, replacing McCabe. See http://www.richmondfed.org/publications/research/special_reports/treasury_fed_accord/background/index.cfm

Chapter 5

[1] Personal interview, Jerry Rubin, August 8, 2009.

[2] Personal interview, Griffith X. Clarke, January 28, 2010.

[3] Dale Keiger, "What Makes Mike Bloomberg So Smart?" *John Hopkins Magazine,* November 1996.

[4] In May 1993, Discount Corporation, a 75-year-old firm whose first board of directors included J. P. Morgan, was acquired by Zions Bancorp, a Utah holding company.

[5] Personal interview, Ben Fargione, January 18, 2010.

[6] Kenneth Garbade, "Origins of the Federal Reserve Book-Entry System," *Federal Reserve Bank of New York Economic Policy Review* (December 2004).

[7] Gordon interview.

[8] "Marine Midland Bank used to get funds payments for anything over $100,000 and Fed Funds checks for anything smaller." (Buckmaster interview).

[9] Clark interview.

[10] That trade log would be run in batch form every few hours, and used by the broker's "back-office" to create paper confirmations of each trade and to settle the trades with the clearing banks. (Purpora interview).

[11] Rubin and Fargione interviews.

[12] Personal interview, Chris Dark, October 19, 2009.

[13] Or as the parlance of the day would have it, they'd meet for "limos, bimbos, and lines." See http://money.cnn.com/magazines/fortune/fortune_archive/1985/06/24/66043/index.htm

[14] Dark interview.

[15] Personal interview, Ed Watts, November 30, 2009.

[16] Not that there weren't regulatory limitations on gift giving and entertainment. In fact, the NASD rule limiting gifts and entertainment has been in effect, in one form or another, since 1937. See http://www.finra.org/web/groups/industry/@ip/@reg/@guide/documents/industry/p018025.pdf. But not until after 9/11 were these limitations well enforced. The NYSE has also had long-standing gift and entertainment limitations, but enforcement actions pre-9/11 typically were limited to infractions regarding payments made to NYSE floor employees. (personal interview, Joseph La Rosa, July 29, 2008).

[17] Shannon D. Harrington and Pierre Paulden, "Credit Seizure? $6 Million Pay Turns on Relationships" (Update 2), Bloomberg.com (accessed December 28, 2000).

[18] Gordon interview.

[19] Rubin interview.

[20] Adam Leitzes and Joshua Stern, "A Pioneer's Perspective," *Forbes*, December 28, 2000.

[21] Michael Moritz, Adam Zagorin, and Alexander Taylor III, "Making a Mint Overnight," *Time*, January 23, 1984. In 1972, before Telerate was to sell stock to the public to raise capital, Cantor Fitzgerald bought a 25 percent interest in it; Cantor would later buy control of Telerate for $3 million, before selling it in 1981 for $75 million.

[22] See http://www.fundinguniverse.com/company-histories/Dow-Jones-Telerate-Inc-Company.

[23] "Garban did its first trade in September 1974. It started in the agency market but that was a very thinly traded market and a very small part of that market traded through the inter-dealer brokers at the time. So it switched to Treasuries about a year later where much more of the market, about 40-50 percent, was traded through the inter-dealer

brokers and there were more issuances. And that turned out to be a smart move, and it started building business." (Purpora interview).

[24] Clarke interview.

[25] Rubin interview.

[26] "If a particular security looked out of line relative to others, a dealer would short the issue and buy another one, then sit there repoing out securities they had bought and reversing in what they had sold until the relationship reverted back to the mean. Then the dealer would take the trade-off, at a profit." (Rubin interview).

[27] Rubin interview.

[28] Testimony of Warren Spector before the Financial Crisis Inquiry Commission, May 5, 2010.

[29] Working Group, "Report to the Federal Reserve Board" (December 2003), 111.

[30] Michael Lewis, *Liar's Poker: Rising Through the Wreckage on Wall Street*, (Penguin Books, 1989), 90.

[31] In 1979, the MBS Clearing Corporation was formed to provide comparison, risk management, and other services for the MBS marketplace. See Ingber, "From Birth to Central Counterparty Status."

[32] "You had the mortgage-Treasury trade-off. That trade lost money for more people than any other trade in the government market over the course of years. Because the two markets don't always act in concert, what would happen is that the market would rally and governments would outrun the mortgage positions. Spreads would widen, and they would have losses on both sides of the trade." (Rubin interview).

[33] Leo Melamed, "The Birth and Development of Financial Futures," presented at the China Futures Seminar in Shen Zhen, Guangdong Province, China, April 25, 1996.

[34] Leo Melamed, *Escape to the Futures*, (John Wiley & Sons, 1996), 240.

[35] Personal interview, Dennis Dutterer (former President of the Board of Trade Clearing Corporation), December 10, 2009.

[36] Telephone interview, Phupinder Gill (President of the CME Clearing House Division), December 18, 2009. The Cantor-CME initiative, known as the Traders' Instant Access Network, or TITAN, would have allowed CME members to play the Treasury-Eurodollar spread, known as the TED spread, right on the exchange floor. The CBOT, in turn, had in 1998, established plans for a Treasury trading partnership with Prebon Yamane, another inter-dealer broker, which never came to fruition. See Robert Hunter, "The TED Spread Soap Opera," *Derivatives Strategy* (August 1998).

[37] See Mark Girolamo's induction speech for Martin L. Leibowitz, Inaugural Hall of Fame Award, Fixed-income Analysts Society. Available at http://www.fiasi.org/1995/44-martin-l-leibowitz.

[38] Thomas R. Keene and Shannon D. Harrington, "Markets Rely on 'Too Much Mathematics,' Wilmott Says," *Bloomberg.com* (accessed September 21, 2009).

[39] By 1985, the number of unregistered firms was estimated to be over 200. See James B. Burnham, "The Government Securities Act of 1986: A Case Study of the Demand for Regulation," *Regulation: The Cato Review of Business and Government* (Summer 1990).

[40] If a government securities broker-dealer was regulated, it was only because that broker-dealer participated in another securities activity that was regulated. General securities broker-dealers that dealt in government securities were regulated in the course of their general securities business, and commercial banks that dealt in government securities were regulated in the course of their banking activities. Although those federally-regulated broker-dealers represented a majority of the government securities broker-dealers, there still remained a substantial amount of government securities broker-dealers that dealt exclusively in government securities and weren't subject to

any form of federal supervision. See R. Lane Sisung, "The Law of Salomon: A History of the Regulation of Government Securities, An Accounting of the Salomon Brothers Scandal, and an Analysis of the Government Securities Act Amendments of 1993," *Loyola Law Review* (Summer 1994).

[41] Testimony of William M. Isaac, former Chairman of the Federal Deposit Insurance Corporation, before the Subcommittee on Capital Markets, Insurance, and Government Sponsored Enterprises, Committee on Financial Services, U.S. House of Representatives, March 12, 2009.

[42] "Lombard Wall had over a billion-dollar repo book, but only $4 million in nominal capital, part of which was given to us by Equimark, a Pennsylvania bank holding company. In reality, the capital of the firm was a little under $1 million. But then you didn't have to mark the repo book. That happened later, and Lombard was part of the reason why." (Rubin interview).

[43] "Markets tend to grow if they serve an economic purpose. But there are a lot of questions – fundamental questions – that often are not settled in them, which in the normal day to day don't matter, but they do in a crisis." (Russo interview).

[44] Repos in government securities had been common for a number of years, but many legal aspects had never been tested until the 1980s. There were no industry standards before then. After the bankruptcy of a number of Govie dealers in the 1980s, the Bond Market Association (then the Public Securities Association) published a Master Repurchase Agreement. This Agreement made clear, among other things, the purchase-sale intent of the parties, and provided a fall back if courts viewed the transactions as loans. See Baxter and Toomey, "Agreements Used by the Federal Reserve Bank of New York."

Another consequence of the 1980s' failures and the subsequent creditor losses on repos was an acceleration of the growth of the tri-party repo market, which became an important mechanism for financing the securities inventories of banks and dealers. Before the late 1970s, all repos were settled on a delivery-versus-payment basis where the parties, at the time of trade, agree to interact directly with each other in the transfer of securities and cash and in the performance of all other repo obligations. After the failures of Govie firms in the 1980s, use of tri-party repos became popular because it meant that an agent bank stood between the dealer and the creditor as custodian, and it protected the latter by exercising independent control over the exchange of securities and funds between the two parties. In a tri-party repo, the parties must have cash and collateral accounts with the same tri-party bank agent, whose key functions are: 1) verifying that the collateral is sufficient and that securities are eligible ones, 2) holding and valuing them, and 3) maintaining appropriate margin. After the repo is entered into, the custodian takes possession of the seller's collateral and transfers cash to the seller. Similarly, it takes in the buyer's cash and confirms to it the receipt of the seller's collateral. The custodian performs these functions in reverse at the end of the transaction. See Garbade, "Repo Conventions," 11-12.

[45] During its four months of operation, Drysdale Government Securities continually acquired securities at a discount, which often was huge, via reverse repos, and sold them immediately in the cash market for a price that included accrued coupon interest income. Drysdale's reverse repo positions came to exceed its repo positions by over a billion dollars and, when its reverse repo customers reduced their positions, the firm went under. See Christopher Byron and Frederick Ungeheuer, "Wall Street's Panic That Wasn't," *Time,* May 31, 1982.

[46] "Chase sent me a letter saying they didn't know any of the trades. But they eventually settled up." (Watts interview).

[47] Stephen A. Lumpkin, "Repurchase and Reverse Repurchase Agreements," Federal Reserve Bank of Richmond, 1998.

[48] The failure in August 1982 of Lombard-Wall, a small Govie dealer, was a significant one. Lombard filed for protection under the Bankruptcy Code. Under the automatic "stay" provisions of the code as well as the temporary restraining order issued by the Bankruptcy Court judge, no buyer could sell the collateral securing a Lombard-Wall repo without court approval. The court, rejecting arguments from the Fed, had determined that the firm's repos should be treated as

secured loans rather than outright transactions, prohibiting sale of the underlying securities as they "belonged" to Lombard-Wall. This led to widespread concern that the court decision would undermine the liquidity of the repo market and helped spur Congress in 1984 to amend the Bankruptcy Code to exempt short-term repos in Treasuries and other securities from the automatic stay provisions of federal bankruptcy law. See Garbade, "The Evolution of Repo Contracting Conventions in the 1980s."

[49] Lion Capital Group, a small New York broker-dealer, filed for bankruptcy in May 1984. It had misrepresented to creditors that their securities were held in safekeeping at its clearing bank, leading to sizeable losses for its clients, which included local governments and school districts. See Garbade, "Repo Conventions," 10.

[50] E.S.M. Government Securities was a small dealer in tax-free bonds, located in Fort Lauderdale, Florida. After attempting to cover up its speculative trading losses by using customer securities and transferring the losses through journal entries to an unaudited affiliate as a receivable, it collapsed in March 1985, leading to sizeable losses for some municipalities and thrift institutions. See "E.S.M. Failure Prompts Study by the Government Accounting Office," *New York Times*, March 21, 1985. ESM had invested its clients' cash in repos, but the clients failed to either take possession of the collateralized securities or have them held by a third party in an account in their name. When ESM failed, the clients were unable to prove that they owned the securities. The ESM failure precipitated the failure, four days later, of the Home State Savings Bank in Ohio, which had been borrowing heavily from ESM for years. Home State's failure led, in turn, to the insolvency of Ohio's state-chartered savings banks' mutual deposit guarantee fund, and a temporary inability of 70,000 Ohioans to have access to their savings deposits. See Burnham, "The Government Securities Act of 1986."

[51] Bevill, Bresler & Schulman Asset Management (BBS), a small New Jersey-based firm, filed for bankruptcy under Chapter 11 after admitting that it could not meet some $140 million in debts to its customers, including about 45 savings and loan associations. The Securities and Exchange Commission sued BBS for fraud, charging

that the firm secretly drained its customers' investments to make up for heavy trading losses. *In re Bevill, Bresler & Schulman Asset Mgmt. Corp.*, 878 F.2d at 747 (3d Cir. 1989).

Instances of insider trading on Treasuries are unusual. One of them involved BBS. In 1988, Robert Rough, a former director of the Federal Reserve Bank of New York, was indicted for tipping off BBS about nonpublic information regarding the Fed's discount rate deliberations. Rough pled guilty to one count of bank fraud and was sentenced to six months in prison. The author of this book testified against Rough at his trial, introducing certain New York Fed telephone records that showed Rough had made calls to BBS from outside the board room right after board meetings.

[52] Thomas Russo, "The Drysdale Affair," *New York Times*, May 23, 1982.

[53] Statement by President Reagan on signing the Government Securities Act of 1986, October 28, 1986.

Congress decided to exempt government securities sales practices from the Treasury's rule-making reach, on the theory that overregulation might result in increased taxpayer cost. Questionable government securities sales practices would need to rise to the level of outright fraud, as defined in the federal securities statutes enforced by the SEC, before legal action could be taken. See Diana Henriques, "Wall Street; Rules for Government Securities?," *New York Times,* September 16, 1990.

[54] Primary dealers were perceived as having a particularly "safe" status also as a result of their acceptance by the New York Fed as suitable counterparties. See Burnham, "The Government Securities Act of 1986."

[55] The Treasury Department was granted authority to adopt regulations applicable to all government securities broker-dealers concerning financial responsibility, protection of investors' funds and securities, record keeping, reporting and audit requirements, and custody of government securities held by depository institutions. See Steven Lofchie, *Lofchie's Guide to Broker-Dealer Regulation* (2005), 10.

[56] The 1993 Amendments removed the statutory restrictions on the authority of the NASD to regulate its members' sales practices with respect to government securities, and provided the bank regulatory agencies with the authority to issues sales practice rules for government securities. See *Lofchie's Guide to Broker-Dealer Regulation*, 11.

[57] Personal interview, Andrew Waskow, November 5, 2009.

[58] The enactment of the GSA laid an important legal foundation for the formation of GSCC in at least two respects. First, the GSA amended the definition of "exempted security" in the Securities Exchange Act of 1934 to include a new section stating that "government securities shall not be deemed to be 'exempted securities' for the purposes of section 17A." Consequently, the GSA required the registration of any entity seeking to perform the role of a clearing agency for government securities, and granted the SEC jurisdiction over such clearing agency activity. Also, the GSA extended Federal regulation of the government securities marketplace to many of the prospective participants in such a clearing agency, such as government securities brokers, government securities dealers and depository institutions.

A registered clearing agency typically performs at least three basic functions:

1. *Comparison*: the process of matching or recording the terms of each side of a transaction. Attendant to a comparison service usually is the ability to correct or resolve differences in reported trades.

2. *Clearance*: the process of preparing compared trades for settlement. This can take several forms, from the most basic (to simply produce individual receive-and-deliver instructions for each trade matched) to more sophisticated (to net all deliver-and-receive obligations in each security on a continuous basis).

3. *Settlement*: the actual exchange of securities and funds.

[59] Representatives of the operations departments of the various brokers and dealers would physically exchange paper confirms at a facility

provided by Bankers Trust Co. – the "Banker's drop" – and immediately bring these back for comparison to their records in the hope of identifying any problems before the opening of Fedwire or, more importantly, before any market-moving news affected a trading decision based on a faulty position.

[60] Every security is represented by a "CUSIP," the 9-character alphanumeric security identifier given to all North American securities.

[61] Goldman Sachs was one of the firms that set up its own netting system; Ed Watts ran its Govie operations function:

> "Our computer system would print up a ticket for every trade. We'd come in the morning and have two huge stacks of computer-generated tickets, one for buys and one for sells, sorted by counterparty and security. The guy who did the Treasury bills would grab his tickets and take out his adding machine and add up for each instrument all the buys and sells by dollar amount and then by par amount and take the net of each. Based on the subtotals, he would come up with either a final buy differential or a sell differential, both dollar amount and par amount, for each counterparty. Then he would call the counterparty and find the guy who was doing the same thing and say, "This is my figure." And he would hope that the other guy had the same number. If so, that would be the one settlement that would settle all the actual trades, which might have been in the hundreds." (Watts interview).

[62] The concept of multilateral netting had sprung out of Wall Street's Paperwork Crisis of the late 1960s:

> "If one broker does 100 trades in IBM, both buying and selling at different prices with a variety of different brokers, there are few opportunities for netting. By interposing a central organization as the counterparty to all trades, all that broker's trades in IBM can settle to one net position, and all money for trades in all securities can settle to a single dollar figure owed to or from the central counterparty." (Depository Trust & Clearing Corporation, "Responding to Wall Street's

Paperwork Crisis," available at
http://www.dtcc.com/about/history).

[63] Tierney became the first Chairman of the GSCC board, with Kelly as Vice Chairman and CEO. Other original GSCC Board members were Herb Levitt of Spear Leeds & Kellogg, Jerry Lynch of Morgan Stanley, Chuck Moran of Manufacturers Hanover Trust Company, and Ron Readmond of Alex Brown & Sons, Inc. In 1989, the author of this book joined GSCC and later became General Counsel. For a complete description of the establishment of GSCC, see http://www.dtcc.com/downloads/products/cs/Development-GSD.pdf.

[64] This game playing only went away after the Fed, in April 1994, began to charge a fee on the intraday credit that it provided to market participants, also known as *daylight overdrafts*.

[65] Watts interview.

[66] GSCC began to match, in an automated fashion, the next-day and future-settling Treasury and agency trades of 30 participants. The comparison of trade data was deemed to have occurred when GSCC made available to its members a report of the comparison results.

[67] It also eliminated risk by providing for the easy resolution of trade data differences.

The Comparison System was successful from the start, with a daily average of over 16,000 sides compared by December 1988 (and over 24,000 sides compared on November 9, 1988, the record date for that year) and an average comparison rate by December of 94 percent. Comparison System participation grew rapidly in 1989, to 56 members by year-end, with a record volume on August 11 of $258.5 billion (representing over 34,000 sides).

The capabilities of the Comparison System also grew rapidly. "As-of" trades (trades compared on or after their scheduled settlement date) were made eligible for comparison in March 1989; their comparison was useful for audit trail purposes. Trade cancellation and replacement features were added in May 1989.

[68] Until May 2009, market convention was that if a seller did not meet its obligation to deliver Treasury securities on scheduled settlement date, there was no penalty. There was monetary incentive for the seller to make timely delivery, as it had to finance the securities while no longer having the benefits of ownership. In September 2008, after the failure of Lehman Brothers, "with short term interest rates close to zero, the time value of money no longer provided adequate incentive and the Treasury market experienced an extraordinary volume of settlement fails...In response, the Treasury Market Practices Group...revise[d] the market convention for settlement fails, developing a 'dynamic fails charge'..." Kenneth D. Garbade, Frank M. Keane, Lorie Logan, Amanda Stokes, and Jennifer Wolgemuth, "The Introduction of the TMPG Fails Charge for U.S. Treasury Securities," *Federal Reserve Bank of New York Economic Policy Review* (October 2010).

[69] GSCC imposed on its members the discipline of having to meet various financial, operational, and other standards.

During the initial weeks of the netting operation, eligible securities were limited to newly issued Treasury notes, allowing participants time to acclimate themselves to the process. The first Treasury bond (the August 30-Year) was added to the system in September. Product eligibility grew rapidly. By January 1990, all non-zero Treasury securities were eligible for the net (and there were 34 netting participants.) In April 1990, the scope of the Netting System was expanded to encompass all forward-settling trades (that were scheduled to settle within 15 days of execution) of netting members in Treasury securities. The following month, the quarterly Treasury refunding was encompassed within the net for the first time, and in July 1990, agency securities become eligible for the net. On February 1, 1991, zero-coupon securities were made eligible for netting. By the end of 1991, GSCC was processing each business day more than 20,000 sides on average, worth over $150 billion.

[70] Susan Kelly, "Fundamental Brokers Temporarily Closes Shop After Sale Talks Falter," *American Banker,* August 25, 1992.

[71] There were various risks and inefficiencies in the repo market at that time. First, repo transactions were confirmed on a non-automated basis

by telephone or fax. Also, the bulk of repo activity was done through the inter-dealer brokers; however, such brokered transactions weren't transacted anonymously but, rather, on a "give-up" basis, exposing a dealer's trading strategies to competitors. Market participants faced the risk that a counterparty would fail to pay back principal plus interest owed or fail to deliver back collateral. Finally, repos required settlement of their start and close legs on a trade-by-trade basis between myriad counterparties with whom a firm was dealing. This practice kept administrative and operational costs high.

In 1995, GSCC began both its repo comparison and repo netting services, which provided a range of benefits such as:

1. Automated comparison of the start and close legs of a repo, including the capture of all the key elements of the transaction. This would facilitate members' ability to monitor repos and maintain appropriate recordkeeping and audit-trail information.
2. Netting and settlement of underlying collateral movements so as to eliminate the need to transfer the majority of such movements, providing significant cost savings and alleviating operational burdens.
3. Pass-through of coupon interest, providing for coupon payment protection.
4. Guarantee of settlement of repo transactions, including payment of coupon interest, with GSCC assuming the role of credit counterparty to each side (as it did for buy-sells).
5. Centralized and standardized daily margin and mark-to-market for each repo position.

GSCC's margining and re-pricing services provided a standardized approach for moving repo cash collateral with interest. They fundamentally changed the marketplace in that participants no longer needed to build margin (typically two percent) into the original value of the repo, but rather could price the repo at the current market value. See Jeffrey F. Ingber, "A Decade of Repo Netting," *Futures and Derivatives Law Report* (February 2006).

[72] Dark interview.

[73] In February 1991, Salomon submitted a bid in the Treasury five-year note auction on behalf of Warburg Asset Management that was unauthorized. The securities were, in fact, purchased by Salomon itself. This was done in order to skirt the rule limiting the amount that Treasury will recognize as bid on a single yield by a single bidder to 35 percent of the public offering amount. Salomon's top executives learned in April that the securities had been purchased for Salomon itself, but didn't promptly inform the Fed or the Treasury. The government's investigations ultimately resulted in Salomon's August 1991 admissions that it had submitted unauthorized customer bids in several auctions in 1990 and 1991, in some cases resulting in Salomon having a large percentage of the issue. That in turn resulted in a "short squeeze" in the issue, wherein the yield on the issue moved considerably out of line with surrounding market rates and the securities were "on special" in the repo market. See Joint Report on the Government Securities Market (1992)

Although the maximum auction award to an individual bidder had been limited since 1962, before 1990 there was no limit on the size of a bid. In the interest of encouraging broad public participation in its auctions, the Treasury announced in July 1990 that it would limit the total bids by a given participant at a given yield or discount rate to 35 percent of the amount offered to the public. See Garbade and Ingber, "The Treasury Auction Process."

[74] The firm was sold to Travelers Group in 1997 and later became a part of Citigroup.

[75] Diana Henriques, "Reluctant Regulator: A Special Report; Free-Wheeling Treasuries Market is at a Turning Point with Congress," *New York Times,* September 3, 1991 (quoting Joseph Grundfest, a former SEC Commissioner).

[76] Michael W. Sunner and Oliver Giannotti, "US Treasury Auction Compliance: How 'Dealer Visits' are Conducted, What's Discussed, and Treasury Expectations for Auction Participation," *Journal of Securities Compliance* (October 2007) and Federal Reserve Bank of New York, "U.S. Monetary Policy and Financial Markets," 97.

[77] Single-price auctions were thought to reduce the Treasury's financing costs, because in a single-price auction, a participant can bid at the minimum yield at which it's willing to buy the security. If the auction stops at a higher yield, it will get the full benefit of buying at that higher yield. In contrast, the multiple-price format encourages a participant to bid higher than its reservation yield in hopes of getting the security on more favorable terms. See Garbade and Ingber, "The Treasury Auction Process."

[78] See Garbade and Ingber, "The Treasury Auction Process." After the scandal, in January 1992, the Federal Reserve Bank of New York made changes to create a more open system of primary dealers. It also discontinued its own dealer surveillance over the primary dealers and disbanded its dealer surveillance unit. See Federal Reserve Bank of New York, "Administration of Relationships with Primary Dealers," January 22, 1992. According to then New York Fed President Gerald Corrigan, "in part because of 'moral hazard' considerations and in part because of legal and regulatory realities, it was important that the Federal Reserve Bank of New York make absolutely clear to the marketplace that the New York Fed does not regulate the primary dealer firms." (E. Gerald Corrigan, "Changes in the Government Securities Market," *Federal Reserve Bank of New York Quarterly Review,* Winter 1991-92.

[79] By the early 1990s, the inter-dealer brokers found themselves in an untenable economic position because of severe cuts in commission rates in previous years. These cuts were caused by primary-dealer pressure, including actions such as the formation of Liberty Brokerage Inc., which was owned by various primary dealers. To make up for lost commission income, the inter-dealer brokers sought to "go national" and expand their customer base beyond the primary dealers. (At the time, there also was a category of "aspiring primary dealer," which was treated as a primary dealer for these purposes. The one aspiring primary dealer was Eastbridge Capital.)

In late 1991, four inter-dealer brokers – Fundamental Brokers Inc., Garban, Liberty and RMJ – announced that they would expand access to their screens to non-primary dealers that were GSCC netting members. This action had been untenable before the Salomon Brothers scandal, as a primary dealer would not continue to do business with a broker that might match it against a "second-tier" dealer on a blind basis. Certain primary dealers were vocal in their opposition to this development, voicing credit concerns, but the inter-dealer brokers, taking advantage of the post-scandal climate (and the intensified scrutiny of primary dealer actions), successfully adopted the standard of status as a GSCC netting member as an objective means of expanding their customer base beyond the primary dealer community. The first non-primary dealer to receive broker screens was the Chicago Corporation (on October 28, 1991), followed by Continental Illinois Bank.

[80] See abstract, "End-of-day Pricing in the U.S. Treasury Market: A Comparison of GovPX and the Federal Reserve Bank of New York," *Journal of Financial Research,* March 22, 2005.

[81] "I remember when some guys from a Japanese firm wanted information on Baldwin Treasury Securities Trading Company. I told them that it's just one 30-year-old guy in a pit who's taking the other side of your $300-400 million trades." (Dutterer interview).
[82] Dutterer interview.

[83] Testimony of Annette L. Nazareth, Director of the SEC's Division of Market Regulation, before the Senate Committee on Banking, Housing, and Urban Affairs, June 17, 2004.

[84] Department of the Treasury, Securities and Exchange Commission, and Board of Governors of the Federal Reserve System, "Joint Study of the Regulatory System for Government Securities" (March 1998).

By 2001, GovPX had created the Repo Index, a comprehensive source of rates and trading volume for the Treasury repo market, and GovPX and Garban-ICAP had teamed up to create AgencyPX to provide pricing, market and other information about the U.S. agency securities market. In 2004, ICAP bought GovPX.

[85] In August 1996, Daiwa Securities America and First Union Capital Markets conducted the first ever government securities trade over the

internet. See Nancy Mandell, "First-ever Government Securities Trade Transacted over the Internet," *Business Wire,* September 4, 1996. Before then, dealers had decided not to use the Internet because of its lack of speed and security.

[86] Bruce Mizrach and Christopher J. Neely, "The Transition to Electronic Communications Networks in the Secondary Treasury Market," *Federal Reserve Bank of St. Louis Review* (November/December 2006). This article reviews the history of the shift to electronic trading in various markets.

[87] Jerry W. Markham and Daniel J. Harty, "For Whom the Bells Tolls: The Demise of Exchange Trading Floors and the Growth of ECNs," *Journal of Corporation Law,* July 1, 2008.

[88] David Barboza, "In Chicago's Trading Pits, This May Be the Final Generation," *New York Times,* August 6, 2000.

[89] Dutterer interview.

[90] Hillary Davis, *A Million a Minute*, (Harper Business 1998), 217.

[91] Purpora interview.

[92] Andrew Rafalaf, "The Death of the Inter-Dealer Broker?" *FinanceTech,* June 1, 2000.

[93] See Schmerken, "E-Bond-Trading Systems Consolidate."

[94] See "2001 Review of Electronic Transaction Systems," Bond Market Association.

[95] "The system would tell each trader what their current position was at any time in each instrument and the trader would be able to manage and hedge his position all day long rather than trade. That was a huge economic benefit for the dealers. You spent time not so much selling to customers but to making yourself safe." (Watts interview).

[96] "Very similar to GSCC. You come up with a net position and then hedge it to keep safe." (Watts interview).

[97] Securities and Exchange Commissioner Laura S. Unger, "Electronic Trading Technology's Impact on the Fixed-Income Markets," presentation at the Bond Market Association's Fifth Annual Legal and Compliance Seminar, New York, October 28, 1999.

[98] Harvey L. Pitt, Chairman, U.S. Securities and Exchange Commission, "The Condition of the U.S. Financial Markets Following the Recent Terrorist Attacks," testimony before the U.S. Senate Committee on Banking, Housing and Urban Affairs, September 20, 2001.

[99] Federal Reserve Bank of New York, 2001 Annual Report.

[100] *The Economic Effects of 9/11,* CRS-7.

[101] See Chairmen's Interview with Warren J. Spector, President and Company-Chief Operating Officer, Bear Stearns Companies, and Thomas L. Kalaris, Chief Executive, Americas, Barclays Capital, *News from The Bond Market Association* (January 2002). See also Gary Gensler, Under Secretary for Domestic Finance, "Remarks to the Bond Market Association," July 13, 2000.

Chapter 6

[1] Telephone interview, Roger Ferguson, May 14, 2010.

[2] During the time that the 9/11 events were occurring, Chairman Greenspan was on a Swissair Flight back to Washington. The plane ultimately returned to Zurich. The next day, with help from Andy Card, White House Chief of Staff, Greenspan was able to fly on a U.S. Air Force tanker from Basle to London and then to Andrews Air Force Base. When that plane entered U.S. airspace, it was met and escorted by two F16 fighters. See Alan Greenspan, *The Age of Turbulence: Adventures in a New World,* (Penguin Press, 2007), 1-4.

[3] The message was sent at 9:44 a.m. See Lacker, "Payment System Disruptions," 9.

[4] See http://www.Federalreserve.gov/Boarddocs/press/general/2001/2001091 1/default.htm. Before the initial attack, the Open Market Trading Desk had decided not to engage in open market operations for that day. Following the attacks, that decision held, as the discount window was considered the most effective means of providing any additional liquidity to the banking system. Discount window borrowing is generally arranged at the end of day, although borrowing can be arranged earlier and banks are often in contact with their Federal Reserve Bank lending officer before a formal request is made. See Lacker, "Payment Systems Disruptions," 13-14.

The New York Fed conducted its normal securities lending operation at noon, but altered its usual limits, essentially eliminating the securities lending cap. See Federal Reserve Bank of New York, 2001 Annual Report.

[5] See http://www.fdic.gov/news/press/2001/pr6401.html. The FDIC's office in New York City was closed.

[6] See http://www/occ/treas.gov/ftp/release/2001-78.txt.

[7] Ferguson interview.

[8] Beginning on 9/11, the Fed also waived daylight overdraft fees and overnight overdraft penalties for many days thereafter. See McAndrews and Potter, "Liquidity Effects," 69-70. On the securities side, the New York Fed acted to make Treasury collateral more readily available to primary dealers. On 9/11, it suspended the $500 million limit on borrowings of SOMA [System Open Market Account] securities by a single dealer, as well as the issue limit of $100 million for a single dealer. Securities borrowings increased from $100 million on September 10 to $8.9 billion on 9/11. See Michael J. Fleming and Kenneth Garbade, "When the Back-office Moved to the Front Burner: Settlement Fails in the Treasury Market After September 11," *Federal Reserve Bank of New York Economic Policy Review* (November 2002).

[9] "Discount window loans soared instantly from around $200 million to a peak of about $45 billion on September 12." (Fed Governor Laurence H. Meyer, speech before the National Association of Business Economics, St. Louis, November 27, 2001).

[10] Grima interview.

[11] Robert Plummer, "Recovering from Disaster: Exchanges Reopen Against Incredible Conditions," *Futures Industry Magazine*, October/November 2001.

[12] Gill interview.

[13] Floyd Norris and Jonathan Fuerbringer, "A Day of Terror: The Markets; Stocks Tumble Abroad; Exchanges in New York Never Opened for the Day," *New York Times,* September 12, 2001.

[14] Personal interview, Tom Hammond, April 15, 2010.

[15] Telephone interview, Bernie Dan, February 12, 2010.

[16] See http://www.sec.gov/news/press/2001-90.txt.

[17] Immediately following the attacks, many firms tried to contact the BMA to ask about the status of the market. See Minutes of Emergency Meetings of the Bond Market Association, September 11-21, 2001.

[18] The Calendar Committee was first organized by the BMA in 1989. Since its primary role was to make recommendations for holiday and early closings, it initially was composed solely of dealer firms. In March 2005, the committee's membership was formally expanded to include inter-dealer brokers, institutional investors, representatives from providers of core clearing and settlement services, business continuity professionals, and other participants in the fixed-income markets. See SIFMA press release, "The Bond Market Association Announces Formation of a New Calendar and Securities Market Emergency Committee," March 31, 2005.

[19] Foster interview.

[20] Repo trading among the dealers continued for a good part of the day, with traders not negotiating rates but just trying to square positions. (Blauvelt interview).

[21] Blauvelt interview.

[22] Personal interview, Micah Green, September 20, 2010.

[23] Schroeder, "Attack Shuts Down U.S. Markets," B1.

[24] Schroeder, "Attack Shuts Down U.S. Markets," B1.

[25] Blauvelt interview and contemporaneous notes.

[26] The story is told in Roger Lowenstein's book *When Genius Failed: The Rise and Fall of Long-Term Capital Management* (Random House, 2000).

[27] Personal interview, Peter Fisher, August 10, 2006.

[28] The group's mission was to give recommendations for legislative and private sector solutions for "enhancing the integrity, efficiency, orderliness, and competitiveness of United States financial markets and maintaining investor confidence." (Executive Order 12631 of March 18, 1988).

[29] Fisher interview.

[30] Telephone interview, James Newsome, March 15, 2010.

[31] Blauvelt interview.

[32] Saltzman interview.

[33] Fisher interview.

[34] Personal interview, Brian Roseboro, September 15, 2006.

[35] Personal interview, Don Hammond, December 29, 2006.

[36] U.S. Department of Transportation, "Effects of Catastrophic Events."

[37] Don Hammond interview.

[38] Personal interview, Yvette Hollingsworth, November 24, 2008.

[39] Roseboro interview.

[40] Santamorena interview.

[41] "That worked very well. Of course, the banks were beyond cooperative. No discussion required." (Don Hammond interview).

[42] Roseboro interview. "We were lucky with respect to auction issues in general, because it's very flexible in terms of the rules structure. So we are in a good position to make whatever changes we need to in an emergency." (Santamorena interview).
The Public Debt Act of 1942 grants the Treasury Department considerable discretion in deciding on the terms for a marketable security. See Frank J. Fabozzi, *Treasury Securities and Derivatives* (Frank J. Fabozzi Associates, 1998), 5.

In addition, Fannie Mae postponed the scheduled announcement of its benchmark bills and notes.

[43] Pursuant to an "auction takedown service" initiated in 1994, designed to provide more safety and efficiency to the auction settlement process, the Treasury Department made most of its auction deliveries to dealers indirectly, through GSCC. See Garbade and Ingber, "The Treasury Auction Process: Objectives, Structure, and Recent Adaptations."

[44] "Thinking about it now, I'm sure we already had many sales in our system which were done by the firms that won the Bills in the auction, so by taking them in we would not have had a big exposure - the opposite might be true." E-mail from Dave Buckmaster to the author of December 18, 2010.

[45] Roseboro interview.

[46] The BMA also determined that the recommendation should address only sales and trading activities, and not settlement or other matters "that cannot yet be assessed."

[47] SEC Historical Society, "Keeping the Markets Open: Lessons Learned from the 1987 Market Break," Washington D.C., November 1, 2007.

[48] Markham and Harty, "For Whom the Bells Tolls."

[49] Gill interview.

Chapter 7

[1] Buckmaster interview.

[2] For example, if Dealer A had sold government securities to Dealer B, it likely did so through one of the inter-dealer brokers (IDBs). As a result, there would be four "sides" to that transaction:

1) Dealer A sold to IDB
2) IDB sold to Dealer B
3) Dealer B bought from IDB
4) IDB bought from Dealer A.

For the entire transaction to be acknowledged as a good one, and ultimately settled, each of the four sides of that transaction needed to be sent to GSCC for comparison with the other sides. The IDB, even though it was "flat" (it had bought and sold the same security in the same amounts), would need to submit two of the four sides, and each dealer would submit a side.

[3] For repos, a large number of which had already been executed that morning, the situation was more complex. The Fedwire had opened at 8:30 a.m., and many repos had "started" that morning. A repo would be started by the dealer that was the seller of securities – if it had the bonds in its "box" or account at its clearing bank – delivering them to the buying dealer for payment. For such repos, the problem then became how to settle the end (or "close") leg of the repo.

[4] GSCC had made available in 2000 a "real-time" trade matching process, which allowed for comparison of trades to occur within minutes of their execution rather than at end of day. However, few members were participating in this real-time environment on 9/11.

[5] Personal interview, Tom Quaranta, February 25, 2003.

[6] Trapani interview. On 9/11, Cantor Fitzgerald and eSpeed, through their London offices, issued a statement regarding the disaster, indicating that those offices "are doing everything possible to assess the situation." Phone numbers were provided both for outsiders to confirm the safety of any potentially affected employees and for friends and relatives to inquire about Cantor Fitzgerald staffers.

[7] Palatnick interview.

[8] Personal interview, Jon Ciciola, May 24, 2005.

[9] Ciciola interview.

[10] Ciciola interview.

[11] One major client that Chase had to finance was its own securities affiliate, JPM Securities Inc.

In one of the day's ironies, after Fedwire closed, Chase also needed about $30 billion to fund its reserve account overnight, given all the securities it was holding, particularly from the unwinding of tri-party repos that morning. Otherwise, it would have been overdrawn at the Fed. BoNY had the opposite problem. It lacked the ability to wire out funds. As a result, Chase bought the $30 billion in the federal funds market from BoNY that night.

"Before September 11, banks held approximately $13 billion in the Fed accounts. In the days after September 11, these balances ballooned to more than $120 billion because some banks (like BoNY) could not move funds out of their accounts." (speech by Fed Vice Chairman Roger Ferguson at Vanderbilt University, February 5, 2003).

[12] Ciciola interview.

[13] On the Fedwire Funds Transfer System, payments are initiated by the sender of the funds. On the Fedwire's Securities Services System, the party sending the security initiates the transactions, which results in the immediate and simultaneous transfer of the security against offsetting payment, known as "delivery versus payment." See Lacker, "Payment System Disruptions," 6.

[14] Grima interview.

[15] Personal interview, Neal Arbon, May 23, 2003.

[16] In the early morning of 9/11, a total of 2,178 trades, for four brokers (Cantor Fitzgerald, Garban, Maxcor/Euro Brokers and Tradition) and one dealer (Refco), with a par value of $71.5 billion, were "administratively compared" by GSCC. There were many dealers that didn't submit data to GSCC on 9/11; however, GSCC only force-compared the trades of Refco, at its specific request.

[17] In administratively comparing the brokers' start-leg repos, the corresponding close legs were automatically included. This resulted in the generation of receive-and-deliver instructions for any netting-eligible transactions that were scheduled to settle Wednesday or later.

[18] "GSCC is novating all trades submitted by taking only one side of trade – this alleviates a significant amount of the settlement risk with all the inter-dealer brokers but increased our risk significantly as a shareholder of GSCC based on the loss sharing provisions. For example, we could be making up phony trades right now and submitting them." (internal Chase email from Joseph Blauvelt to Mark Werner, subject: "Funding update," September 11, 2001, at 8:53 p.m.

[19] Purpora interview.

[20] The only broker that GSCC was able to obtain records from on 9/11 was BrokerTec.

[21] See "GSCC Summary and Detailed Chronology of GSCC's Actions Following the September 11th Terrorist Destruction of the World Trade Center." The 2171 fails assumed by GSCC were those of BrokerTec, Cantor, Garban, GFI, Hill Farber, Liberty, Maxcor/Eurobrokers, and Prebon.

[22] GSCC was able to receive the information on the broker fails from the clearing banks. Although communications with Chase were briefly interrupted as Chase moved from one backup site to another, the clearing corporation still managed to obtain data from Chase in the ordinary course. As for BoNY, while its staff had to vacate their buildings near the World Trade Center, the bank's systems kept running automatically. At 5:20 p.m., when Seven World Trade Center collapsed, causing the stoppage of Verizon's activity at 140 West Street, GSCC's communication connection with BoNY went down. By then, as a precautionary measure, GSCC had already downloaded all broker fails as they existed at BoNY. In addition, on 9/11, for some transactions, instructions had been submitted by the brokers to their clearing banks, but the delivery was not made by the dealer and, subsequently was not re-delivered to the dealer on the other side of the trade.

[23] When a broker executed a trade, it would normally immediately transmit instructions to its clearing bank to receive the transaction from one dealer and deliver it to the other. Later, near the end of the day, it would transmit the transaction to GSCC which, assuming it compared to a valid dealer trade, would be responsible for the "close" leg at some time in the future.

[24] Cosgrove interview.

[25] Cosgrove interview.

[26] Buckmaster interview.

Chapter 8

[1] Cutler interview.

[2] Personal interview, Dina Deluca, May 7, 2003.

[3] Within two weeks, the bulletin board had grown "as big as a wall." See Jerome Charyn, "9/11: The Enduring Salute," *New York Times*, September 11, 2005.

[4] Jim Dwyer and Lawrence K. Altman, "After the Attacks: The Morgue; Loads of Body Parts Hint at Magnitude of Grisly Task," *New York Times*, September 12, 2001.

[5] N.R. Kleinfield, "After the Attacks: The Mood; A City Awakes, Only to Reflect On a Nightmare," *New York Times*, September 13, 2001.

[6] Dwyer and Altman, "After the Attacks: The Morgue."

[7] Personal interview, Brian Macwilliams, June 10, 2010.

[8] See http://www.g-gej.org/6-1/photography.html

[9] "Many apartments sustained extensive damage: blown out windows, ash-filled rooms, belongings coated in dust, and furniture singed by fire. Displaced residents, some living in temporary housing for months on end, could not return until the City's Department of Environmental Protection cleaned and tested indoor air quality to ensure residents returned to safe homes – and even then, many remained without power or phone lines. The catastrophe also caused the temporary closure of seven downtown public schools, displacing approximately 9,000 students. Members of the National Guard stood on corners, and residents had to show identification in order to get home. Many businesses struggled to reopen or keep their businesses afloat." Email announcement from Joe Daniels, President and CEO of the National September 11 Memorial and Museum at the World Trade Center Foundation, Inc, subject: "9/11 and its Impact on the Lower Manhattan Community," October 29, 2010.

[10] Kirk Johnson and Eric Lipton, "After the Attacks: The Canyons; First Inspections Show Most Buildings are Structurally Sound," *New York Times,* September 14, 2001.

[11] Plummer, "Recovering from Disaster."

[12] Interview with William J. McDonough, prepared by Emily Walker (January 21, 2004). See http://www.scribd.com/doc/20583251/Mfr-Nara-t8-Frbny-Mcdonough-William-J-1-21-04-00711.

[13] There were 178 buy-sell transactions, with a par value of about $9 billion, submitted to GSCC at the end of the day on September 12, a minuscule amount compared to the 41,421 buy-sell transactions, with a par value of $486.5 billion, submitted to GSCC on September 10, a normal trading day.

[14] Telephone interview, Lee Olesky, September 13, 2010.

[15] Oztan interview. Dealers attempted to settle all repo trades due to settle on September 12. If securities were bounced back or if the dealer was unable to reach the client, then the trade was rolled at the previous day's rate. (Blauvelt contemporaneous notes).

[16] Purpora interview.

[17] Personal interview, John Schipano, July 12, 2010.

[18] Donnelly interview.

[19] SEC Historical Society, interview with Harvey Pitt, May 12, 2008. Available at http://c0403731.cdn.cloudfiles.rackspacecloud.com/collection/oral-histories/Pitt051207Transcript.pdf.

[20] See http://www.sec.gov/news/press/2001-90.txt

[21] Annual Meeting of the SEC Historical Society, "Crisis and Resolve," 2005.

[22] Annual Meeting of the SEC Historical Society, "Crisis and Resolve," 2005.

[23] From September 12 to September 20, the Association's website received 1.7 million hits. (Blauvelt contemporaneous notes).

[24] See http://www.cftc.gov/opa/press01/opa4567-01.htm

[25] Kelsey interview.

[26] Minutes of Emergency Meetings of the Bond Market Association: September 11-21, 2001.

[27] Substantial volumes of maturing commercial paper hadn't been accepted for payment by the appropriate issuing/paying agent on September 11, September 12, and September 13, with a peak maturity value of $45 billion in commercial paper not honored on that Wednesday. In other words, on those days, issuing/paying agent banks "refused to pay" presented paper. See Depository Trust & Clearing Corporation and the Bond Market Association, "Discussion Paper: Issues and Recommendations Regarding Commercial Paper Settlement Practices" (March 2003).

Fed Chairman Greenspan, speaking at the American Bankers Association's annual convention on October 23, 2001, stated, "The resulting shortfalls in the coverage of billions of dollars of maturing paper were managed by rolling fails into the next day's settlement or by drawing on bank lines, causing bank assets to balloon for a few days."

[28] Author's personal recollection and Minutes of Emergency Meetings of The Bond Market Association: September 11-21, 2001

[29] Perna and Volpe interviews.

[30] Greenberg interview.

[31] William Cohan, *House of Cards: A Tale of Hubris and Wretched Excess on Wall Street* (Doubleday, 2009).

[32] Joseph Kahn, "Bush's Man on Wall Street Pushed For Reopening," *New York Times* (September 21, 2001).

[33] Also, the dollar fell sharply against both the Japanese yen and the Euro, and the prices of oil and gold soared. See Liz Alderman and

Nicola Clark, "Terrorist Attacks Send the World's Market's Plunging," *New York Times,* September 12, 2001.

[34] SEC Historical Society, interview with Harvey Pitt.

[35] Sodano interview.

[36] Schroeder, "Attack Shuts Down U.S. Markets," B1. Ironically, while the NYSE closed on its own, the SEC could have ordered the closing of an equities exchange only with the signature of the President of the United States. "The drafters of the Exchange Act never contemplated that the President would be assassinated." (Securities and Exchange Commission, interview with David Silver, April 21, 2006, available at http://c0403731.cdn.cloudfiles.rackspacecloud.com/collection/oral-histories/Silver042106_interview.pdf.

"I remember being told a story from a source that I considered creditworthy that the markets were closed just as the correct and complete story was getting around that only Jack Kennedy was killed and there were no members of the Cabinet killed which had been a rumor at the time. The story continued to go on to say that the reason the markets were closed was because they had stabilized and were starting to turn around on the breaking of the complete story. It could look to some that the markets were rallying on the news of the death of a President. I also remember being told that before the markets had reopened the Fed went around to the primaries requesting that they be told of any sizable sellers who might come in." (Clarke interview).

[37] On the MBS side, the upcoming settlement day for Class-A MBS securities also placed a load on the system.

[38] During this time, "a brokerage firm used approximately 33 different documents to execute and record a single securities transaction." (Nelson, "Crisis In and Out of the Financial Markets"). See also Larry E. Bergmann, Senior Associate Director, SEC Division of Market Regulation, "The U.S. View of the Role of Regulation in Market Efficiency," presentation at the Annual International Securities Settlement Conference, February 10, 2004.

[39] As stated in 1992 by the Bachman Task Force (formed to evaluate changes to the clearance and settlement system), "time equals risk." See Securities and Exchange Commission Concept Release 33-8398; 34-494405: Securities Transactions Settlement (2004). Available at http://www.sec.gov/rules/concept/33-8398.htm.

[40] Grima and Arbon interviews.

[41] Minutes of Emergency Meetings of the Bond Market Association: September 11-21, 2001.

[42] The press release also contained the following other recommendations:

> 1) Commercial paper transactions originally scheduled for settlement on September 11 and September 12 that did not settle should settle on September 13. Commercial paper transactions scheduled for settlement on September 13 and later should settle as originally scheduled.
>
> 2) Class A-MBS securities should settle on Monday, September 17 as originally scheduled.
>
> 3) The 48 hour notification day for MBS should be extended by an additional 24 hours, through September 14 at 3 p.m., "although parties are encouraged to deliver as early in that period as possible."
>
> 4) Good delivery for MBS pools, where pool information was communicated on or before 3 p.m. on September 14 would be September 17. Good delivery for pool information communicated after 3 p.m. on September 14 would be September 19.

[43] "We were scrambling like crazy and focused on getting back downtown. I had my futures people sneak through the police lines. I don't know how they did it." (Watts interview).

Chapter 9

[1] Costa interview.

[2] Charlie Rose's interview with John Mack on PBS (September 17, 2001).

[3] In an interview on Fox News with Neil Cavuto eight years later, Dick Grasso said, "Economics are important. People are more important…The thought that we could save one more life by staying closed…was a driver." (available at http://www.foxnews.com/printer_friendly_story/0,3566,550064,00.html).

[4] In an interview with the SEC Historical Society, Harvey Pitt said, "My biggest fear, which didn't get allayed until September 17, was if we got the markets back up and running, would they collapse again?"

[5] Federal Reserve Bank of New York 2001, Annual Report.

[6] Stewart interview.

[7] In an odd breach of security, one of the janitors gained access to the building's internal speaker system and announced an evacuation, which he was not authorized to do. (Interview with William J. McDonough, prepared by Emily Walker).

[8] Interview with William J. McDonough, prepared by Emily Walker.

[9] GSCC had $266 billion in fails versus only $584 million the previous day. See GSCC Summary of Clearance Report for September 11 to September 18, 2001.

[10] Buckmaster interview.

[11] GSCC and SIAC had developed alternative FTP and e-mail facilities, using SIAC's internet connection, to exchange data files with participants. GSCC development personnel worked with Chase staff to write and test code for loading at Chase in order to conduct settlement. Chase used that code to load as many receive-and-deliver orders as possible on behalf of the brokers.

[12] On each of September 12 and September 13, GSCC suspended its margin process. It did, however, make a margin call each day on one member, Refco Securities, because of its high leverage. The calls were satisfied. (Notes of Marc Golin from Monday, September 17, 2001).

[13] Buckmaster interview.

[14] "We knew what had been returned, but for anything that was rolling onto a new one we didn't have the ability to make sure that the transaction had taken place as it should have. And any Fed settlement that had occurred that morning, we had no way of knowing what had actually transpired because we had no transaction journals. We had to basically go in and reconfirm fails with all of our counterparties manually." (Donnelly interview).

[15] Cutler interview.

[16] On September 12, MBSCC, GSCC's sister company, netted and issued balance orders for Class-A MBS, as it was scheduled to do. Output was made available by 2:45 p.m.

Chapter 10

[1] Saltzman interview.

[2] Lacker, "Payment System Disruptions," 7.

[3] Richard Oliver and Stuart E. Weiner, "The Role of Central Banks in Retail Payments: The Central Bank as Operator" (prepared for a conference sponsored by the Federal Reserve Bank of Kansas City, November 9-10, 2009).

[4] Pristin, "After the Attacks: Utilities."

[5] Keith Epstein, "Triage: Can Bleeding Red Cross Heal Itself?" *Contribute Magazine,* February 7, 2008.

[6] Recollection of Thomas Russo, Annual Meeting of the SEC Historical Society, "Crisis and Resolve," 2005.

[7] Sarah D. Scalet, "IT Executives From Three Wall Street Companies – Lehman Brothers, Merrill Lynch and American Express – Look Back on 9/11 and Take Stock of Where They Are Now," (*CIO,* September 1, 2002). Available at www.cio.com

[8] Recollection of Stuart J. Kaswell, provided to the SEC Historical Society on May 27, 2005. Available at http://c0403731.cdn.cloudfiles.rackspacecloud.com/collection/papers/2000/2005_0527_Sept11_Kaswell.pdf

[9] After a few years in the Woolworth Building in lower Manhattan, the SEC's Northeast Regional Office relocated to the World Financial Center. (recollection of Wayne Carlin , Annual Meeting of the SEC Historical Society, 2005).

[10] Citigroup was created as a result of the Gramm-Leach-Bliley Act (also known as the Financial Services Modernization Act of 1999), which had broken the barriers between commercial and investment banking. Salomon Brothers soon became a part of Citigroup Global Markets Inc.

[11] Steve Lohr, "After the Attacks: The Reaction; Financial District Vows to Rise from the Ashes," *New York Times,* September 14, 2001.

[12] Will Acworth, "Recovering from Disaster: Futures Industry Fights Back from Terrorist Attacks," *Futures Industry Association Magazine,* October/November 2001, and telephone interview, Will Acworth, February 1, 2010.

[13] Thomas C. Baxter, Jr., executive vice president and General Counsel of the Federal Reserve Bank of New York, "Oversight of the Extended Custodial Inventory Program," testimony before the U.S. Senate Committee on Banking, Housing and Urban Affairs, May 20, 2004.

[14] "We used every existing vehicle for injecting liquidity and even invented a new one – the use of large swap lines with foreign central banks to inject dollar liquidity," stated Fed Governor Laurence H.

Meyer in a speech before the National Association for Business Economics, St. Louis, November 27, 2001.

[15] See http://www.federalreserve.gov/boarddocs/press/general/2001/20010913/default.htm.

[16] Remarks by Federal Reserve Vice Chairman Roger W. Ferguson, Jr. at the conference on Bank Structure and Competition, "Implications of 9/11 for the Financial Services Sector," Chicago, May 9, 2002.

[17] See http://www.treas.gov/press/releases/po610.htm.

[18] Kathleen Day and John M. Berry, "Stocks to Trade Monday with Special Rule; Big Firms Can Buy Shares Back to Halt Plunge," *Washington Post,* September 14, 2001, E01.

[19] Sodano interview.

[20] Pitt, "The Condition of U.S. Financial Markets Following the Recent Terrorist Attacks."

[21] Annual Meeting of the SEC Historical Society, 2005.

[22] Annual Meeting of the SEC Historical Society, 2005.

[23] Gasparino, *King of the Club*, 162.

[24] Telephone interview, Don Kittell (executive vice president of the Securities Industry Association), March 8, 2010.

[25] Pristin, "After the Attacks: Utilities."

[26] Randich, "Electronic Communications Networks in the Wake of September 11th."

[27] Personal interview, Steve Randich, January 24, 2007.

[28] Interview with William J. McDonough, prepared by Emily Walker.

[29] For the day, 12,997 buy-sell transactions (about a third of normal), worth $149.5 billion, and 2,892 repo transactions (about a sixth of normal), worth $121.5 billion, were submitted to GSCC for comparison.

[30] Nicola Clark, "U.S. Government Bond Prices Rise as Trade Resumes," *New York Times,* September 14, 2001.

[31] Repo volumes through BrokerTec were $4 billion (internal Chase email from Joe Blauvelt to Mark Werner, James Paterson, Glenn Havlicek, Colin McKechnie, and Michael Garrett, subject: "Update-Day 3," September 13, 2001, 6:43 p.m.

[32] Jonathan Fuerbringer, "As Activity Resumes in the Bond Market, Investors Send Interest Rates Plummeting," *New York Times,* September 14, 2001.

[33] See http://www.ebi.com/sept11/updatesarchive.asp

[34] See http://www.ebi.com/sept11/updatesarchive.asp

[35] Kim Koster, "From the Brink – The Road to Recovery." *Duke Magazine*, November-December 2002.

[36] "I remember that Garban got in touch with us [Nomura]. Because they apparently lost all their data. And I got on the phone with someone from there, and we quickly agreed that he wanted to see all his trades and his obligations on a daily basis. And we created yet another spreadsheet of all Garban's trades and settlements and whether they were matched or not matched. And we would e-mail it to them every day. And gradually that allowed them to get their books in order, because they had no clue as to where they were. So it was a major broker that we helped through that whole crisis." (Donnelly interview).

[37] Purpora interview.

[38] In one of several statements issued by Cantor Fitzgerald and eSpeed on September 13, Chairman Howard Lutnick said, "Our first priority remains the whereabouts and welfare of our employees and their families. There are currently 320 people on our safe and accounted for

list, and we are doing everything possible to verify the accuracy of this list. At this point, we have no confirmed information on employees having been rescued from our floors. We expect to publish a verified list on Friday. I would direct all family members and friends to any one of our websites, which have the most updated information available."

[39] Micah S. Green, President, Bond Market Association, statement before a hearing of the New York State Assembly, October 8, 2002.

The Statement from Cantor Fitzgerald and eSpeed read in part:

> Cantor Fitzgerald and eSpeed (NASDAQ:ESPD) confirmed that their trading systems were fully operational on the reopening of the U.S. Treasury market. Since the Tuesday tragedy in the United States, the companies have been operating continuously in both the European and Asian bond and equity markets. The firm's multiple locations in the U.S. and overseas, and system redundancies have enabled it to maintain trading of its financial products.

[40] E-mail from Joe Blauvelt to Mark Werner, September 11, 2001.

[41] "I did not make the decision to reopen," an exhausted Mr. Lutnick said on Thursday. "I interviewed a broad range of my staff, and that is what they wanted to do. In part, they simply were not going to let somebody defeat them," he said. Diana B. Henriques and Jennifer B. Lee, "After the Attacks: The Trading Firm; Flinty Bond Trader Leads His Firm Out of the Rubble," *New York Times*, September 15, 2001.

[42] Six of eSpeed's top technology executives had planned to go on a fishing trip that day. The trip was canceled because of bad conditions in the Atlantic, but fortunately too late to get the participants to their desks before the first plane hit. See Noelle Knox, "Cantor Fitzgerald Howard Lutnick Notes," *USA Today,* July 22, 2009, and Meryl Gordon, "Howard Lutnick's Second Life," *New York Magazine*, December 10, 2001.

[43] Edward Cone, "Cantor Fitzgerald - Forty Seven Hours," *Baseline Magazine,* October 29, 2001.

[44] Cone, "Cantor Fitzgerald - Forty Seven Hours."

[45] GSCC "Summary of Clearance Report for September 11 to September 18."

[46] Additionally, outstanding fails were marked to the market daily, but those fails may have already settled.

[47] GSCC Summary and Detailed Chronology.

[48] Trapani interview.

[49] Personal interview, Sal Matera, May 15, 2006.

[50] In August 2000, the CBOT and Eurex, a large European futures and options exchange based in Frankfurt, Germany launched a joint electronic trading platform known as A/C/E (for "alliance/cbot/eurex"), allowing CBOT and Eurex members to trade each other's derivatives products. This would be a supplement to the CBOT's open-outcry trading.

[51] Dutterer interview.

[52] Minutes of Emergency Meetings of the Bond Market Association, September 11-21, 2001.

[53] Arbon interview.

[54] The third alternative of not identifying to the system any transactions as settled, so that the end-of-day process could be run, would have incorrectly labeled thousands of transactions as fails to settle, setting back and potentially crippling the ongoing cleanup effort.

Chapter 11

[1] Telephone interview, Ira Polk (CFO of Man Financial), April 10, 2010.

[2] Jonathan Fuerbringer, "AFTER THE ATTACKS: THE COMMODITIES; Hoard of Metals Sits Under Ruins of Trade Center," *The New York Times,* (September 15, 2001).

[3] James E. Newsome, Chairman of the Commodity Futures Trading Commission, testimony before the U.S. Senate Committee on Energy and Natural Resources, January 29, 2002.

[4] Another reason for the push to reopen quickly was that the September gold options were set to expire on Friday. See Plummer, "Recovering From Disaster."

[5] See Plummer, "Recovering From Disaster," and Acworth, "Recovering From Disaster."

[6] See Acworth, "Recovering From Disaster." Man Financial, a derivatives broker, handled much of the volume generated during the Friday session. Recalled Ira Polk, Man's Chief Financial Officer, "We had thought a lot about how to handle the volume, since we were a big player in the energy sector. A lot of the firms used an omnibus account. They would put all of their customer trades into that one account, and then reallocated trades. We decided to set up all of our large accounts so that as soon as it traded we could direct right into their specific account. We set up about 600 accounts. So that Friday, when the Nymex reopened, we were in good shape as opposed to other FCMs, by avoiding using an omnibus account in allocations." (Polk interview).

[7] The *Washington Post* reported that major securities firms and corporations had reached "an extraordinary agreement to prop up prices by buying shares if a flood of sell orders threatens to send markets into a free fall... Federal securities regulators have made it clear they will permit these and other market practices that might raise legal questions in ordinary circumstances, the sources said." See Kathleen Day and John M. Berry, "Stocks to Trade Monday with Special Rule; Big Firms Can Buy Shares Back to Halt Plunge," *Washington Post,* September 14, 2001, E01.

[8] SEC Rule 10b-18 provides a "safe harbor" for companies and their affiliated purchasers from liability for manipulation when they repurchase the company's shares of common stock (in other words, they will not be deemed to have violated anti-fraud provisions of the Securities Exchange Act of 1934). The repurchases must fall within the four conditions of the rule. These cover the manner of purchase, the time of the repurchases, the prices paid and the volume of shares repurchased.

[9] The Commission also provided certain other types of relief to registered investment funds and public companies.

[10] The emergency order, with some modifications, was twice extended by the Commission to cover the period to October 12, 2001.

[11] Broker-dealers also lobbied the Commission for other regulatory options that could provide additional liquidity to the market: 1) for purposes of the securities lending collateral requirements of Rule 15c3-3 (the "Customer Protection Rule"), an expansion of the categories of securities that could be pledged as collateral; 2) an expansion of the categories of securities that could be held in the "special reserve account" for the benefit of customers; and 3) the facilitation of lending between broker-dealers and their affiliates by relaxing margin restrictions that apply to those circumstances. See Minutes of Emergency Meetings of The Bond Market Association, September 11-21, 2001.

[12] Annual Meeting of the SEC Historical Society, 2005.

[13] Broker-dealers could also disregard the days when the markets were closed in calculating the amount of deposit required in their "Special Reserve Bank Account for the Exclusive Benefit of Customers" arising from aged fails in government securities transactions and from unresolved reconciliation differences with accounts or clearing corporations or depositories involving Govies.

[14] This relief was subsequently extended by the Commission to permit all days from September 17 to October 19, 2001 to be disregarded from the calculations.

[15] The Commission didn't implement other suggestions received, such as prohibiting all short selling, moving to ten-cent quotation increments, and extending settlement cycles in the equity and corporate debt markets. See testimony of Harvey L. Pitt, "The Condition of the U.S. Financial Markets Following the Recent Terrorist Attacks."

[16] Kelsey interview.

[17] Michael J. Fleming and Kenneth D. Garbade, "Repurchase Agreement with Negative Interest Rates," *Federal Reserve Bank of New York Current Issues in Economics and Finance* (April 2004).

[18] Internal Chase email from Joe Blauvelt to Mark Werner, September 14, 2001, 5:14 p.m.

[19] On the morning of September 13, at the specific request of Queen Elizabeth II, the band at the Changing of the Guard ceremony at London's Buckingham Palace played the "Star Spangled Banner" instead of "God Save the Queen." A crowd of thousands watched in person; many wept.

[20] An exception was made for trades done with BrokerTec, which remained fully automated and retained full connectivity.

[21] Most of the brokers still didn't have an ability to communicate their activity to GSCC or the clearing banks; it would have been difficult anyway to do comparisons between the brokers and dealers. (Buckmaster interview).

[22] Internal Chase e-mail from Joe Blauvelt to Colin W. McKechnie and Michael Garrett, September 14, 2001, 4:20 p.m.

[23] A number of callers argued that the Association should bite the bullet and recommend that T+5 settlement continue for all trades done during the week of September 17. That notion was tabled.

On Wednesday, September 19, 2001, the BMA hosted a conference call for traders and lawyers to discuss moving OTC options on Govies from their normal T+1 settlement cycle to T+5, to reflect the change made for cash Govie trades. The BMA concluded that it would not make a recommendation about the settlement of option trades but, rather, that the parties to each bilateral contract should agree among themselves as to when settlement should occur. (internal GSCC e-mail from Nikki Poulos to Kate Connelly, subject: "Conference call today, September 19, 2001.")

[24] Corporates and munis settled on a T+3 basis. There also was a legal impediment for certain non-exempt securities. SEC Rule 15c6-1 provided for a T+3 settlement cycle, unless otherwise expressly agreed to by the parties at the time of the transaction. The SEC had not waived this Rule.

[25] GSCC Summary of Clearance Report for September 11 to September 18, 2001.

[26] Palatnick interview.

[27] Perna interview.

[28] The WorldCom-managed communications project established a Verizon connection after the close of the Fedwire. Shortly thereafter, terminal, file transfer, and MQ connections were re-established over that circuit. Once the MQ connections were restored, the file of clearance instruction sent by BoNY could not be read, so all messages were routed to an exception list. GSCC development staff had to write, test, and implement code to read the information from the list. See GSCC Summary and Detailed Chronology.

Chapter 12

[1] Perna interview.

[2] Gustav Niebuhr, "After the Attacks: A Day of Worship; Excerpts From Sermons Across the Nation," *New York Times,* September 17, 2001.

[3] "After the Attacks," *New York Times*, September 14, 2001.

[4] Somini Sengupta, "After the Attacks: The Methods; Hairbrushes, Razors, and High-Technology Identification," *New York Times,* September 17, 2001.

[5] Randy Kennedy, "After the Attacks: The Landscape; Business Will Resume on Drastically Redrawn Map," *New York Times,* September 17, 2001.

[6] Randich interview.

[7] Richard W. Stevenson with Jonathan Fuerbringer, "After the Attacks: The Economy; Nation Shifts its Focus to Wall Street as a Major Test of Attack's Aftermaths," *New York Times*, September 17, 2001.

[8] Brian E. Albrecht, "Grass-Roots Pride Day Shows Resolve," *Plain Dealer,* September 14, 2001.

[9] Andrew Y.S. Cheng, Letter to the Editor, *New York Times,* September 17, 2001.

[10] The call was for members of the Calendar Committee, the board, and the Primary Dealers Committee. Representatives of the Federal Reserve Bank of New York, the SIA, and the Emerging Markets Traders Association also were invited to participate. See Minutes of Emergency Meetings of the Bond Market Association, September 11-21, 2001.

[11] Blauvelt contemporaneous notes.

[12] By day's end, there would be only two dealers and one broker from whom GSCC still had not received trade data submissions (internal GSCC e-mail from Marc Golin to Kate Connelly, subject: "Member Data Submissions," September 17, 2001, at 3:53 p.m.

[13] Blauvelt contemporaneous notes.

[14] Minutes of Emergency Meetings of the Bond Market Association: September 11-21, 2001.

[15] Macwilliams interview.

[16] See http://www.ehstoday.com/news/ehs_imp_35096.

[17] Kennedy, "After the Attacks: The Landscape."

[18] See http://www.siferry.com.

[19] Stephen S. Roach, "The Economy, Too, Will Recover," *New York Times,* September 18, 2001.

[20] 15 men from Engine Company 54, Ladder 4, Battalion 9 died on 9/11. See http://www.newyorkfire.com/nyfd/e54memorial.jsp.

[21] The S&P 500 was down 4.93 percent. Airline stocks were hit particularly hard, falling more than 40 percent on average. See Jake Ulick, "Dow Enters Bear Market, Nasdaq Off 6.8% from High in Orderly Selloff," *CNN Money.com,* September 17, 2001.

[22] Jamie B. Stewart, "Challenges to the Payments System Following September 11: Remarks before the Bankers Association for Finance and Trade," April 25, 2002.

[23] In 1998, the AMEX had merged with NASDAQ, but the partnership wasn't a happy one. In 2004, AMEX members bought out the NASD. In 2008, the AMEX was acquired by NYSE Euronext, and is now known as "NYSE AMEX Equities."

[24] Sodano interview.

[25] Sodano interview.

[26] "After the Friday of the February 1993 bombing, they were going to keep us out of the building for two weeks. Since there wasn't electronic trading then, we would have lost the trading floor and might have lost the exchange to overseas markets or Chicago. We convinced them to let us in on the Monday following the Friday of the bombing. We were able to salvage trading with the help of our Philly hot site, though only two hours a day initially for about a week. Then about two weeks later they were able to put up a structure outside to allow heating, air conditioning and electric to be flowing to the trading floors.
    That was not a situation we ever wanted to get into again. So we came up with a new plan, to establish a backup trading floor. I put

together a plan and presented it to our board. They weren't too happy with it, because of the expense. They thought it would be unnecessary and a dust collector.

I demanded that the board bring in a consultant, Deloitte, which took three months to do an analysis that cost about $300,000. They agreed with our assumptions that we need to establish a backup site, as well as a hot site that backed up our facility more so than what we had. The consultant calculated that the exchange had lost about $300,000 a day in fees, and the community that it serves lost a few million dollars a day, after the '93 bombing. With that, the board said to go ahead." (Gambaro interview).

[27] Telephone interview, George Haase, April 28, 2010.

[28] Elton Robinson, "Two years after 9/11: New NYBOT Trading Floor in Action," *Farm Press,* November 14, 2003.

[29] Haase interview.

[30] "With a low ceiling, the noise generated from open outcry is louder than usual. American flags line the walls; makeshift booths are crammed with telephones and clerks." (Plummer, "Recovering From Disaster.")

[31] Gambaro interview and Bennett Voyles, "Thinking About the Unthinkable: Lessons Learned in Security in the Wake of 9/11," *Futures Industry Magazine,* March/April 2002. In 2006, NYBOT became a unit of the Intercontinental Exchange, known as ICE.

[32] Haase interview. Mayor Giuliani had assigned a Deputy Mayor to help the NYBOT. On Thursday, September 20, one of the phone switches in the backup site blew up. "We called our vendor, Siemens, who immediately reallocated one of theirs and had it flown to New York. The Deputy Mayor helped arrange for a New York City helicopter to fly it to the site. A Siemens technician and the IT staff engineered, installed, and tested the new box and by Sunday, September 23, it was up and running with all the same phone lines plus additional capacity. If not for the Mayor's Office's help, we would

have had half the phones on the trading floor out and we probably wouldn't have been able to trade." (Gambaro interview).

[33] Gambaro interview

[34] Ironically, the following year, NYBOT would negotiate an agreement to move into the NYMEX facility on the trading floor of the Commodity Exchange (COMEX), a subsidiary of the NYMEX. "As COMEX was then using the entire 25,000-square-foot space, the relocation necessitated that we first move them, without interruption, to one side of the floor, and then build out the vacated area for our own ongoing use. It took almost one year. We started trading there, without incident and with record volumes, on September 4, 2003." (Gambaro interview).

[35] Newsome interview. Over the next few weeks, Man Financial, a futures commission merchant that had been headquartered in the World Financial Center, set up an office with 75 to 100 people in the NYMEX building as its main operation. "We had to go back into Two World Financial Center four times, with groups of 10 to 15 strong, able-bodied people. They carried down our service equipment that we relocated to the NYMEX building. In that way, we were able to set up relatively quickly and get the operation organized and working, with help from Chicago and London. At one point, the FBI were very helpful. They let us use their black Suburbans to help us move equipment." (Polk interview).

[36] Gill interview, Dan interview, and telephone interview, John Damgard (President of the FIA), February 01, 2010.

[37] Telephone interview, Dennis Murray, March 15, 2010.

[38] General collateral repos were done in the 3 ½ to 2 ¼ range. Repo specials' rates were varied, depending on the hot issues. (internal Chase e-mail from Joe Blauvelt to Mark B. Werner, Colin W. McKechnie and Michael Garrett, September 17, 2001, 5:30 p.m.)

[39] GSCC Summary of Clearance Report for September 11 to September 18, 2001, and internal Chase e-mail from Joe Blauvelt to Mark B. Werner, Lawrence Forte, Kevin J. Finnerty and Tom Connors, September 17, 2001, 12:42 p.m.

[40] Internal GSCC e-mail from Marc Golin to Kate Connelly, subject: "Disaster Chronology," September 19, 2001.

[41] GSCC Important Notice 68.01, subject: "Reconciliation Processing Procedures," September 17, 2001. The margining process also was abnormal. On Friday, Clearing Fund calls were made to all nine participants with deficiencies. As of Monday morning, GSCC was unable to confirm whether three of the nine had satisfied their deficiencies. (Marc Golin's notes from Monday, September 17, 2001).

[42] Members also were asked to fax to GSCC a list of any deliveries that they believed their company had made, as well as a complete list of all outstanding fails.

[43] Lanston had for many years been owned by the Industrial Bank of Japan (IBJ). In 2000, IBJ, Fuji Bank, and Dai-Ichi Kangyo Bank merged to form Mizuho Holdings Inc. The Lanston name was no longer used, and it withdrew from the New York Fed's list of primary dealers. See http://www.newyorkfed.org/newsevents/news/markets/2000/an000417.html

[44] Personal interview, Bill Hughes, July 13, 2006.

[45] As usual, representatives of the Treasury, Fed, SEC, and SIA also participated, and the discussion opened with status reports from the major clearing houses and banks.

[46] The group also agreed that: 1) the moratorium on collateral substitutions should continue, in order to provide relief to GSCC and the clearing banks; 2) while significant progress had been made in the reconciliation process, the T+5 recommendation for Govies should continue for the remainder of the week to give the market another weekend for reconciliation, and delay the time when back-offices and clearing banks had to confront "double-settlement" days, in which

settlements from the temporary T+5 and T+3 regimes would be handled at the same time; and 3) if the early close and settlement recommendations became overly restrictive as a result of market resilience, they could be revised to reflect market conditions. See Minutes of Emergency Meetings of the Bond Market Association, September 11-21, 2001.

[47] Amy Waldman, "A Nation Challenged: Rosh Hashanah; Rabbis Revise Sermons to Soften a Stark Prayer," *New York Times,* September 18, 2001.

Chapter 13

[1] Clark interview.

[2] Recollection of Ed Kwalwasser, head of regulation at the New York Stock Exchange, Annual Meeting of the SEC Historical Society, 2005.

[3] Blauvelt interview.

[4] McAndrews and Potter, "Liquidity Effects," and internal Chase email from Joe Blauvelt to Mark B. Werner, subject: "Bank of England," October 19, 2001.

[5] "Euro-Brokers Guts It Out to Recoup Bond Business; Resolve Restores Pre-September 11 Levels," *Crain's New York Business,* March 4, 2002.

[6] Stewart interview.

[7] Olesky interview. In late September, Vin Mavaro, a Battalion Chief with the New York Fire Department, found in the rubble of Ground Zero a baseball that had been a promotional item for Tradeweb. The baseball, which amazingly was still in good shape, had been signed by Tradeweb's original members. Mavaro contacted Tradeweb, and the story later was carried on the *Today* show. Ultimately the baseball ended up in the Baseball Hall of Fame. See Wayne Coffey, "Baseball Lifts His Spirit: Fireman's Find Finds Hall Home," *New York Daily News,* November 8, 2001.

[8] "Another problem we came up against was that BoNY's TJs didn't have our participant IDs on them, just a Fedwire address. At that point in time, our Oracle data base only had the trade components, not Fedwire addresses. So we had to construct a set of tables that mapped the physical string of a Fedwire address into an actual participant. That might sound easy, but sometimes the string was truncated, and not always unique." (Matera interview).

[9] GSCC Summary and Detailed Chronology.

[10] As a result of the initial suspension of funds settlement with accounts from September 11 to September 21, GSCC had outstanding compensation claims of $279,000 that were paid. Those claims would be offset by funds in GSCC's account at BoNY during the period; GSCC generated over $340,000 in interest on the funds it was holding at BoNY. The remaining $61,000 was used to offset the $39,000 final difference amount. See GSCC Summary and Detailed Chronology.

[11] There had been tense discussions between the two clearing banks and the brokers regarding the validity of those costs. GSCC normally assumed financing costs that a inter-dealer broker incurred only if it could not turn around a late-in-the-day delivery through no fault of its own; regarding the 9/11 financing costs, GSCC management suggested to its board that this might be an expense that should be mutualized since it might be difficult to determine the party at fault. Staff noted that, if the clearing banks were not reimbursed for their costs, they might be less likely in the future to assume them in a crisis situation.

[12] The author was General Counsel of GSCC at the time and involved in the handling of the dispute.

[13] Perna interview.

[14] Grima interview.

[15] "I called a friend of mine at HSBC, John Burrus. As luck would have it, they had disaster recovery space at 111 Pavonia and at 545 Washington Boulevard, two buildings right here." (Purpora interview).

[16] Schipano interview.

[17] Purpora interview.

[18] "The reason why Bloomberg had that space available is that he had used the ground floor as a sales office. Right after 9/11, he converted that sales office into a rest station for the emergency workers. They took all the furniture, phones, conference rooms out and put Lazy-Boy recliners, showers and kitchens in. The bathroom was unbelievable, it looked like Duane Reed. It had boxes of shaving cream, razors, and toothbrushes, you name it. Free food and TV. He did that for months. We would see out of our window these waves of firefighters and others walking up West Street to the building." Purpora interview.

[19] "The construction crew head explains that Bloomberg has three construction crews working 24 hours a day in eight hour shifts. He adds that, by mid-November, you can tell us where you want the desks. And you know, by the first week in December, we moved our non-operations staff in Manhattan and Jersey City there…Before then, we used Nextel and personal cell phones. We used to buy about 20 cell phones a day, because the brokers would leave the cell phones by their desks, and the cleaning staff just took them. We were in that site for a year, until December 2002 when we moved to Jersey City." (Purpora interview).

[20] Settlement fails jumped from $1.7 billion a day in the week ending September 5 to $190 billion a day in the week ending September 19. See Michael J. Fleming and Kenneth D. Garbade, "When the Back-office Moved to the Front Burner: Settlement Fails in the Treasury Market After 9/11," *Federal Reserve Bank of New York Economic Policy Review* (November 2002).

[21] Fleming and Garbade, "When the Back-office Moved to the Front Burner."

[22] Before 1999, the New York Fed rarely lent securities outright to market participants. However, in the interest of aiding the smooth functioning of the government securities market, the Fed implemented a formalized securities lending program that made available a large

portion of its securities holdings on a daily basis. See Thomas C. Baxter and Robert B. Toomey, "Agreements Used by the Federal Reserve Bank of New York in Reserve Asset Investment and Monetary Policy Implementation," available at http://www.cemla.org/pdf/legales/leg-06-Baxter.pdf.

Pursuant to this program, from September 11 to September 13, the Federal Reserve loaned $22 billion worth of securities to broker-dealers that needed securities to complete settlement of failed trades. The Federal Reserve subsequently relaxed restrictions on its securities lending, which led to a sharp increase in borrowings by the end of September. "Our post-September 11th lending was extraordinary in many dimensions. Prior to September 11th, the Desk lent about $1.5 billion per day during the first eight months of the year. In the days following September 11th, we frequently lent multiples of that number, and at the peak, we lent $13.4 billion, more than 2.5 times the previous record. The lending also was extremely broad. On a typical day prior to September 11th, we might lend four or five issues. On September 11th, we lent 69 issues." (Dino Kos, Manager of the System Open Market Account and executive vice president, "The Repo and Securities Lending Markets," presentation before the Bond Market Association Repo and Securities Lending Conference, December 6, 2001).

[23] Fleming and Garbade, "When the Back-office Moved to the Front Burner."

[24] Internal Chase e-mail from Joe Blauvelt to Carolyn Monroe-Koatz, subject: "Specials," October 2, 2001.

[25] Greg Ip and Gregory Zuckerman, "Treasury Sale Averts a Crisis in 'Repo' Market," *Wall Street Journal,* October 5, 2001.

The Treasury Department made two other significant decisions soon after 9/11. In October, it suspended issuing the 30-year bond (the "Long Bond"), owing to four years of rising budget surpluses and the desire to reduce cost by borrowing at shorter maturities. The 10-year Treasury note began to replace the 30-year Treasury bond as the most-followed U.S. debt instrument. (However, given the costs of the war on terrorism, demand from pension funds and other large, long-term institutional investors, a need to diversify the Treasury's liabilities, and the recession, by February 2006, the Long Bond was back.)

Also, in December 2001, the Treasury Department created "Patriot Bonds," formerly Series EE Savings Bonds, to help finance the war on terrorism and provide a way for citizens to show their support for the effort. See Gail Makinen, "The Economic Effects of 9/11: A Retrospective Assessment," Report for Congress, September 27, 2002.

[26] Fisher interview. "In October, when BoNY was still having problems getting back sufficiently on-line, we were extremely worried. So we took the extraordinary step of having a special reopening. And held our breath a bit to hope that it would help the situation, and it did. If that had not helped, there would have been major concern, particularly with the quarterly refunding just a few weeks away." (Roseboro interview).

[27] Charles Gasparino and Gregory Zuckerman, "Treasury Bonds Enter Purview of U.S. Inquiry Into Attack Gains," *Wall Street Journal,* October 2, 2001.

[28] Jason Bram, James Orr, and Carol Rapaport, "Measuring the Effects of the September 11 Attack on New York City," *Federal Reserve Bank of New York Economic Policy Review* (November 2002).

[29] Remarks by Under Secretary of the Treasury Peter R. Fisher to the Futures Industry Association, Boca Raton, Florida, March 14, 2002).

[30] Leslie Eaton, "Attack Gave a Devastating Shove to the City's Teetering Economy," *New York Times,* September 8, 2002, and New York Metropolitan Transportation Council, "Demographic and Socioeconomic Forecasting Post September 11th Impacts" (2002). In the spring of 2002, the Federal Job Creation and Worker Assistance Act was enacted. It included authorization for up to $8 billion in tax-exempt financing to help reconstruct buildings and infrastructure damaged in the attacks.

[31] See http://www.disabilitylawblog.com/2009/07/articles/disability-claim-reassessment/former-government-bond-trader-and-911-survivor-receives-more-than-one-million-dollars-in-longterm-disability-benefits.

Chapter 14

[1] Randich interview.

[2] Tobias Guldimann, managing director and Deputy Risk Officer of the Credit Suisse Group, presentation at the joint conference of the Board of Governors and the Federal Reserve Bank of Boston, "Capital Allocation for Operational Risks," November 15, 2001.

[3] See Michael E. Bleier, "Operational Risk in Basel II," *North Carolina Banking Institute* (2004).

[4] Don Kittell, executive vice president, Securities Industry Association, "Recovery and Renewal: Protecting the Capital Markets Against Terrorism Post 9/11," testimony before the Subcommittee on Capital Markets, Insurance and Government Sponsored Enterprises, Committee on Financial Services, U.S. House of Representatives, February 12, 2003.

[5] Lackritz interview.

[6] On November 1, 2006, the Securities Industry Association and the Bond Market Association merged to form the Securities Industry and Financial Markets Association (or SIFMA).

[7] In April 2003, the senior market regulators issued "Sound Practices to Strengthen Resilience of the U.S. Financial System," a paper laying out their expectations about business contingency steps that key market participants would be expected to implement. Available at http://www.sec.gov/news/studies/34-47638.htm.

[8] Sandra Krieger, senior vice president and Head of Domestic Reserves Management and Discount, Federal Reserve Bank of New York, "Assessing and Managing Operational Risk," presentation at the Risk Roundtable sponsored by Oliver, Wyman and Company, Wharton Financial Institutions Center, April 18-19, 2002.

[9] Chris Steele, "Rethinking Business Continuity Planning," *Site Selection: Online Insider,* October 21, 2002.

[10] "When they come knocking, our inspections staff will ask for a copy of contingency plans, and likely will ask questions about alternative physical facilities, backup records storage, and backup communications systems" (Voyles, "Thinking About the Unthinkable").

[11] Securities and Exchange Commission Release No. 34-49537; File Nos. NASD-2002-108 and SR-NYSE-2002-35 (April 7, 2004).

[12] NASDAQ customers tested connectivity from their backup sites to NASDAQ's primary site in Connecticut and its backup site in Maryland. The NASDAQ was a host and allowed customers to confirm their ability to fall over to their backup systems. Previously, NASDAQ had accommodated individual requests for testing whenever NASDAQ conducted its own. See Elena Varon, "NASDAQ Tests Everyone's Disaster Recovery Plans," *CIO Magazine,* September 1, 2004.

[13] Landon Thomas Jr., "A Farsighted New Fortress Mentality on Wall Street," *New York Times,* September 10, 2004.

[14] Dan Verton, "For Wall Street, 9/11 Lessons Three Years in the Making," *InfoSec News,* September 9, 2004.

[15] The exception was certain products, such as options spread trades, that are more involved (they might have multiple legs to them) and remained for the time being more efficiently executed on the floor. (Haase interview). In 2000, 85 percent of all U.S. futures trading volume was handled in trading pits. By 2010, that was down to 12 percent. See Mary Pilon, "Trader is Keeping Hands in History," *Wall Street Journal,* July 10, 2010.

[16] "We cannot wait for a 'cyber 9/11' before our government realizes the importance of protecting our cyber resources" (opening Statement of Senator Susan Collins, "Protecting Cyberspace as a National Asset Act of 2010," U.S. Senate Committee on Homeland Security and Governmental Affairs, June 15, 2010).

[17] New York Metropolitan Transportation Council, "Demographic and Socioeconomic Forecasting Post September 11th Impacts," 3.1-3 (2002).

[18] Jack Lyne, "Bank of New York Adding as Many as 800 Jobs in Syracuse," *Site Selection,* July 19, 2004.

[19] Landon Thomas Jr., "A Farsighted New Fortress Mentality on Wall Street"; Charles V. Bagli, "As Companies Scatter, Doubts on Return of Financial District," *New York Times,* September 16, 2002; http://www.tenantwise.com/reports/World Trade Center_relocate_032002.asp.; Ricardo Kaulessar, "New York City Firms Find New Home in Jersey City," *Jersey City Reporter,* July 4, 2010.

[20] Roger W. Ferguson, Jr., Vice Chairman of the Federal Reserve, remarks at the conference on Bank Structure and Competition, "Implications of 9/11 for the Financial Services Sector," Chicago, May 9, 2002.

[21] Seidenberg Speech (December 3, 2001).

[22] See http://www.netscout.com/docs/success/NetScout_success_SIAC_NYSE_Euronext.pdf.

[23] Suburban Emergency Management Project, "Has U.S. Financial Infrastructure Protection Improved Since 9/11?" (October 28, 2004). Available at http://www.semp.us/publications.

[24] Walsh, "Leadership on 9/11: Morgan Stanley's Challenge."

[25] Almost seven years to the day after 9/11, researchers from the universities of Greenwich, Ulster and Liverpool released the findings from a three-and-a-half-year study of the evacuation process in the World Trade Center. After interviewing 271 survivors, the researchers found that congestion on the stairs was the main cause of delay, even though the towers were less than one-third full at the time of the attacks. Computer simulations suggest that if the North Tower had

been fully occupied at the time of the attack, over 7,500 people would have died in that tower alone. See University of Greenwich, "Evidence of Survivors of 9/11 Will Help Save Lives in Future High Rise Evacuations," September 9, 2008 (available at http://www.gre.ac.uk/pr/articles). Other findings were that the vast majority didn't flee as soon as the alarm was raised; rather, they stayed behind waiting for information or carrying out at least one additional task, including saving their work, shutting down computers, changing shoes, phoning their family, collecting belongings, and visiting the bathroom. See Lee Glendinning, "9/11 Survivors Put Off Evacuation to Shut Down Computers, Study Finds," *Guardian,* September 9, 2008 (available at http://www.guardian.co.uk).

[26] Randich interview.

[27] "Interagency White Paper on Structural Change in the Settlement of Government Securities: Issues and Options," Federal Reserve Docket No. R-1122, S.E.C. File No. S7-15-02.

[28] Micah S. Green, President of the Bond Market Association, statement before a hearing of the New York State Assembly, October 8, 2003. The Association noted that "given the conversion costs of restructuring the current system, and given concerns with the ability of an alternative system to support a deep and liquid trading market, the Association believes that the majority of the industry's and the regulatory community's efforts should be focused on addressing the risks present in the current system and not on fundamentally altering the existing structure, at least in the short term…Enhancing the Federal Reserve to provide clearance and settlement for Government securities arguably would present the greatest reduction in the risks that currently exist in the clearance and settlement system. However, the ability of (and the propriety of) the Federal Reserve to extend sufficient intraday financing is unclear. In addition, while some costs may be reduced, others (such as DOD fees) may significantly increase. Another issue of potentially significant concern relates to the responsiveness by the Federal Reserve to the industry in relation to calls for a reduction in fees or the implementation of innovative practices." See BMA letter of August 19, 2002 to the Board of Governors and SEC re Docket No. R-

1122, "Interagency White Paper on Structural Change in the Settlement of Government Securities: Issues and Options."

[29] The idea of allowing dealers direct access to the Fed has long been debated. While having its merits, the concept is unworkable without the Fed providing the full panoply of services that the clearing banks offer. Also, the Fed has been opposed to counterparty credit exposure to individual dealers, and dealers have been reluctant to open up their books and allow the Fed to see their positions.

Chase also recommended that the industry begin considering the adoption of compatible technology by clearing banks and the development of a real-time repository for data from clearing banks. Successful completion of this initiative "would permit a clearing bank, and an existing or newly created utility, or the FRB, to back up a clearing bank that was not able to operate from its primary or contingency sites." (letter from Chase to Jennifer J. Johnson, Secretary, Board of Governors of the Federal Reserve System, and Jonathan G. Katz, Secretary, Securities and Exchange Commission, August 12, 2002).

[30] Personal interview, Michael Urkowitz, March 20, 2010.

Made in the USA
Charleston, SC
19 June 2012